INVESTMENT IN BLOOD

FRANK LEDWIDGE

INVESTMENT IN BLOOD

THE REAL COST OF BRITAIN'S AFGHAN WAR

YALE UNIVERSITY PRESS
NEW HAVEN AND LONDON

For information about this and other Yale University Press publications, please contact:

U.S. Office: sales.press@yale.edu   yalebooks.com
Europe Office: sales@yaleup.co.uk   www.yalebooks.co.uk

Set in Minion Pro by IDSUK (DataConnection Ltd)

Printed in Great Britain by TJ International Ltd, Padstow, Cornwall

Library of Congress Cataloging-in-Publication Data

Ledwidge, Frank.
   Investment in blood : the real cost of Britain's Afghan War / Frank Ledwidge.
      pages cm
   ISBN 978-0-300-19062-5 (cl : alk. paper)
1. Afghan War, 2001—Participation, British. 2.   Afghan War, 2001—Casualties—
Great Britain. 3. Afghan War, 2001—Economic aspects—Great Britain. 4. Afghan War,
2001—Casualties—Afghanistan—Helmand. 5. Afghan War, 2001—Campaigns—
Afghanistan—Helmand. 6. Civilian war casualties—Afghanistan—Helmand.   I. Title.
   DS371.412.L44 2013
   958.104'7341—dc23
                                                                        2013002859

A catalogue record for this book is available from the British Library.

10 9 8 7 6 5 4 3 2 1
2017 2016 2015 2014 2013

Contents

Acknowledgements

I have spoken to very many people in the course of researching and writing this book and taken up their time. It is difficult to do justice to everyone, but here goes.

I have been fortunate to have had the opportunity to speak to dozens, perhaps hundreds of veterans of Afghanistan, British and other NATO, of all ranks and levels of experience ranging from four-star rank to almost newly minted private soldiers, marines and airmen over the last two years. It is not often remarked but nonetheless true how respectful service personnel are of views other than their own. Whilst not all share my opinions, I am proud to say that they are all my comrades and it has been a privilege to hear their views, each and every one of them. Most of them are still serving and it would help no one to name them. They know who they are.

Similarly many civilians I have met in the course of my work have been kind enough to give me their time to sit down and talk matters over. It has been fascinating to hear the often trenchantly expressed views of civil servants, consultants (who get a bad press, but are almost uniformly highly impressive people), diplomats, academics, aid workers and human rights researchers. Some of them I cannot name here as they are still working for a government which does not encourage free expression in its servants.

I am fortunate to have several Afghan friends, both from my own time in the country and afterwards. We do not hear their voices nearly as often as we should, but I hope those who have been kind enough to speak to me on or off the record see their views accurately represented here.

Bob Churcher, a Helmand veteran of many years whom I am fortunate to count as a friend, has been immensely encouraging and helpful. He may be rivalled in his knowledge of Helmand's people and ways by Michael Martin, who was kind enough to show me his PhD thesis, soon to be a ground-breaking book. Literally no British man or woman knows more than Ken Guest about Afghanistan and its history and people. I thank him for giving me hours of his invaluable insight and the benefit of his decades of deep involvement in the country. RAM Seeger has been involved in Afghan affairs for many, many years and has been a superb sounding board and conduit of information and advice. Likewise Lucy Morgan Edwards, with her years of work in the country, has been something of a bulwark and essential support. If only senior figures had listened to them and people like them, we would not be in the mess we are today.

Journalists, academics and aid workers who have aggregated hundreds of years in Afghanistan provided information, help and moral support over the years. They include Ben Anderson, Samim Bromand, Jean Mackenzie, Carsten Jensen, Heidi Kingstone, Nagieb Khaja, Aziz Ahmad Tassal, Jonathan Steele, Caroline Wyatt, John Hilary, Rune Henriksen, Lucy Morgan Edwards, Nadene Ghouri, James Fergusson, Matthew Willis, Cynthia Alkon, Rosemary Hollis and Javed Ziary. Rebecca Stewart and her team's work in revealing the unspeakable state of thousands of Helmandis driven from their homes by our war deserves many awards for courage both moral and physical.

My academic colleagues at RAF Cranwell, Doctors Peter Lee and David Gates, provided essential information and perspective. Professor

Anatol Lieven gave richly of his time in discussing international and regional consequences arising from the war. My old college friend (and now Professor) Paul Robinson, an authority on the Soviet period of Afghanistan was good enough to allow me a preview of his and Jay Dixon's new book on the Soviet civilian effort in Afghanistan. Professor Paul Rogers, whose prognoses concerning British military adventures and adventurism have proved almost unerringly right over the last decade, also gave me time to talk.

Military psychiatrist Dr Ian Palmer provided an expert perspective on Post-Traumatic Stress Disorder and was very generous with his comments on my rather inexpert understanding of this potentially lethally damaging condition. Dr Hugh Milroy, Chief Executive of Veterans Aid and himself a former senior RAF officer, was typically and effectively forthright about the realities facing veterans.

On the economic front I was immensely fortunate to have the assistance of Professor Keith Hartley of York University. He was kind enough to introduce me to Neil Davies, former Chief Economist to the Ministry of Defence. Without the assistance of these two leaders in the field of defence funding and economics, I honestly don't know what I would have done.

Chris Langdon put me in touch with John Sloboda and his team who discussed a way forward for reporting of civilian casualties; one can only hope it goes beyond discussions at the UN.

Retired Commodore Steven Jermy provided the strategic insight of someone who has been at the forefront of national policy. Expert on army structures and reform Rupert Lescott gave his insight into the way the army might change. Nick Lunt provided the knowledge and viewpoint of a strategic communications guru.

I am also very grateful to my friends Dr Michael Finn and the heroic Alex Donnelly for their support and help. Legendary veteran of the Second World War Dr Stephen Weiss, whom I am extremely proud to call a friend, put matters into necessary perspective. All have endured many hours of discussion on the matters raised in this book. My friend and comrade from Iraq James Milton was kind enough to allow me to publish his poem which opens the book. To hear him recite this and other poems before an audience is to tap into an ancient tradition.

I made many Freedom of Information requests in the course of researching this book. May I say here that the efficiency of the teams dealing with these requests in government departments with which I dealt, the MOD, FCO, DFID and Department for Health was exemplary. I would also like to thank the cadets, military staff and librarians of RAF Cranwell where I worked during most of the time I was writing this book. There can be no more congenial place to work, if not for the cadets then for the staff!

My editor Phoebe Clapham has combined her usual patience, realism and incisive critical faculty in helping me bring this book to market. Similarly I marvel at the forbearance, professionalism and efficiency of my copy-editor Clive Liddiard. Clearly any mistakes are the result either of my own negligence or of my not having listened to these consummate highly skilled professionals. Without my superb agent Andrew Lownie, I would be nowhere.

Finally my wife Nevi and son James have put up with many months of research, writing and generally being unsocial. Their love, support and care are the basis for all the work I have been able to do and my thanks to them are boundless.

To my mother

Children of a Lesser War

We were children of a lesser war,
A petty conflict, nothing more,
There'll be no bluebirds over
The White Cliffs of Dover
For us,
There'll be no fuss.

Just a footnote in our history,
No Vera Lynn, no mystery,
No turning back the evil tide
Of Nazis in the countryside,
Just tattered gaps in people's lives,
Grieving wives.

No fly by at the Cenotaph
Or sing songs where people laugh
Through the Blitz,
Defying Fritz,
We envy them that cause,
Not like our wars.

No equals in Afghanistan,
No tussles man to man,
No Luftwaffe in Iraq,
No Bletchley Park,
Just car bombs and smell,
A cut price hell.

No Winston, just windbags
No victory with waving flags,
Just body bags and sad parades
Until a sordid peace was made
With nothing solved,
Nothing gained.

James Milton

Introduction

One summer's day in 2010, I was walking down a staircase in the London Underground; next to me was a young baby being lifted in her pram down the steps by her parents. I don't know what it was about this particular child, but as I glanced into the pram I had a flashback to Helmand, where I had served as a civilian advisor in 2007.

In late October of that year I was walking from my rather pleasant, air-conditioned office in the Provincial Reconstruction Team (PRT) in Lashkar Gah, the provincial capital, down to the security gate. The PRT was essentially a large fort on the outskirts of town, and was used by both military and civilian staff. I can't remember what I was supposed to be doing at the gate – probably meeting an Afghan lawyer or a prosecutor. But anyway, as I approached the heavily guarded base entrance complex, with its search bays and armed soldiers, a young woman in British military uniform, a medic, ran at full pelt across my path carrying what appeared to be a bundle of rags streaked with brown. I walked on, wondering what it was all about, as generally very little running went on in this camp – except for recreational or fitness purposes, and this woman was emphatically not out for a jog.

Every evening in those air-conditioned offices, so far removed from the poverty outside our high-tech walls, there would be a briefing about the day's events in our 'area of operations'. Among the several SIGACTs (significant actions) of the day there was mention that there had been an 'unfortunate incident' in Lashkar Gah: a baby had been shot in the head by one of our soldiers in an accident at a checkpoint in the town. The child had been brought to our base, but unfortunately nothing could be done. The bundle of rags the young medic had been carrying had been covering the dead or dying baby, and the brown streaks had been the baby's blood. The servicewoman had evidently received the baby at the gate and was doing all she could to get him to some kind of medical care. There had been no time to put him on a helicopter to the main field hospital across the desert at Camp Bastion.

There was little comment on the incident among either the soldiers or the civilians in the camp: we all took the view at the time that it was 'one of those things'. The next day, I saw a heavily bearded man dressed in Afghan clothes waiting outside the office of the 'Crown Agents'; I found out later that he had come to claim compensation for his dead child. He was brave even to enter the camp, as the Taliban were known to track the comings and goings from the camp, and took a dim view of those perceived to be collaborating. He was one of the very few that year to claim compensation.

I had not given the incident a thought since then until I saw the baby on the London Underground; but I thought of little else for the rest of that day. When I got home, I searched the famous WikiLeaks cache of reports of SIGACTs, called the 'Afghan War files', to see if there was any reference to the accident. There were hundreds of reports relating to incidents involving British forces, but I could find no reference to the baby's death. Maybe the report had been classified too high to register on the American system that had been obtained by WikiLeaks; or maybe it had not been considered 'significant' enough to report. At home I had my own young child. How many others, young and old, had 'we' killed?

In a war like the one we were fighting, those who serve are very much in it together. I had believed in the mission when I went there, and my job placed me front and centre in it. I was as responsible as any soldier for what we were doing. It is simply not acceptable for the likes of me to pass responsibility for the horrors we were perpetrating to those who were placed on the trigger end of rifles or the other, even more savage or destructive weapon systems we operate. Infantry soldiers are, after all, implementing the strategy to which – for better or worse – we, the British people, had either explicitly or implicitly acceded.

At the time, the dead baby incident did not change my mind about what we were doing. In the early days of our mission I was inclined to put our signal lack of success down to a shortage of helicopters or armoured vehicles. After all, this was the message being put out in firm tones and unequivocal terms by our senior officers. The real turning point for me was a conversation with an American journalist, who – unusually for Western journalists in Afghanistan – lived and worked entirely separate from the foreign armies. She lived 'outside the wire' and talked largely to 'real' Afghans. Sometimes she would visit our base in Lashkar Gah to speak to officials there. At the security post she would unwind her various shawls to reveal herself as a blonde American. The British soldiers on guard were always left 'gobsmacked': surely no non-Afghan could actually live out there? The woman's name was Jean MacKenzie, and she had been a friend of mine ever since I had worked as a human rights lawyer in Central Asia. She was with a body called International War and Peace Reporting – a well-regarded non-governmental organization (NGO) which trains local journalists in war zones to report fairly and in a professional manner. Jean made it very clear to me that most of the people 'outside the wire' disliked us with varying degrees of intensity. We were regarded as invaders and as (at best) incompetent or (at worst) malevolent in the way we had made promises on development and then clearly failed to deliver on them. Most of the people inside (and indeed outside) the wire that I spoke to were government officials or police officers. They were reluctant to criticize us to our faces, and in any event such topics rarely came up in the conversations we had, which were largely to do with matters of law and order – or what approximates to it in Afghanistan. I always thought we were the good guys. It came as something of a shock to realize that very many of the civilians among whom we were fighting did not see us that way at all.

The international military campaign in Southern Afghanistan, under the auspices of NATO, had begun in the full expectation that it would succeed in bringing the benefits of 'good governance'. The British had chosen Helmand as 'their' province, a place about the same size as Bosnia and with a population roughly same as Northern Ireland's. The defence secretary in 2006 had told the first troops deployed that he hoped their mission would proceed 'without a shot being fired'. It took only a few weeks for that to be revealed as a very rash hope indeed, as one town after another was swept by battles between the newly confident Taliban and the newly arrived British soldiers.

As the mission in Afghanistan plummeted downhill, I changed my view – as did many others. Soon enough, the presence of British soldiers in a remote and not particularly important part of a Central Asian country will be the subject of a brief chapter in books on British military history and will comprise a few lines of text in political histories. The politicians and high-ranking officers who ran this misbegotten campaign will move on to other jobs. The legacy of Helmand will fade. It will be something from which we must 'move on'. But for all the taxpayers who paid for the war in Helmand, the expense will not cease when the last Chinook leaves an abandoned Camp Bastion in the so-called 'Desert of Death': as this book will demonstrate, the financial costs are ongoing and will not peak for many years. Nor will that final helicopter's departure mark the end of the war for the soldiers or for the civilians among whom they fought: for the wounded and disabled on all sides of the war, the pain and loss will last a lifetime. For some of our professional soldiers and reservists – man for man and woman for woman surely the very best in the world – Helmand may well be the pinnacle of their professional lives; for others, Helmand will have brought disaster and permanent injury. And for all too many of their families and friends, it has already brought bereavement and sorrow without end.

The UK did not fight the war in Helmand on its own. Denmark's forces fought a very costly campaign in the central part of the province – the first foreign war that country had fought for over two centuries. With 42 dead, in proportion to the size of its contingent it suffered more fatalities than any other country. In 2009, just as had happened in Basra a year earlier, the US armed forces in the shape of 20,000 marines bailed out a British contingent that had shown itself 'not up to the task' of securing the province. Despite the key contributions of these two allies, however, it will be the British who are primarily associated with the Helmand campaign – a campaign described by the UK's own ambassador as 'half-baked' and 'probably a strategic mistake'.[1]

Britain has fought four wars in Afghanistan, and most of them have been 'strategic mistakes'. The first was in 1842 and ended in arguably the most humiliating retreat in British military history. The second (1878–81) included a major defeat at the hands of the Afghan army (Maiwand, 1880) that is largely forgotten by British soldiers but is well remembered by Afghans. That war attained few of its political objectives. The Third Afghan War (1919) succeeded in its military aims, but since it resulted in Britain's complete removal from all influence over Afghan foreign policy, the Afghans regard it as a victory. Britain's Fourth Afghan War has gone on far longer and has cost far more than any of the others.

War is not (or should not be) only about fighting: the objectives it seeks must be in proportion to the losses sustained or the damage caused. This is at the heart of the ancient precepts of 'just war' theory that run through every major belief system, both religious and secular.

In order to assess whether a war is just, it is essential for us to comprehend fully the likely costs and to ensure that there is an equally firm realization that the gains will, put bluntly, be worth it.

This book will detail what the war in Afghanistan has cost us. It will also look at what it has cost the people of Helmand and examine the extent to which the war has in fact achieved any of its aims. Since 2006, no British government has seen fit to tell its people how much we have spent on the war. This book will provide the figures, using information in the public domain. Similarly, there has been no accounting by any government department of what it will cost to treat our wounded veterans, the men and women we have sent into often acute danger; this book will provide an estimate of that cost. During the period of the British occupation of Helmand, the army was fond of telling itself and the media that it was in Helmand to 'protect the people'. Yet at no point were any efforts made to enumerate the casualties that the British and other armies caused among non-combatants. This book contains a first attempt to do that.

The war in Afghanistan has cost Britain more money and claimed more casualties than any other foreign involvement since the Second World War – apart from Korea, which was a conventional war against a conventional opponent, with artillery and armour used on both sides. It is, then, entirely right to wonder what it was for.

Ultimately, in every tradition in the world, war is so terrible that it must be fought only for the very clearest and best of reasons. The principles behind 'just war' theory are often complex. However, they may be summarized by the simple words: 'We fight for a better peace.' What have we gained from these appalling wars? How much has it all cost? And has this sacrifice made a better peace? These are the questions that this book tries to answer.

The book is divided into three parts: Part I deals with casualties; Part II with the financial cost; and Part III looks at what might have been gained or lost by our efforts.

Part I begins with a look at the background to Britain's involvement in Afghanistan – at the reasons behind the presence of a very significant proportion of our soldiers in a desert in Central Asia (chapter 1). I will describe the process by which a fairly small mission, supporting very limited development objectives in a relatively benign part of the country, developed into a force fighting a full-on war in a province that is deeply hostile to the presence of any (but particularly British) troops. Moving from questions of politics and principle to hard-edged reality in chapter 2, we then survey the cost of Britain's involvement for those who have actively taken part in those efforts. We are by now achingly familiar with the formula: 'The MOD [Ministry of Defence] has announced the death of a soldier from the . . . Regiment in the Nad Ali District of Helmand.' Such statements have provided a relentless drumbeat to the war in Helmand (and indeed in Iraq) since 2003. The Fourth Afghan War has cost more than 440 lives, each loss representing a shattered family. We have also sustained thousands of other casualties. Some of those are all too visible: the maimed, blind, paralysed. But some injuries are not so visible. We look here at the consequences of this war for our own troops.

'We killed a lot of people, I think. Many of them might have been the wrong people.' Those are the words of a decorated army officer friend. I go on to examine in chapter 3 who those people might have been and how many of them there were. The UK army neither keeps records nor attempts to estimate the number of civilian casualties it has inflicted as 'collateral damage'.

Part II attempts to answer the question: 'When all the bills are in, how much will the war in Afghanistan have cost Britain in financial terms?' Making these assessments for the UK is far harder than for the US.

In the US, the question of how much citizens are paying for activities carried out on their behalf is commonly thought to be a vital matter of public interest. By contrast, in the UK military costs are hidden in documents that are largely kept free from public or parliamentary scrutiny. Such estimates as exist in the public domain are so riddled with inaccuracies and gaps as to be functionally almost useless.

Chapter 4 details the vast logistic effort to transport and sustain a medium-sized town in the desolate centre of the Desert of Death in Helmand.

We move on in chapter 5 to look at the care given to our wounded soldiers and at how charities displace the duties of society as a whole towards those we have sent into mortal danger. The costs incurred in caring for those people are huge and will extend far into the future; they may well be as great as the cost of fighting the war itself. This expense should be borne by the state, which sent these soldiers into danger. Here we assess what exactly the long-term and ongoing cost of caring for these men will be.

All of this effort and violence was originally designed to establish 'security', within which development could take place. Chapter 6 looks at the civilian effort in Helmand. What has it achieved and at what cost? We look at where the billions of pounds of taxpayers' money have gone in Afghanistan.

DFID proclaims its aim as 'helping the poorest of the poor': Afghanistan has been by far its largest area of operations in the world. I will ask how much British money has really gone to help those whose lives have been devastated by British military activities and will try to provide an answer.

In Part III, we look at what has been achieved in return for the money and human suffering. We were told in the United Kingdom that the war was being fought for our security, to prevent Afghanistan from once again becoming a haven for terrorists who threaten our way of life. Chapter 7 will describe what the British presence has actually done for Afghanistan, and particularly Helmand. Have Afghan people's lives been significantly improved? Is that change 'sustainable' (a seriously overused word)? And what about opium, a key reason for the army's presence in Helmand? In chapter 8 we examine whether, in fact, we have been rendered safer by our troops' activities. Security is, of course, a very broad topic, and so we go on to look at what the war in Central Asia has cost us in wider security terms – having armed forces that are skewed towards a single campaign and a defence policy that is focused on an opaque group of terrorists at the expense of perennial and far more serious threats. Were we really acting in the national interest, or in the interests of the so-called 'special relationship'?

Britain's leading economist of conflict and war, Professor Keith Hartley of York University, has this to say: 'Economists start by viewing conflict as a rational act resulting from an assessment of both costs and benefits for the nation involved. On this basis conflict is justified if its benefits exceed its costs.'[2] The key phrase here is 'rational act': economists see conflict and war as something derived from considered calculation by those who make the decision to go to war. We must hope that this is true.

Professor Hartley suggests, as any sane person would, that the calculations on which a decision to go to war is founded must be based upon knowledge available before the conflict. Prior to entering a conflict, a rational actor would attempt to determine the probable costs. Hartley points out that 'vote-sensitive governments either ignore or underestimate the costs of conflict'. The Iraq War, for example, was initially estimated to cost £1 billion. At its baleful end, the true costs were seen to be well over ten times that figure. In Afghanistan (and specifically Helmand, where politicians at least did not expect a shooting war), the costs have soared to levels that no one could have expected. As we will see, the Afghan conflict developed in a way that was not entirely rational.

Once the costs have been measured (something that really can only be done at or near the end of a conflict), the question arises of benefits, and we can ask whether the costs are balanced by the benefits. This book poses the question; again it is for the reader to decide.

Finally, I would like to say a brief word about the policy I have adopted in this book in analysing the costs. In my estimates of financial or human costs, I have counted only things that can be firmly evidenced (mostly by the government's own statistics). I have decided not to go down the route of looking at costs that are borne at two or three removes from the battlefield. I have chosen not, for example, to try to estimate the macro-economic effects of the Afghan War on the world's economy or on that of the UK. Equally, I have not attempted to estimate the second- and third-order effects (and their costs) of, for example, the possibly thousands of veterans with post-traumatic stress disorder (PTSD) and other conditions. (Here I am thinking of the effects of homelessness or loss of work through depression.) With respect to financial matters, my objective is simple. It is to determine how much we have paid and are going to continue to pay in cash terms for the war and its immediate effects. The figures I arrive at are to be considered minimum estimates, most of which are based on the government's own estimates. They are baseline figures.

Similarly, concerning the strategic consequences, I have erred on the conservative side. I have concerned myself with measuring losses and costs against declared aims. I have not dealt, for example, with the moral costs to a media excessively concerned with pandering to an over-confident military hierarchy. Similarly, I have not looked in detail at the cost to Britain's military reputation of its failure in Afghanistan. At the global level, I have not dealt in detail either with the further damage done to the appalling reputation we have in the Muslim world by our failed occupation of an Islamic country, or with what economic damage that reputational problem may do to our long-term interests.

I take the view that matters are bad enough without projecting too far into the future and engaging in speculation concerning the future of Afghanistan or elsewhere, however reasonably founded. To see how bad things are as matters currently stand, please read on.

PART I
THE HUMAN COST

CHAPTER 1

Helmand and the 'Angrez'

Here in this extraordinary piece of desert is where the fate of twenty-first century world security will be decided.[1]

Background to the Afghan War

In the 1960s and early 1970s, Afghanistan was a well-loved stopover on the hippie trail. And Helmand – for those who ventured to such a backwater – was a very pleasant, quiet spot that had a potential for real growth and wealth, thanks to the huge American investment that had been ploughed into the province.

On my own first trip to Kabul in 2007, the woman sitting next to me on the plane had been on that trail. Still wearing a floaty 1970s dress, she told me how relaxing and pleasant the whole experience had been; how Chicken Street had had much of the same appeal (and indeed clientele) as any of the dozen chilled-out locations in Asia that are today favoured by young people trying to 'find' themselves. Helmand province, with its lush, fertile orchards, had been regarded as a particularly chilled-out place, where marijuana could be smoked in the shade of the pomegranate trees. My companion's stories ended abruptly when the pilot of our UN aircraft warned us on our approach to Kabul that we were about to start a corkscrew movement to avoid anti-aircraft missiles. Things have changed radically since the 1970s.

For us, the war and all its attendant chaos and atrocity started on that unforgettable day in September 2001. Of course, for the inhabitants of Afghanistan it started long, long before that. For many of its people there had been constant war, struggle and displacement since 1979, when the Soviet army intervened to stabilize the new regime of Babrak Karmal after a somewhat Byzantine power struggle that threatened to drag Afghanistan into civil war.

The Soviets, unlike their Western successors, had in fact been invited by what passed for the legitimate government. That government was composed of an alliance of squabbling quasi-Marxist officers who had seized power from King Zahir. The Russians were not at all pleased with their would-be protégés, as Zahir had at the very least presided over a stable and peaceful country. They were not at all happy with the idea that Afghanistan might return to the kind of chaos that had been the norm in their southern neighbour earlier in the century. The Soviet leadership – advised by the pragmatic and experienced spy Yuri Andropov – was well aware that the cabal that had installed itself in Kabul had no popular basis at all. The last thing the Soviet Union needed was a country riven by internal conflict on the southern frontiers of its Muslim Central Asian republics. Like the Western invasion of 2001, the key objective in 1979 was to guarantee stability – in this case to ensure that any conflict between modernizers and traditionalists did not turn seriously bloody and begin to infect the potentially fractious Central Asian republics with ideas unpalatable to socialism. Alongside (and in Soviet eyes complementary to) that ambition was – perhaps eerily – a desire to create a more modern country. A former UK ambassador to the USSR and Russia, Rodric Braithwaite, has written the classic study of that period, entitled *Afgantsy*.[2] He takes the view that: 'The Soviets came in believing they could re-engineer other people's societies, releasing Afghans from their medieval backwardness. They didn't transform Afghan society any more than we are going to.'[3]

Against them was ranged a ragbag of militias and tribal groups that called themselves the mujahedin – 'holy warriors'. These were supported by Pakistan, which had been given *carte blanche* to channel US funds to whatever group it thought should have them. Contrary to popular belief (and such largely fictional films as *Charlie Wilson's War*), the Central Intelligence Agency (CIA) had little idea of what was actually going on in Afghanistan. What the CIA did do, however, was contribute to what amounted to an Islamic international brigade of enthusiasts, feckless youth and fanatics to assist the mujahedin. The leader of one of these Arab groups was Osama bin Laden.[4]

As with so many such interventions – from the British in the nineteenth century to Bush and Blair in the twenty-first – good intentions paved the way to hellish outcomes. There followed a decade and a half of resistance, counterinsurgency Soviet-style (i.e. savage) and civil war. Over a million people were killed, four million lost their homes, and Kabul – which had, let us recall, provided a popular and very pleasant backpacking destination in the 1970s – was wrecked.

After the Soviets pulled out, the government they had installed, under Mohammad Najibullah, lasted until 1992. During that time, though under attack by the mujahedin, Kabul still had functioning institutions such as universities, schools and hospitals. After the fall of Najibullah's government in 1992, civil war and large-scale gangsterism brought chaos, fear and insecurity to most Afghans. Kabul became a battleground for warlords (mostly former mujahedin), at the cost of tens of thousands of ordinary Afghan lives. These are the same men who today rule Kabul and those parts of Afghanistan not under Taliban control. Under those warlords, the country descended in the early 1990s into a form of Hobbesian chaos.

It was the Taliban, led by Mohammed Omar, an obscure cleric from the southern Pashtun Uruzgan province, and heavily supported by the

Pakistani intelligence service, that brought some semblance of order in 1994. ('Taliban' means 'students' in Persian: these men saw themselves as religious scholars.) By the end of that year they controlled most of Southern Afghanistan. While they established the most basic and severe form of justice and order, which had been seriously lacking over the previous two decades, the Taliban made the fatal error of allowing those former Arab fighters against the Soviet occupation to stay and base themselves in the country. One of those groups was run by that same somewhat dilettante scion of a wealthy Saudi family who had shown up in the mid-1980s. This group now called itself 'the Base' ('Al Qaeda' in Arabic), and the rest is – if not yet history – most certainly well-established current affairs. In October 2001, with the assistance of US and (to a lesser extent) British special forces, the 'Northern Alliance' of various largely Tajik and Uzbek warlords took Kabul. Following a Loya Jirga (grand meeting) of selected Afghan leaders, Hamid Karzai – quite the darling of the international media at the time – was installed as president. He surrounded himself with many of those leaders – war criminals by any standard – who had ruined Afghanistan in the early 1990s.

For perhaps two years, the international presence, including the military group known as the International Security Assistance Force (ISAF), conducted a low-key programme of reform. With the Taliban licking its wounds in Pakistan and biding its time, casualties were few and hopes were high.

The British in Afghanistan, 2001–06

Ever since September 2001, Britain had been the key ally of the United States in Afghanistan. The country had, as its leader Tony Blair said shortly after 9/11, stood 'shoulder to shoulder' with the US in its fight against 'terror'. UK special forces and British marines had played a major part in the failed hunt for Osama bin Laden (who, it turned out, had decamped to Pakistan). In December 2001, the British agreed to 'take the lead' on counternarcotics in Afghanistan. The Germans would train the police, and the Italians would, it was planned, lead justice development.

The British army and marines deployed units to Kabul from 2002 in order to assist in the newly constituted ISAF. At this stage, the US armed forces were not heavily involved in the NATO effort, as they were conducting their own Enduring Freedom operation without the assistance of the rest of NATO (and indeed without much mutual awareness). British troops in those early years were primarily involved in patrolling the streets of an essentially benign capital city. Hopes were high that the foreign presence would significantly improve the country, and the foreign soldiers were tolerated – and indeed welcomed by many people.

British focus shifted from Afghanistan in 2002 when Prime Minster Blair decided to support the US in what was a somewhat more controversial campaign.

The Iraq factor

In March 2003, following a long lead-in, the United States and UK invaded Iraq. In the first phase of the operation, thousands of Iraqi civilians were killed throughout the country, as were possibly tens of thousands of often helpless Iraqi conscript soldiers. After a brief but effective battle, the British army established itself in Basra city and the four provinces of Southern Iraq. Unfortunately, in those provinces of Basra, Muthana, Maysan and Nasiriyah some 1,694 civilians were killed and 6,184 injured.[5] As Britain's disastrous campaign in Southern Iraq unfolded, at least another 3,334 civilians were to die in its 'area of responsibility' and more than a thousand were wounded. Meanwhile 179 British soldiers were killed.

The material damage sustained by the Iraqis (and indeed by the 'coalition' soldiers) was bad. From the perspective of Afghanistan, there were two consequences, both of which were seriously (if not terminally) damaging to the Afghan campaign.

First, there was the diversion of military, civilian and technical resources from Afghanistan to Iraq. From being a priority in US foreign policy, Afghanistan quickly slipped to being seen and treated as something of a sideshow to the *real* campaign, which was being ramped up in Iraq. For a crucial five years, the Iraq campaign sucked military and civilian resources away from Afghanistan.

The second consequence was more insidious, but equally damaging: the invasion of Iraq changed Afghans' perception of the Western presence. By 2003, Afghans were beginning to realize that it was not quite the panacea it had initially seemed. It was evident to many that much – indeed most – of the vast amounts of money being thrown into Afghanistan was ending up in the bottomless bank accounts of Western consultants and Afghan politicians. As author Nadene Ghouri, a long-time resident of Afghanistan, remembers:

> anger was building, but attitudes changed overnight with the invasion of Iraq. Before that, the Western soldiers were not regarded as invaders or even occupiers. In 2003 for the first time even Afghan intellectuals started talking about the 'invasions' of Iraq and Afghanistan. Prior to that there had been no talk about it in these terms. Iraq was a huge factor in changing the perception of the Western intervention. Suddenly people started talking about oil and energy. They felt there was a link between what they perceived as an energy grab in Iraq and what they were doing in Afghanistan.[6]

For six years, the British army engaged in what would turn out to be an ill-fated and ultimately humiliating battle in the southern Iraqi city of Basra: by 2006, it was hunkered down in an airfield and one remaining base in the city, occasionally fighting its way in and out of its other bases for supplies – and being attacked every time it did so.

The following year, the British retreated to the huge base at Basra airport and did a deal with a ragtag set of militias: now they ventured out of their base only with the permission of those groups. In the eyes of Britain's American allies, its reputation for effectiveness in so-called 'low-intensity wars' lay in tatters. Defiant, quixotic references to successes in Northern Ireland and Malaya were treated by US army officers as just 'so much tripe'.

In 2009, the US Marine Corps took over from an embarrassed British military presence. In US eyes, the long battle for Basra was something of a fiasco. The embarrassment engendered by it would have consequences far beyond the borders of Iraq.[7]

Meanwhile back in Afghanistan . . .

Back in Afghanistan, now regarded as something of a military back-water, most of the few hundred British soldiers were based in Kabul, where they assisted in securing the city. On 28 January 2004, Private Jonathan Kitulagoda was on patrol in the eastern suburbs of Kabul. He was 23 years old and a Territorial Army soldier, a part-time reservist who had recently graduated with a degree in marine navigation. As his small convoy overtook a taxi, the driver of the taxi detonated a bomb. It was one of the first suicide attacks ever in Afghanistan: even in the savage days of Soviet occupation the practice had been virtually unknown. In the 'war on terror', Private Kitulagoda was the first British casualty of hostile action.[8] His death caused little comment at the time.

In July 2004, a British Provincial Reconstruction Team was set up in the northern Afghan province of Balkh. The idea of the PRT, initially developed in Iraq, was to combine civilian and military staff in a seam-less cooperative effort to bring development; for two and half years it worked – if not well, then at least without serious problems. Only one soldier was killed during that mission in the north: Lance Corporal Steven Sherwood was shot in October 2005. He was the second soldier

to be killed in the four years of British involvement. It was at this time
that the decision was announced that there would be a large-scale
deployment of British troops to the almost unheard-of province of
Helmand in Southern Afghanistan.

By this time, the Taliban were beginning to show signs that they had
not gone away. Since 2002, NATO had had the intention of eventually
spreading out from its bases in Kabul and the north into the Pashtun
provinces of Southern Afghanistan – Taliban country. At a NATO
conference in 2005, it was decided that Canada, the Netherlands and
the UK would each take 'security responsibility' for a province. After
some argument and confusion, it was decided that the Netherlands
would send troops to Uruzgan, Mullah Omar's home province; Canada
would 'take' Kandahar, where Mullah Omar and the Taliban had their
capital; while the British would be given responsibility for Helmand –
largely, it would appear, because Tony Blair liked the idea of the British
visibly taking the lead on the opium problem.[9]

Consultation on the deployment was very limited. Matt Cavanagh
was part of the Downing Street team dealing with Afghanistan when
these decisions were made. He is clear about who had given what
advice: 'the Chiefs [of Staff] advised that . . . taking on the largest and
potentially most difficult province . . . as part of ISAF's move into the
south was an appropriate level of ambition for a country with the UK's
military capabilities and its place in NATO and the world. Indeed the
Chiefs came close to arguing that *only* Britain could play this role.'[10]
Rather more prosaically, the army had its own reasons for wanting a
large-scale deployment: it was threatened with cuts – particularly to its
many infantry battalions. In written evidence to the UK House of
Commons Foreign Affairs Committee, a former UK ambassador to
Afghanistan, Sir Sherard Cowper-Coles, said:

the then Chief of the General Staff, Sir Richard Dannatt, told me in
the summer of 2007 that, if he didn't use in Afghanistan the battle

groups then starting to come free from Iraq, he would lose them in a future defence review. 'It's use them, or lose them.'[11]

This comment was later strongly denied by Dannatt.

But there was another problem. Having been seen to have failed in Iraq had dealt a great blow to the army's self-image – and, just as importantly, the image it had enjoyed in US eyes. It is vital for British soldiers to be seen to be at least as professional and effective as the Americans, towards whom the British had had a somewhat patronizing and paternal attitude – at least until matters started to deteriorate in Basra in 2004. By 2006, the British were seen to have seriously failed in Basra, and the US was presented with the distinctly unwelcome problem of trying to bail them out. General Sir Richard Dannatt, head of the British army at the time, put the problem thus:

> There is recognition that our national and military reputation and credibility, unfairly or not, have been called into question at several levels in the eyes of our most important ally as a result of some aspects of the Iraq campaign. Taking steps to restore this credibility will be pivotal – and Afghanistan provides an opportunity.[12]

'How the pros execute counterinsurgency'

'The British planned to show the Americans . . . how the pros executed counterinsurgency.'[13] That is how Rajiv Chandrasekaran, the author of a history of the US presence in Helmand, has put it. The British prided themselves that while they could no longer compete with the Americans in firepower or sheer combat power, they were still masters of the supposedly subtle military art of 'counterinsurgency'. Afghanistan was to provide the opportunity and Helmand the location.

Not all British officers agreed with the deployment to that particular province. As General Richards, commander of ISAF in 2006, put it:

'Where's Helmand? It's not important. Kandahar is what matters.'[14] These were words he surely regretted in 2010, when, as chief of defence staff, he took over responsibility for running Britain's campaign there. So where indeed is Helmand, and was it important?

Helmand

This province, the largest of the 34 in Afghanistan, takes its name from the River Helmand, which rises in the Hindu Kush, west of Kabul. The river flows through Helmand and sweeps west again, through the 'Desert of Death', before itself dying in the marshes around Lake Hamoun in Iran. Its course through Helmand province is marked by quite extraordinary lushness and fertility, and it is on the river's banks that upwards of 90 per cent of Helmand's people live – in towns such as Gereshk, Sangin and Garmsir, now famous as battlefields for the British.

The British are (or were, until their recent military discomfitures) inclined to believe that their own history inclines them to a special awareness of history generally – one reason why they believed in their prowess in guerrilla warfare. Yet not more than one in a thousand of those soldiers or civilians who served in Helmand had the slightest idea of the province's rich and ancient heritage.

The capital of Helmand is the town of Lashkar Gah. The term means literally 'Army Camp': it was here that the armies of the Ghaznavid rulers of this part of Central Asia were based whenever the kings came down out of Kabul to avoid the cold winter. The monarchs themselves were quartered a few kilometres to the south of modern Lashkar Gah, at the great fortress of Bost, still an impressive archaeological site. The nobility built great mansions in Lashkar Gah itself, which can still be seen a few hundred metres up from the main bridge across the Helmand – huge, looming, sand-brown ruins leaning over the river. Like so much else in this country, these are the sorts of places that make one think 'if only it were safe enough, tourists would love it'.

The glory days did not last long. The Ghaznavids went the way of all Central Asian dynasties in the late twelfth century – destroyed by invaders. Over the centuries, various Mongol or Persian armies passed through or across what is now Helmand; but none stayed. Although situated on some fairly well-used and ancient smuggling routes from the badlands of Baluchistan and the Arabian Sea, Helmand has never really been on Afghanistan's beaten track for travellers, save for a few hippies in the 1960s and 1970s. Its towns and fertile areas were always in the shade of the great centre of Kandahar, three days by mule and camel (or half an hour by Chinook helicopter). Many Kabulis simply cannot understand why the West has got itself so heavily engaged in what they regard as a remote backwater filled with illiterate farmers and religious fanatics.

The British passed through Helmand twice during their many wars and border campaigns in imperial days. Their first visit was in 1840, on their way to Kabul to install a king of their own making. This episode ended badly, with the disaster of the 1842 retreat from Kabul – a strong contender for the most ignominious of Britain's nineteenth-century defeats. In 1878 they came again. While it may be a footnote in the history of Britain, that particular visit is well remembered in Helmand.

Especially well remembered is the Battle of Maiwand, which took place about eight miles east of Gereshk. There had been some significant fighting around there in late 1878 and early 1879 as the British made their way to Kabul in the Second Afghan War. A British paratrooper told me how, while on patrol in Helmand's second town of Gereshk in 2006, he was approached by an old man. 'You're back again,' the man said. 'Here to burn our bazaar, I suppose.' 'We've done no such thing,' the paratrooper replied. 'Indeed you did, when you came through here with General Burrows. But we saw him off.'

Indeed they did see him off at Maiwand, where an Afghan army defeated a British brigade of 2,000 on 27 July 1880 (in another prime candidate for worst defeat of the nineteenth century; though it is probably outdone by the defeat at the hands of the Zulus the year before, at Isandlwana). Forgotten (if it was ever known) by most British servicemen, for Afghans Maiwand is a combination of Agincourt and Waterloo. Every Afghan knows the story of Maiwand, not least because there is also more than a hint of Joan of Arc: the best-known hero of this battle, not excepting the Afghan commander Ayub Khan, is Malelai, who supposedly encouraged the wavering lines of Afghan soldiers by removing her veil – Islamic green, of course – and reciting a poem which included the lines:

> Young love if you do not fall in the battle of Maiwand;
> By God someone is saving you as a token of shame.
> With a drop of my sweetheart's blood,
> Shed in defence of the Motherland,
> Will I put a beauty spot on my forehead,
> Such as would put to shame the rose in the garden.

Malelai was killed in the battle; her grave, known and tended to this day, is near the battlefield at her home village. There are few towns without a Malelai School, and the name is very common among girls. Understandably less well remembered, it should be said, is the fact that later in 1880 a British army met and comprehensively defeated the Afghans at Kandahar.

Be that as it may, all Afghans remember that the British (or the 'Angrez' as they call them) have been here before. And Afghan memory of them is not positive. As we will see, some British officers were well aware of the 'Maiwand Factor': it had no small influence on what was to happen to the next British army to arrive in Helmand 126 years later.

Little America

The West's next encounter with Helmand was a result of one of those very odd examples of how the global economy is interlinked. The fur trade had been predominantly run and organized by European Jews, but after the Holocaust its focus shifted to New York. The year 1946 saw an increased demand for Astrakhan coats – made from the fleeces of fat-tailed sheep. In place of the pelts that had previously been traded through Europe, the US clothing industry looked elsewhere. Afghanistan had a very rich supply of the right kind of sheep, and began to sell the fleeces at a handsome profit. As a result, the country found itself with a considerable surplus of cash. King Zahir Shah decided to invest this money in a large and fantastically ambitious project: he wanted to build a dam to improve the situation of the Pashtun tribes of the south and entrench their political strength nationally, thereby securing his own position. The dam would be constructed on the Helmand River, and the company selected to build it was Morrison-Knudsen, the same firm that had built the famous Hoover Dam in Colorado. The result was the construction of two dams, one of them the Kajaki Dam, which was to provide electricity to Kandahar.[15]

The king's investment was supplemented in 1952 by the US government, which was keen to use its economic strength to counter Soviet influence. Building on what had already been done, the Helmand Valley Authority was set up (based on the concept and organization of the Tennessee River Valley Authority). With a controlled and regular source of water came 300 miles of canals and channels, and millions of acres of newly fertile land. The authority acted essentially as a centralized integrated planning authority.

As well as inviting the US to assist in building the two dams on the rivers Helmand and Argandab, the Afghan government embarked on a big programme of resettling some of the Pashtun tribes that lived on the border with what was by then Pakistan. Driven by Prime Minister Daud, a cousin of the king, the idea was to strengthen the position of the Pashtuns politically, thus creating a far more coherent and settled group. The newly sedentary border Pashtuns would farm the freshly irrigated fields in what we now call the Green Zone. Importantly, however, this move sowed the seeds of serious future conflict. The major changes in land ownership that ensued did not go down at all well with other groups, which believed they had a right to the land that was being transferred. In Pashtun culture, land, women and gold are the perennial sources of conflict, and these land grants are still the subject of fighting and feuding.

Lashkar Gah

At the centre of the huge projects organized by the Helmand River Authority was the new, planned city of Lashkar Gah, built next to the palaces of the Ghaznavid nobles that still dominate the riverbank. The famous Marxist historian Arnold Toynbee visited Helmand in May 1960, as the city was being completed. By then the town had over 8,000 inhabitants living in American-style suburban homes surrounded by lawns; it had a co-educational secondary school and one of the country's best hospitals. Toynbee saw the new city and its vast engineering projects as 'a piece of America inserted into the Afghan landscape. The new world they are conjuring up at the Helmand river's expense is to be an America-in-Asia.' Quoting the Greek tragedian Sophocles, he went on: 'The craft of his engines surpasseth his dreams.'[16]

When I arrived in Lashkar Gah in 2007 to work as the justice advisor to what was, by comparison with previous international assistance projects, an emaciated and extremely half-hearted British effort, Lashkar Gah was a city of 200,000. There was still something of the American planned model town about it: the grid-pattern street plan, the rather leafy character of some of its streets and the remaining suburban villas. But much of it was by then a dusty and depressing husk of the original intentions.

Outside the city, though, the legacy of the dams' construction was apparent everywhere. For several kilometres on either side of the river, the canal and channels dug by those engineers half a century before had created a rather bucolic, fertile oasis in the Dasht e Marg – the so-called 'Desert of Death' of Southern Afghanistan. At this time, most of the newly settled farmers grew wheat – a crop that (like its successor, opium) requires a good deal of regular and controlled water.

The last Americans left in 1979, when the other superpower arrived in Helmand.

The Soviet legacy

The Soviets arrived, initially on a six-month mission to stabilize the Afghan government, which had embarked on another round of revolutionary reforms. One of the reforms of the new Afghan government (Law No. 8 of 1978) was intended to give land to families that had previously been landless sharecroppers. The reform was arbitrary and poorly thought out. One militia leader said that 'the mother of problems we have now is the land redistributions [at that time]'. These land conflicts overlaid those from the 1950s, feeding the tribal and group rivalry.[17]

At about this time, one particular Helmandi family was beginning to accumulate real political power. It was led by Nasim Akhundzada, a little-known cleric who, in 1981, issued a fatwa legalizing the production of opium poppy.[18] In due course, the family became the centre of resistance to the Soviet presence, fighting the Soviet army on much the same ground as those groups we call the Taliban were to fight the British two decades later.

The Soviets continued the US pattern of building the infrastructure, although at nowhere near the same rate. They improved the roads that had originally been constructed with US help, and erected bridges, schools and hospitals. But their focus was not so much on physical infrastructure as on the training and development of cadres of loyal Afghans. Hundreds of Helmandis were selected to go to the Soviet Union, some of them for years, to train as police and military officers, lawyers, doctors and administrators. Most came back with a lasting regard for the Soviet efforts at least (if not for the results of those efforts in Afghanistan). For it was unambiguously the Soviet objective to drag Afghanistan out of what it regarded as primitive tribal ways and into something approximating to the twentieth century.

Those who were taken to the Soviet Union and trained up later formed the backbone of US and British efforts once again to restructure the country. Almost all the senior Afghan police officers, prison officers, military officers and prosecutors with whom I had dealings in Helmand had been trained in the Soviet Union and spoke perfect Russian. Their perspective on what the Soviets did for their country is very different from our own.

There was resistance to Soviet occupation in Helmand, as elsewhere in Afghanistan. However, the usual characterization of the resistance as either ideological or religious is seriously open to question.

Michael Martin is probably the leading British expert on the history and human geography of Helmand. He speaks fluent Pashto and has conducted extensive on-the-ground research into Helmand's recent history, talking to dozens of Helmandi notables about the long war in the province from 1978 until today. No one I have met more accurately represents the old British tradition that gave rise to the intensely involved and aware frontier political officers – the 'politicals' – of the British Raj from the early nineteenth century to 1947.

Martin sees the anti-Soviet 'jihad' in Helmand as an 'intensely complicated private sphere of actors, groups, motives, cleavages and alliances. Each of the areas [of Helmand] had a slightly different mix of local factors.'[19] To give an idea of the complexity, major tribal groups include Alizai, Noorzai, Barakzai, Ishakzai, Alikozai, Popalzai, Pirzai, Hasanzai and Khalozai (these are just within the Durrani Federation);[20] there are many others, and all are subdivided according to clan, location and allegiance. Powerful warlord dynasties grew up in that period – notably the Akhundzada family (see above), which belonged to no major tribal group but had – and continues to wield – huge regional influence. Each of these groups had, in turn, factions that belonged to various so-called mujahedin parties, such as the Hizb-e-Islami or Harakat or their various splinter factions. Alliances and rivalries were built and dissolved as disputes over drugs or land played themselves out.

On the 'government' side, there was an almost equally complex web of tribal, financial and political loyalties, with the Soviet army occasionally conducting operations when the government (or what passed for a government) lost control of one or other *hukamat* or district centre (there are 14 districts in the province, their boundaries constantly shifting). The Soviets, like the British after them, focused their attentions on what they called a 'cummerbund' around the main towns of Lashkar Gah and Gereshk.

Mujahedin groups were infiltrated by the intelligence service Khad, or more often were simply bought off. Groups drifted into or out of the 'government's' orbit as it suited them. At one point, there was even what amounted to a mini civil war between Northern and Southern Helmand.[21] Any characterization of the period as 'Soviets versus mujahedin' is very far off the mark indeed. There was little if any ideology about it, at least in Helmand. To a very great degree, the same might be said of today's war.

Relative stability: Helmand under the Taliban

After the Soviet Union pulled out, the war continued – just without direct Russian involvement. The Russians had left a huge amount of military ordnance, and this was used to continue the fighting and squabbling between tribes and parties for opium 'tax' revenue and land. By this time, opium and the huge revenues to be derived from it had become a major factor. Helmand – along with the rest of the country – sank for several years into rule by tribal (or more accurately militia) warlords, including the Akhundzada family. Former 'government' party and military leaders reinvented themselves as militia commanders.[22] This time is remembered as one of anarchy and fear, with the roads controlled by gangs of feral 'mujahedin' militiamen. At this stage further land thefts took place, serving to fuel the fires of conflict.

It was partly a perceived need to correct this appalling mess that brought support for the Taliban, a group of religious zealots backed by the Pakistani government. At the time of their takeover in 1994, they were regarded by many as a salutary correction to the excesses of those militia leaders. At the very least, the Taliban brought a sense of security – the roads were safe and travellers were no longer preyed on by bandits, who had targeted anyone without the requisite money or armed protection. The local squabbles over land ceased for the moment, as the Taliban would tolerate no form of dispute resolution other than their own. The warlords were unable to conduct attacks on their rivals. Michael Martin summarizes matters thus: 'Helmand was stable under the Taliban.'[23] The now notorious (to us) 'conservative values of the Taliban were similar to the conservative values of rural Helmand. This is an important point as it runs counter to the prevailing overarching public narratives about the Taliban: that they forced their rules on an unwilling population.'[24]

By the late 1990s, people were starting to lose their enthusiasm for the Taliban, which had instituted a system of conscription. Men were still being sent to what seemed an interminable war against the Northern Alliance.

In 2001, as we saw above, the US and its allies installed the Karzai family in the Arg Palace in Kabul. The Karzais were closely linked by marriage to the influential Akhundzadas, and the president soon brought in the warlord Sher Mohammed Akhundzada (known to foreigners as SMA). Helmand, with its relatively fine network of irrigation channels and its proximity to Pakistan, now secured its position as the world centre of opium and heroin production. Former Taliban fighters were incorporated, or reincorporated, into the various new militias that warlords were reforming, and some of the old factional battle lines were redrawn. Some of these militias became factions in the 'police'. Government land, stolen by various warlords over previous decades, was distributed to their followers. US 'special forces' set themselves up near Gereshk, leading to the new local term 'special-porce' (*sic*). They set about bribing anyone who was able to bring in former Taliban or Al Qaeda. 'The US troops did not understand how fractured the society was in which they were operating: the cleavages and alliances of the private sphere. They also failed to understand how offering bribes would cause people to denounce anyone they were having a feud with or even random innocent people to collect the bribe.'[25] Many ended up in Guantanamo Bay.

Alliances were built and rebuilt with international drug-trafficking figures both inside and outside Afghanistan, and militia and 'police' commanders began to set up their own heroin laboratories. It was partly this that brought the province once again to the attention of the British.

Where were Mullah Omar's Taliban, the men Helmandis call *aslee* ('real') Taliban, when the British entered the province in force in 2006? They were there, but not in great numbers: British special forces operators I spoke to told me that their patrols prior to the large British deployment in 2006 were occasionally interrupted by shootouts and ambushes. But Helmand was not a stronghold of the Taliban. This was due largely to the fact that, as governor, SMA and his colleagues and rivals had made sure that tribal and narcotic networks were so arranged that there was little opportunity for them to gain real power. Many of those who would later become 'Taliban' fighters[26] were employed by Akhundzada in his personal militia. No one would describe Akhundzada as an agent of good governance. The uncomfortable fact of the matter was, though, that he could strike deals that ensured the Taliban had few effective units. As one British team reported after a reconnaissance mission in 2005, in preparation for the UK deployment: 'There's no insurgency there now, but if you want one you can have one.'[27] The British army was soon to ensure that it had an insurgency.

The British military campaign in Helmand

Born in confusion and institutional dishonesty, the campaign in Helmand was to dominate the lives of tens of thousands of British soldiers, sailors, airmen and marines, as well as several hundred civilians, for a decade. The British move into Helmand was part of the expansion of NATO forces known as 'Phase IV' – the 'move south'. The central idea was to expand the Karzai government's control beyond Kabul. While it was up to the military to decide on the scale of the operation, Helmand was (as we saw above) specifically selected by Blair for the British contribution because he had been told, rightly, that it was the centre of the opium trade.

The British operation to secure this expansion was dubbed 'Herrick' (not after the seventeenth-century poet; like the names of all British military operations it was computer generated). Before troop deployment, the UK government applied pressure on President Karzai to dismiss Akhundzada and install someone more ostensibly amenable to its objectives. The British had taken grave exception to his having been found in possession of 9 tonnes of opium: given that they had taken on responsibility for counternarcotics, that was hardly going to allow a good relationship to develop (even if the whole affair was a misunderstanding, as Akhundzada asserted). 'He needs to go', said the British; 'He's an effective bulwark against the Taliban, so he ought to stay', argued the US, on the well-trodden basis that 'he may be a son of a bitch, but he's our son of a bitch'. On this occasion the British prevailed and Akhundzada was replaced. As President Karzai put it in 2009: 'We removed Akhundzada on the allegation of drug-running, and delivered the province to drug runners, the Taliban, to terrorists, to a threefold increase of drugs and poppy cultivation.'[28] But we are getting ahead of ourselves . . .

It is probably strictly true that the British army did not go to Helmand looking for a fight. Certainly the original UK 'Joint Plan for Helmand', known as the 'Helmand Plan' and produced jointly by military and civilian advisors, did not allow for any serious fighting. In theory, the army was there to support that plan. The original intention was to concentrate forces around the two major towns of Lashkar Gah and Gereshk and focus development assistance there, as part of a framework that was to involve all arms of the British and Afghan governments in an overarching or 'comprehensive' approach. This was the 'Helmand Lozenge' – an unwitting rehash of the Soviet 'cummerbund' we saw above. The 'Helmand Plan' was not the only one: it formed part of a vast network of plans and strategies. The UK's 'Hierarchy of Plans' (see below) serves to illustrate just how impressive this was.[29] It was, incidentally, to get far larger.

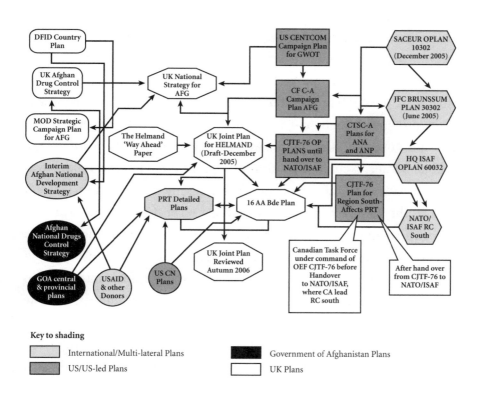

Annex 10A: The Hierarchy of Plans for UK Operations in Helmand 2005

The journalist and author of *No Worse Enemy*, Ben Anderson, writes:

The comprehensive approach looked perfectly feasible in PowerPoint presentation, when the beneficiaries, who weren't consulted, were viewed as automata. When applied to an actual society, especially one as fragmented, traumatised and complicated as Helmand's it rarely lasted longer than the first ten minutes of a *shura* [meeting with local Afghans].[30]

PowerPoint presentations were, and are, very regular indeed, although after a look at the UK's 'Hierarchy of Plans' reproduced above, 'feasible' might not be the first word that springs to mind.

All that notwithstanding, a serious problem had arisen to derail the smooth running of the plans formulated by the various international forces: no consideration had been given to the enemy. The removal of Akhundzada had rendered several thousand former members of his personal militia unemployed.[31] At the same time, coincidentally or otherwise, the Taliban had run up their flags in several outlying towns of the province. Where had all these 'new' Taliban fighters come from? The old governor had the answer: 'I sent 3,000 of them off to the Taliban because I could not afford to support them but the Taliban was making payments. Lots of people, including my family members, went back to the Taliban because they had lost respect for the government. The British bore the brunt of this because the Taliban became the defenders of Helmand.'[32] It is clear now that the term 'Taliban' even then was somewhat moveable. One of Michael Martin's informants told him 'he was not scared of [Mullah] Omar's Taliban (*'aslee* Taliban') but he was terrified of Sher Mohammed's Taliban.'[33]

The new governor, Mohammed Daud, a Helmandi landowner installed by the British, had been told that the UK had deployed 3,500 men. As indeed it had. But in a modern army, a very small proportion of a force is available for fighting 'outside the wire', and in fact the British commanders had only about 200 men available to undertake such activities.[34] Nevertheless, in response to Daud's demands for action, the decision was taken to move troops to occupy the outlying towns. This episode, now known as the 'Charge up the [Helmand] Valley', proved very unwise. The soldiers sent to these remote places found themselves undermanned and under siege, fighting battles of a ferocity and savagery unknown since the Korean War, against thousands of 'Taliban' of whom British military intelligence had been ignorant. One reason they did not know of these 'new' insurgents was that many of them had, until just a few months before, been on the staff of Sher Mohammed Akhundzada.

Many of them were fighters for other warlords, and others were simply men defending their villages against soldiers they perceived to be invaders. Helmandis had not reacted well to the presence of British soldiers, the hated 'Angrez'. First there was the 'Maiwand Factor'. A story related to Michael Martin illustrates this very well:

A young intelligence officer asked [an official] what the Helmandis thought of the British in light of their shared history. The provincial official replied that the Helmandis hated them, and the Britisher went red, embarrassed. Not wishing to offend his guest, the official continued, 'but that was then, and this is now . . . now you have come to help' . . . Yet he was thinking 'why are they *here*?'[35]

But this was not just the 'Maiwand Factor': it was also a simple aversion to occupation – which is what the deployment of a brigade of infantry looked like. The British had abandoned their measured and possibly (on its own terms) workable 'Helmand Plan' and instead, responding to the governor's importunate requests, had sent their few available soldiers to garrison several widely scattered towns throughout the province. These troops acted as magnets for local Taliban units, recently reinforced with Akhundzada's newly unemployed militiamen.

Mini-sieges erupted across the province, and British units found themselves involved in their own little 'Rorke's Drifts', heroically holding off savage hordes. These fights – which saw British numerical weakness more than compensated for by huge amounts of air-delivered high explosives and an attendant depopulation of the towns at the centre of the fighting – set the scene for the rest of the British time in the province. The heaviest fighting occurred around the town of Sangin, where the provincial head of the secret police had established his own private prison. This man, called Dado, was deeply unpopular, and many locals joined the fight against him – and against the British soldiers who were seen (to some extent justifiably, albeit unwittingly) as supporting him. To complicate matters further, Dado was a major player in the regional narco-trade. The British had effectively blundered into a drugs turf war with neither the knowledge nor the awareness to deal with it.

These impossibly complicated matters were even further confused by tribal dynamics – something that a senior officer involved in planning the Helmand operation told me 'we completely ignored'.[36] We will look at the failures of the British counternarcotics mission in chapter 7 below. Suffice it to say now that the situation the British found themselves in was akin to a poker game where a group of seasoned professionals was joined by a rich, overconfident 'greenhorn'. This newcomer was not leaving any time soon, and he could benefit whoever used his strength to best advantage. And so the parties played him into the game. In this they were assisted by the newcomer's confidence that he was a true expert. It did not go well for the British.

The British army deploys its brigades in six-month rotations. With each tour, the situation became worse, and each brigade adopted new 'strategies'. One brigade might focus on 'mowing the lawn': clearing areas that would again be occupied by Taliban, who would then need to be cleared again – just like mowing a lawn. One reason these 'Taliban' returned was that they were, in fact, local farmers and they had nowhere else to go; they were defending their homes against foreigners.

Body counts would feature regularly as a measure of success. That brigade might then be followed by one that focused on a less 'kinetic' approach, with 'influence' as its keynote.[37] The next brigade might again concentrate on body counts, and so on. All claimed to be 'doing counterinsurgency', a 1950s vintage tactic supposedly focused on 'protecting the population'. Clearly the six-month rotation did not lend itself to awareness of what was an almost impenetrably complex political ecosystem.

But the population wanted primarily to be protected against heavy fighting. It wanted 'security' – and security meant being safe not just from the 'real' Taliban, but from all forms of military action. All too often the fighting was caused by unsuccessful efforts on the part of the British army to protect the people by attacking those they believed to be 'real' Taliban. As we shall see, these assaults – and the inevitable Taliban responses – caused the death of thousands of people. A soldier who was heavily involved in the operation in its early days estimated that in the first 18 months up to 6,000 people were killed in Helmand.[38]

The Taliban that they and, later, the Americans fought were often largely Helmandis – not 'Pakistanis' or Afghans from other provinces.[39] As we have seen, Helmandis called those *aslee* Taliban. Many of the men NATO was fighting believed they were engaged in the kind of territorial defence against a well-armed, superbly trained foreign aggressor that in other circumstances (such as the French resistance) might be regarded as heroic. One commander of a British training team attached to the Afghan army said that he was often fighting what amounted to a 'neighbourhood watch'.[40] They were, to all intents and purposes, the same kind of people who had fought the Soviet army. Of course, in those days the anti-Soviet resistance were our heroes. The same kind of tribal complexities and local considerations that prevailed in the days of the Soviet occupation – and indeed in the period afterwards – prevailed during the British and US occupation. Tribes were fighting tribes, rivalries were played out and feuds were continued, and the British were played into some of them. To make matters worse, the British were almost entirely oblivious to the fact that they were seen to be supporting a totally discredited government, dominated by what Michael Martin describes as a 'warlord polity'.[41]

As one baleful year made way for the next, the situation of an undermanned British garrison grew worse. At one point, the British were taking 150 casualties a week, most of them wounded.[42] Despite the heavy fighting, control of much of the province passed to the 'real' Taliban, with their ramshackle but efficient courts and their administration, which certainly outperformed the Karzai government in terms of effectiveness and relative probity. Michael Martin summarizes matters thus: 'The British intervention had been a godsend for the Taliban movement. The presence of foreigners, particularly the British, who engaged in judicious [sic] use of firepower reminiscent of the Soviet military, made funding and recruitment non-issues for them.'[43]

It was only with the US surge in 2009 and 2010 that matters began to improve slightly for the British, largely because many of the problems they were dealing with were passed on to the US Marine Corps. Once again, as in Iraq, the British had been bailed out by US troops, which could have been used elsewhere with far greater effectiveness to the overall mission. The problems that were handed over included the narco-town of Sangin, which had cost the British army a third of its casualties. As one government advisor put it, the American surge 'relegated Britain from being the dominant player in the south, to the custodian of a relatively small slice of Helmand'.[44]

This did not impress a US military command that was keen to take advantage of the temporary uplift in forces provided by President Obama's surge. For ultimately, the province was no more important to the overall effort in the country than it had been when General Richards asked 'Where's Helmand?' The commander of all international forces in 2009, General Stanley McChrystal, echoed Richards when he asked: 'Can someone tell me why the [US] Marines were sent to Helmand?'[45]

As with Richards in 2006, to his way of thinking the really important front was Kandahar: that was where the war would be won or lost. Kandahar was by far the largest city in Southern Afghanistan – indeed it was Afghanistan's second city. It was there that Mullah Omar had begun his mission in the early 1990s, and there that he had set up his capital. And the city was still the heartland of Mullah Omar's Taliban. Why then, thought McChrystal, was a far smaller force being sent to the metropolis of Kandahar than to Helmand? The reason was stark and simple, as McChrystal must have known: the British had been overwhelmed in the province and the men they called 'the Taliban' essentially ran it.

Town after town was handed over to the US forces, including Sangin. There, in a microcosm of the overall mission, the British had engaged in hopeless and repetitive operations against villages quickly reoccupied by Taliban and others resisting the British – Sisyphean operations, one commentator called them.[46] The Americans understood that the 'British were sensitive about needing an American rescue' and so little was made of it in public. But as the WikiLeaks files showed, in private US government officials were very clear about what had happened: the UK was 'not up to the task of securing Helmand'.[47]

The British 'strategy'

Although now outnumbered two to one by US forces, the presence of the British forces dragged on. They rested their efforts on three pillars: first, reforming and training the Afghan security forces; second, ensuring that Afghan governance (the term 'governance' is a development term co-opted by the military) was 'credible'; and third, economic development. They continue to call this set of aspirations a 'strategy'.[48] The first pillar – rendering the Afghan armed forces capable of securing the province – is regarded by many ordinary British soldiers as little short of ridiculous. Many Afghans take the same view. A very senior

Afghan army officer told me that 'the ANA [Afghan National Army] is far less capable than the [Soviet-trained equivalent] army of 1989'. He went on to say that there was little that was 'national' about the army; when NATO left, the army's coherence would disappear and it would fragment into militias with various ethnic and factional interests.[49] For several years the ANA's desertion rates have run at up to 30 per cent per year.

By the end of 2012, and after ten years of development, only one of the ANA's 23 brigades was capable of acting independently – and even then only with US or foreign advisors.[50] Much of the army is now either infiltrated or (just as importantly) suspected of having been infiltrated by 'real' Taliban. This infiltration has produced the so-called 'green on blue' attacks, when Afghan police and soldiers have killed and injured foreign troops. These had become so prevalent by September 2012 that the British decided to scale down their cooperation with the ANA.[51]

The second arm of the British 'strategy' – developing 'governance' – depended largely on Governor Mangal (Daud's successor). He was a competent technocrat, and the British thought they could work with him. But in September 2012 he was dismissed by President Karzai and replaced with General Naim Baloch, formerly of the National Directorate of Security (the intelligence service set up and initially trained by the KGB in the 1980s). A senior British official has described the general as being 'rather too close to Sher Mohammed Akhundzada'; the British 'did not welcome' this development (something of an understatement).[52] In terms of influence over how Helmand would develop, Mangal's dismissal was the last straw.

As for the third element of the 'strategy', Helmand's economy depends almost entirely on opium. The province produces nearly half of the world's opium, and until that changes, any other forms of 'economic development' are bound to fail. The British had barely begun to understand the economics, let alone the deeply complex human geography of Helmand.

Then, with the end of the war in Iraq, UK and US special forces, and other assets such as reconnaissance satellites, were moved to work on Afghanistan, and especially Helmand. A new military approach was introduced: the 'capture or kill policy'. Tactically, it was based on high-tempo operations, primarily against the makers and planters of the improvised explosive devices (IEDs) that were causing NATO forces such high casualties. This drew assets away from trying to understand what was really driving the 'insurgency'. As we will see in chapter 3, there was at least as much killing as capturing. 'Taliban' fighters at ever-lower levels were targeted. 'This had very little strategic effect on the "Taliban" movement . . . but often killed "Taliban" fighters who were no more than resistance figures for their communities.'[53]

This tactic, like so much else in the current phase of the Afghan War, was more than a little redolent of the desperate days of the Vietnam War, when the CIA instituted Operation Phoenix to target key Viet Cong officials. After that war, in 1975, a US veteran, Colonel Harry Summers, returned to Vietnam as part of a delegation. While there, he met a North Vietnamese counterpart, one Colonel Tu, who spoke some English. 'You know, you never defeated us on the battle-field', said Summers. 'That is true', replied Tu. 'It is also irrelevant.'[54] The British army won every battle it fought in Helmand. That is also irrelevant.

Perspectives

In the words of Britain's former ambassador to Afghanistan, Sir Sherard Cowper-Coles, the whole Helmand campaign had been a 'half-baked effort' and 'probably a strategic mistake'.[55] By the end of 2012, Helmand had cost the US more casualties than any other province – indeed, more Americans had been killed in Helmand than British soldiers.[56] A mission that had begun with high hopes of resurrecting Britain's military reputation in the eyes of its American allies had resulted only in reinforcing the American view that the British were not to be relied upon. By 2012, the British were drawing down their presence in the province. By the end of 2014, they will have withdrawn almost all their combat troops, leaving just a few from the special forces and trainers.

The British reputation in Helmand as rapacious and malevolent 'Angrez' did not improve as the years went on. Even in 2007, as a member of the British Mission, I was surprised to be told that many, if not most, Helmandis believed the British were failing deliberately, so bad did things seem.[57] The reasoning was simple: everyone knew that the British were technically highly capable and well organized. Similarly, everyone knew that the British had promised development and reconstruction – after all, they had taken over the Provincial Reconstruction Team HQ from the Americans. Yet there had been very little sign of such promises being fulfilled. 'We shouldn't be surprised', went the reasoning, 'they are failing on purpose. They are taking their revenge for the beating we gave them at Maiwand.'

Suspicion of the British became even stronger. Many began to believe that they were working closely with what Helmandis called the *aslee* Taliban – the 'real' Taliban – as opposed to the local militias comprised mainly of Helmandis, which the British called 'Taliban'. This reasoning seems to be based on the fact that Britain has very close historical ties with Pakistan. Indeed, many Helmandis believe that Britain never gave up effective control of the country. All Afghans – and especially Helmandis – believe, to some degree rightly, that the Pakistani Inter-Services Intelligence is behind the 'real' Taliban. Therefore the British *must* be aware of (and indeed be behind) much of what the 'real' Taliban do. These stories culminated with the rumours in 2009 that the British army was transporting Taliban fighters in helicopters to the north of Afghanistan.[58] As their time in Helmand went on, further rumours did the rounds concerning weapons supplies. Some local Taliban commanders themselves were convinced by them, and were said to be outraged when the British broke what the Taliban thought was a 'deal' and attacked them![59]

All this plays into a larger narrative of the West, and particularly Britain, dividing Islam, in order to weaken it – and of course (in the British case) eventually to restore the Empire. Clearly not everyone believes these nonsensical stories. Nonetheless, they gain enough traction in a society that has a largely oral tradition and that is by nature suspicious of foreigners, especially the 'Angrez'. I was told by a senior NATO intelligence officer and a very senior diplomat separately that President Karzai himself believes them.

It is ideas like this that the British will leave behind. There will be little talk of any British legacy of democracy and human rights.

The British intruded into a civil war of 30 years' duration without the slightest understanding of that environment. So what now? One thing is almost certain: barring a comprehensive political settlement involving all relevant actors *including* Pakistan and Iran, that war will continue. It will, however, continue without major British involvement. It may well be that the 'real' Taliban has a role to play in Helmand and indeed Afghanistan. It is far more likely, however, that the underlying dynamics which have always been present will reassert themselves. The warlords and their families will continue to feud over the vast opium revenues, and land disputes will continue to drive smaller-scale squabbles and vendettas.

At the height of their involvement in Afghanistan, UK forces – the second largest of all international deployments – constituted about 9 per cent of the international force there. They occupied less than 1 per cent of the country's territory, which contained about 1 per cent of its population. Of Afghanistan's 400-plus districts, they believed they had 'stabilized' three – all of them in just one of the country's 34 provinces. Those three districts had, of course, been 'stable' (insofar as the word is applicable to Afghanistan) before the British arrived. They believed that Helmand, regarded by most Afghans as remote and politically insignificant compared to the key cities of Kabul and Kandahar, was 'the decisive campaign of the whole war'.[60] It will be up to history to decide whether this was the case – or whether the British (and the Americans who bailed them out) were gulled by a savvy Taliban, supported by Pakistan's extremely capable Inter-Services Intelligence, into focusing huge tactical efforts on a strategically irrelevant area dominated by 'narco-lords'.

In February 2013 on a visit to the UK, President Karzai expressed the view that Helmand had been 'the wrong place' for British forces to be sent, and that for all the claims of the British to improved 'security', the situation there had been better before the British arrived. In saying this he was surely only stating what was obvious to most residents of Helmand.[61]

CHAPTER 2

Military Suffering

It's all forgotten now, isn't it – the war in Iraq? To all intents and purposes, the British ended their involvement in 2009, dropping the problem of Basra into the lap of the Americans. How long ago it all seems – those daily reports of British soldiers, their lack of helicopters, the horrendous attacks involving sinister new 'improvised explosive devices' . . .

Occasionally there will be a reminder of that ill-starred war: Tony Blair might pop up somewhere in the UK, where a protestor will loudly denounce him as a war criminal; new allegations might emerge of the abuse of detainees or worse (or old allegations might be litigated in the courts).

Helmand still occasionally – and often literally – explodes into public awareness with some appalling disaster befalling a small group of British soldiers. However, as Caroline Wyatt, a senior BBC journalist with extensive experience of reporting the Afghan War, told me: 'It is getting harder and harder to get Afghan stories on air or on the screen.'[1] Media coverage now is generally reduced to the baleful, dutiful ritual of reciting the secular litany: 'Today another soldier from the . . . Regiment was killed in an explosion in Southern Helmand. His family has been informed.' Two days later, there will be the naming: 'The Ministry of Defence today named Private ... as the soldier who was killed in an explosion on Sunday. His commanding officer has said that Private ... was an example to his platoon ... it is the end of what would have been a fine career. Our hearts go out to his girlfriend Emma and their daughters Rosie and Genna.'

After over 600 deaths in Iraq or Afghanistan, most soldiers who have served there know someone who has been killed. In those tight little family-like groups, the regiments, every dead soldier is remembered, by name, by each of his comrades. In more amorphous units, people will remember the young officer in the bar, or the soldier who used to drop into the office at the depot occasionally for a coffee.

Here I would beg just a moment of personal reflection. I was part of a small, close-knit group, one of the most heavily deployed units in the Royal Navy. We, in turn, were part of a larger tri-service outfit, whose people were constantly moving in and out of operational tours.

We were based with our sister units at a large army base in eastern England. One August, my ship (a so-called 'stone frigate' – a shore base, but none the less naval for all that) hosted a royal visit. Clearly, security is a vital part of any royal visit, and we were fortunate to have the assistance of a superb team of soldiers. What was for us, frankly, a rather protocol-ridden, awkward and largely unnecessary palaver was for them 'another day at the office'.

I was one of the two people responsible for organizing the visit. The base security officer (for whom the word 'impossible' did not exist) detailed one of his NCOs to oversee the security element of the trip. Corporal Bryant was someone whose easy competence reflected a huge amount of training and professionalism. She was someone who was clearly heading for success – early success. Everything went well and smoothly on the day, largely thanks to Corporal Bryant. She was waiting for her deployment to Afghanistan, she told me afterwards. We wished her well.

In mid-June 2008, I was travelling on a train and casually glanced at a newspaper front page. There was Corporal Bryant. She had been killed a couple of days earlier, with four other soldiers in Helmand. Corporal Sarah Bryant was the first female soldier to be killed in the Afghan War. On a previous tour in Iraq, her American commanding officer had called her 'a credit to the British Army'. She was exactly that.

I knew other soldiers killed in Helmand. I remember Private Damian Wright and Private Ben Ford of the Mercian Regiment, who would breeze into the tearoom at the Helmand PRT every day or so, always ready with a joke. They were killed by an IED in September 2007. At drinks in their memory, their friend told me how strange it was to wake up every day and not see 'Wrighty' in the next camp-bed, ready with a witty remark. Ford's practical jokes marked him out, he said.

The loss of these highly professional people leaves a gap in the army. That gap will (callous but true) be filled. All who deploy on operations know that ultimately they are replaceable and that the operations clocks will not stop if they are killed. The organization will move on. That is not the case for the families of the dead. For them the gap will never be filled.

The wounded

In *The Three Trillion Dollar War*, a masterly study of the cost to the US – and indeed the world – of the Iraq War, Linda Bilmes and Joseph Stiglitz make the essential point that almost every successive major war brings a higher survival rate for those wounded. In the Second World War, 1.6 men were wounded for every man killed; in Vietnam (for the US) the figure had grown to 2.6. In the recent Iraq and Afghan wars, the ratio of wounded survivors to dead soldiers is more than seven to one.[2] There are a number of reasons for this. In our recent wars, the use of body armour to cover vital areas has significantly reduced fatalities.

There has, however, been a commensurate increase in amputees: those who would, in times gone by, have been killed by blast or shrapnel now suffer traumatic amputation, leaving torsos relatively unscathed. As in previous wars, medical science has worked hard to improve the chances of soldiers' survival. Combat trauma medicine is now right at the forefront of the world of 'accident and emergency'. Within that field, there is nowhere better in the world of trauma medicine than the hospital at Camp Bastion, the huge British base in the southern Afghan desert. With a staff of 254, including 85 Americans and 15 Danes, this so-called 'field hospital' works at an almost incredible pace. In one week, a Cambridge researcher saw 174 casualties brought in, including 23 who needed amputations;[3] more blood products are used here than in the whole of Scotland.[4] As a result, a staggering 98 per cent of those who make it to the hospital survive.

How many wounded have we sustained?

How many British servicemen have passed through the safe hands of this and other field hospitals in Afghanistan? The bare figures on the number wounded and on the broad degree of severity of injures are published regularly by the Ministry of Defence. As of 18 January 2013, some 2,076 soldiers had been admitted to field hospitals in Afghanistan, categorized as 'wounded in action'; 293 UK personnel had been categorized as 'very seriously injured' (VSI – 'of such severity that life or reason is imminently endangered');[5] and a further 300 as 'seriously injured' (SI – 'where there is immediate concern but life or reason is not imminently endangered').[6] Clearly, if there is no 'immediate concern', a soldier will not be categorized as either SI or VSI. Consequently, a traumatic amputation or shooting where there is no immediate concern for the survival of the soldier would not be categorized as SI or VSI: he would be 'wounded in action'. In addition, 4,368 military and civilian personnel have been admitted for non-battle-related injuries or illness.

There have been 6,440 aeromedical evacuations of UK military and civilian personnel.[7]

By early 2013, 440 soldiers had been killed and more than 2,600 had been wounded with varying degrees of severity. Thus the 1:7 figure mentioned by Stiglitz and Bilmes holds as true for British as it does for American soldiers – testament to the skills of the medics and the effectiveness of the body armour now issued to soldiers. The raw figures reflect the intensity of combat in Helmand. There is no doubt that the British casualty figure – already high relative to other such campaigns – would have been even greater had it not been for the technical advances in body armour and medical care. In previous wars, the level of savagery encountered might have produced fatalities in the low thousands rather than the mid-hundreds (which in any event is a considerable figure for a deployed force of less than 10,000).

A colleague of mine, Dr Peter Lee, a former RAF chaplain, was contacted by a major serving in one of the units involved in heavy combat. The officer wrote:

At midnight the first inbound medevac [helicopter with wounded from a battle – a sort of airborne ambulance] of the day will be given the letter A, the next the letter B, etc. until you run out of letters and begin all over again with AA. Guys are talking about hitting RR [i.e. 44 missions] in a 24-hour period – most of which will carry multiple casualties from IED strikes. And that's happening day after day.[8]

While the Ministry of Defence is necessarily open about overall numbers, when it comes to the nature of injuries suffered by these hundreds of seriously injured soldiers, it is far more coy. Dr Lee submitted a Freedom of Information request to try to determine how many soldiers had suffered from amputations and the severity of such injuries. Official figures indicated that there had been 247 soldiers who had suffered traumatic amputations.[9] Dr Lee then asked for a breakdown of the number of limb amputations and an indication of their severity.[10]

The reply was instructive:

> The information you requested on a detailed breakdown of the number of limb amputations falls within the scope of the Freedom of Information qualified exemption, section 26 . . . any release of more detailed information such as the specific type of amputation would enable the enemy to build up a fuller picture of the effect of the conflict on the UK forces which could threaten operational security.[11]

This, of course, is an instance of the old saw 'might provide aid and comfort to the enemy'.[12] And generally speaking, it targets those who are set to provide embarrassment and discomfort to the Ministry of Defence and its servants and agents, rather than aid and comfort to the enemy. It is occasionally used to prevent the publication in army journals of articles by serving officers on matters of professional interest. The enemy knows full well that its IEDs produce casualties and it is well aware of the nature of those casualties – not least because civilians suffer the consequences, as well as soldiers. It beggars reasonable belief that revealing the number and nature of such injuries would be of any benefit to the enemy. Rather what we have is a desire to conceal from the public the true nature and number of casualties.

In similar vein, nowhere in the MOD statistics is there any indication of the nature of any injury, beyond a global figure for amputations.[13] But there are very common injuries which may, over time, prove extremely serious. One such – an injury that is common among soldiers in Iraq and Afghanistan – is traumatic brain injury. This is caused by the tremendous shock of improvised explosive devices; even if there is no obvious physical injury, the brain may be severely damaged. The scale of such injuries is of serious public concern in the US, where in 2008 a leading medical journal, the *New England Journal of Medicine*, published a study of infantry soldiers who had returned from Iraq. It concluded: 'of 2,525 soldiers, 124 (4.9%) reported injuries with loss of consciousness, 260 (10.3%) reported injuries with altered mental status'.[14]

In other words, over 15 per cent of infantry soldiers suffered what might euphemistically be called a very serious blow to the head. In 2008, in the thick of both campaigns, 585 British men and women suffered such injuries. Even this was a figure that, it was thought, might be the 'tip of the iceberg'.[15] And far more have experienced such 'blows to the head' since. As one expert put it, there are serious concerns that this form of injury, which 'can lead to long-term problems – from depression and anxiety to violence and relationship break-up', all too often goes undiagnosed.[16]

Post-discharge care

Wounded soldiers are generally well taken care of while in the armed services and have access to the best medical care. They are often permitted to remain in the services, despite their injuries. Their real problems start when they leave.

Those who have never served in the armed forces (and indeed many who have) believe that the services are like a family and 'look after their own' – that soldiers display lifelong loyalty to each other in a way that is not found in other professions. Indeed there is some truth to this (as we shall see). However, when it comes to the Ministry of Defence, the key interest is not loyalty, but money; and when a soldier comes between the MOD and its money, there are few limits to the ministry's ruthlessness.

One of the young men in my unit, 'Peter', had been recruited as a very talented graduate and speaker of Arabic and Persian.[17] His intellect, physical fitness and prize-winning performance in junior officer training ensured that he was regarded as an extremely promising young officer. He was expected to go on to complete commando training, and after one or two tours in so-called 'special duties' would be a candidate for selection to the Special Air Service (SAS) or the Special Boat Service (SBS). But this was not to be: in 2006, he was seriously injured in a bomb attack. After completing initial rehabilitation at the Defence Medical Rehabilitation Centre in Hedley Court, he decided that he did not wish to remain in the service – not that the injury caused by the IED would have allowed him to do so anyway. Unable now to become a journalist or a diplomat (as he had hoped) and physically incapable of joining one of the reserve special forces units, he needed to acquire some means of support. In applying for compensation for his injuries, his first port of call was the Ministry of Defence.

Initially he was told that, as a reservist, he was not entitled to any compensation or to a pension of any kind. This was incorrect, but it required lawyers to set matters right. His excellent solicitors advised him that, because of the nature of the incident (which would not have occurred if proper procedures had been followed), he would be entitled to further compensation. Over the next three years – even after it admitted that negligence had been a major factor – the MOD fought tooth and nail to reduce its financial obligations.

Peter's solicitors sought out leading medical experts to testify as to his diagnosis and prognosis. The MOD wanted to show that Peter's injuries would not unduly affect his 'quality of life'. But it found itself unable to track down any genuine experts to testify that his injuries were not serious – largely because they were. The only 'expert' they could find who was prepared to testify had received his doctorate not from a reputable British university, but from a war-torn state in West Africa, in less than the time it generally took. Peter recalls being interviewed by this man. Upon learning that Peter used to enjoy martial arts, the 'expert' asked why he could not continue with this pursuit, perhaps taking on others with the same condition. Peter replied: 'I have a compound fracture of the skull; I am not going to allow someone repeatedly to punch or kick me in the head, particularly as I cannot easily defend myself.'

The MOD also attempted to play down Peter's military potential and his skills. It searched high and low in Peter's military records for evidence to substantiate its contention that his potential had been exaggerated, and at last had found something. All potential officers have to undergo a three-day residential selection course, where they must perform a number of exercises. In all but one of these, Peter had scored well above average – indeed he had excelled. But in a single, rather trivial test (concerned with his ability to convey a piece of wood from one side of a gym to another) his score had been below average. As a result, according to the MOD, Peter was a 'substandard soldier'.

Most officers have long forgotten their initial interviews, conducted at desolate military bases long before actual training starts. The results of these tests are never, ever referred to once the officer is trained: good or bad, they are completely irrelevant to actual service of any kind. On combat service, Peter had met and exceeded all the expectations of his chain of command. It now took months – during which time statements were laboriously gathered from every officer under whom Peter had served (including me) – to show that, in fact, he had been a superb soldier.

The whole process took three years – three years of worry for a man who was already seriously damaged and at risk from the evils that beset the newly severely disabled. It took huge moral courage and strength on his part to continue to assert his rights in the face of a vast organization with unlimited resources. In the end justice was done. But as he says:

I was lucky. I was fortunate in having good friends and good education. I was able to access good lawyers and have the support of a wide
network of competent and supportive friends. Not many soldiers
have these advantages. If I had been alone it was the sort of thing
which could have driven me over the edge; after everything that had
gone before, the pain and disabilities, this was the kind of thing that
can break you.

Peter has used some of the money he was awarded to set up a website
for injured soldiers, in an attempt to ensure that they have the same
access to expertise and care as he had.

There is no doubt that Peter's case is not unusual. Hundreds, if not
thousands, of wounded servicemen and servicewomen have experienced the same obstructive approach.

In the course of my legal work I have also come across veterans who
have received no compensation or assistance of any kind. One man I
remember had lost his best friend in a shooting and had himself
suffered severe hearing loss from IED explosions; he was clearly not
coping well, but he had received no help whatsoever. This was largely
because he had not asked for it, and indeed many veterans do not. Yet
there is plenty of assistance available – if you know where to look. We
examine the role of charities in chapter 5.

Injuries you cannot see – the reality

In the First World War it was known as 'shell shock'. The most famous
of the hundreds of thousands of sufferers were the poets Wilfred Owen
and Siegfried Sassoon, whose experiences were recounted by Pat Barker
in the *Regeneration* trilogy. In the Second World War the term was 'war
neurosis'. In the classic work *Second Chance*, infantryman Stephen
Weiss describes fighting his way up Italy, and then, when his unit had
been overrun, behind the lines with the French resistance. Six months

of heroic combat and daily fear of death proved just too much for him: when the American army fought its way through the German lines and it was time for him to return to his unit, he ran 'as all men will, some sooner than others'. He was saved from a 20-year jail sentence only by the fortuitous arrival of a forward-thinking psychiatrist.[18] But many were not so lucky. In the equally savagely dangerous world of RAF Bomber Command, post-traumatic stress disorder (PTSD) was known as 'lack of moral fibre' and its consequences were immediate demotion and public shame. Vietnam and the Falklands brought new terminology and new victims. The mental health charity Combat Stress is still assisting no fewer than 200 Falklands veterans who still suffer PTSD more than three decades after the war.[19]

No one is unmarked by their involvement in war. For tens of thousands of people in the United Kingdom, their war-time experiences are, and will remain, the central event in their lives.

Every single day, thousands of men and women in the UK gaze into the middle distance and recall their time in Iraq and Afghanistan. Whether they were clerks at one of the big bases or infantrymen in constant danger of being maimed or annihilated, they all reflect daily on what they were doing and why. But many feel there is no point in talking about it to outsiders – anyone who was not there will only wonder 'what all the fuss is about'. They may sense that in some way their experiences are beyond the comprehension of any 'normal' person. Or they may believe (often correctly) that other people simply do not want to know.

A former soldier may engage an old friend in conversation and experience a surge of relief – 'Wow, someone *is* interested!' But then the friend will abruptly change the subject, perhaps after mention of something that is totally alien to a civilian – maybe the recollection of a shooting or the relived fear of being hit by a mortar bomb while asleep. After a while, the soldier will wait until he is with former comrades to talk about his or her experiences; as those old comrades drift away, the veteran will not talk to anyone at all, and the occasional 'melancholy moment' will be put down to moodiness – the inquiry 'What's wrong with you now?' eliciting a muttered 'nothing' as he turns away. Eventually the former soldier will keep his thoughts to himself. Sometimes these will be bottled up for years; sometimes there will be an occasional outburst.

This is *not* post-traumatic stress disorder: it is an entirely normal, ordered processing of experience, much like any other. Post-traumatic stress disorder is far more severe. The term entered the psychiatric lexicon in the 1980s. The symptoms can take many forms: re-experiencing what happened; reliving the trauma (or conversely an inability to remember anything at all about it); 'hyper-arousal symptoms' such as insomnia, irritability or excessive alertness; survivor guilt; and, of course, anger and hostility to the system that originally put the person in that position.[20] These are all common symptoms after any traumatic event; what triggers a diagnosis of PTSD is likely to be that they last longer than a month.

Like most mental disorders, PTSD is the result of a complex interplay of factors: seldom is it the simple cause and effect to be found in physical trauma. The experience of someone being in a situation where he thinks he is about to die may be a serious contributory factor, but it is unlikely to be the only factor. Within the services, there are all sorts of psychological supports available – these stem from the bonding and 'belonging' that is created by training and working under adversity, from friendships and from shared responsibilities. But these supports are lost when an individual leaves the armed forces.

PTSD, once diagnosed, is very often successfully treated. Treatment can range from cognitive behavioural therapy (where patients are guided through their responses to trauma), coping strategies and art therapy, all the way through to individual trauma-focused therapies. Detailed programmes can include occupational therapy and extensive counselling. In the UK, patients might be invited to attend residential sessions at dedicated centres run by the specialist charity Combat Stress or at 'breakaway centres', run cooperatively by Combat Stress and other service charities.[21] Of course the key problem lies in identifying those suffering from PTSD, especially in a population that is not renowned for seeking help.

How many will suffer from PTSD?

In the US, study after study of wars – from the US Civil War in the 1860s,[22] through the two world wars and Vietnam – suggests that 3–4 per cent of combat veterans suffer from full-blown PTSD and that it can take many years before it manifests itself. 'Some take longer, some much shorter, but ten years is a reasonable average', says former military psychologist Professor Ian Palmer.[23] He makes the point that we have to be careful about quoting huge numbers – for example, the US Department of Veterans Affairs suggests that up to 18 per cent of veterans from Iraq or Afghanistan could be suffering from PTSD:[24] 'One problem facing us all is the increasing tendency in the psychiatric profession, particularly in the United States, to turn painful yet normal and ordinary human psychological processes following life events into serious clinical "diagnoses".'[25]

Palmer believes that one compelling reason for being wary of such figures is the need to protect the interests of veterans as a whole: 'There are dangerous urban myths around. One of them is that ex-soldiers come out of the services damaged and dangerous. In other words, overstating the PTSD problem carries with it the serious risk that servicemen might be stigmatized.'

Nonetheless, even with the figure of 3–4 per cent suggested by historical evidence, we are faced with thousands of people who will be seriously affected long after their exposure to combat or other forms of unusual stress. Some authorities even place the figure as high as 6 per cent.[26] Only time will tell which figure is most accurate; but whichever it is, it represents a great deal of suffering for a great many people. Over 190,000 people have served in operations in or around Iraq or Afghanistan,[27] and a figure of 4 per cent implies around 8,000 sufferers. It needs to be remembered that PTSD is a medical condition and must be treated as such.

It is important to be clear that the armed forces are, with respect to mental health, remarkably fit. The army, in particular, resembles a group of tribes and functions like a family. As in most families, there are good and bad members, and people remember their relationships and experiences differently. Again as in most families, there comes a time when the members have to leave home, and some handle this better than others. Losing the support of the family can be damaging. The figures bear out the essentially healthy atmosphere of service life. The Defence Statistics Agency publishes quarterly figures on those assessed for mental health disorders. The 'UK Armed Forces Mental Health Report' shows that less than 0.5 per cent of servicemen present with mental health issues in the normal course of affairs.[28] This is far lower than for the rest of society, where problems such as depression clog up doctors' surgeries. Some figures suggest that as many as 25 per cent of adults experience diagnosable mental conditions each year.[29]

Is there a 'veterans' time bomb' ticking?

There is a general perception in some quarters of the media that soldiers' experience of combat is very likely to result in some form of serious medically definable condition, and that vast numbers of such cases constitute a ticking 'time bomb' of mentally scarred and damaged soldiers.

The *Daily Mail* has reported that 500 servicemen a month are asking to be treated for traumatic disorders after serving in Afghanistan and Iraq.[30] It repeated the old saw that more veterans of the Falklands campaign have killed themselves than were killed in combat – a claim for which there is absolutely no reliable evidence whatsoever.[31] Allan Mallinson, who served as an army officer and now contributes to the

Daily Mail, wrote there that 'perhaps up to 25 per cent of the homeless' are veterans.[32] The fact that he qualified the statement with 'perhaps' and 'up to' may be significant, but it nonetheless reflects a commonly held view that military service produces homeless people.

In 2009, the National Association of Probation Officers produced a shocking survey, which claimed that 8,500 ex-servicemen were in prison (almost 10 per cent of the total prison population), and that many thousands more were on probation.[33] Partly in response to this and other claims, the highly respected Howard League for Penal Reform researched the question of how many veterans were in jail. It concluded that, in fact, about 3.5 per cent of prisoners were ex-servicemen (and many had left the forces a considerable time earlier).[34] The figure was lower in Scotland, where about 1.7 per cent of prisoners had a service background. The Howard League points out that the issue here is not the propensity for soldiers to commit crime (indeed, statistics suggest that servicemen in general are *less likely* to commit crime than are others of their background and age group).

However, for those with extensive combat experience there does seem to be an increased likelihood of violent offending. Evidence published in the medical journal *The Lancet* indicates that, of the 13,856 serving and ex-serving military personnel studied, as many as 20 per cent of those under 30 with particularly frequent exposure to combat had committed violent offences at some point during their lives, as against 6.7 per cent of other males of similar age.[35]

These statistics are difficult to draw definitive conclusions from, as many of these men were violent before they entered the military. As Professor Simon Wessely of Kings College London, one of those who conducted the study, puts it, 'The military don't select chess-playing choir boys. They select people who often come from difficult and aggressive backgrounds and they're the ones who are most likely to end up in the parts of the military that do the actual fighting.' However, the study does suggest that a small but significant association between exposure to traumatic events while deployed and subsequent violent offending. Post-deployment alcohol misuse and PTSD and other mental health problems were also strong predictors of violent offending.[36] It should be stressed, however, that the Kings College study makes it very clear that the vast majority of soldiers make a healthy transition to 'normal' life.

Providing help

Dr Hugh Milroy of the leading charity Veterans Aid sums up the situation thus:

> Media output suggesting that those leaving current operations could be heading straight for prison has created a widespread public perception that is simply not supported by research or Veterans Aid's considerable experience – and as a key frontline charity for veterans in crisis in the UK, we would be seeing this. The reality is that the vast bulk of those leaving military service make a seamless transition to civilian life.[37]

The true challenge is not that Afghanistan (or other) veterans are more likely to commit offences, but that they need to have access to help and advice (such as that offered by Veterans Aid) whenever they need it. There is no doubt that, despite the resilience and toughness of our ex-servicemen and women, many of them will need extensive help. This is owed to them by a state that has used them and, in many cases, simply let them go. That same state has made little effort actively to ensure that these men and women have the care they need – instead that care is devolved to the 'third sector'.

Veterans want (and have earned) at least the same privileges as everyone else: they want dignity, work and a place in society. The truth is that they are at least as capable as any other element of society. The insinuation in much of the recent media coverage has been that the population at large should treat ex-soldiers with suspicion and distrust, yet paradoxically regard them as 'our heroes'.

The legacy of Afghanistan (and indeed Iraq) has been tragic for hundreds of families and soldiers. Their anguish will be lifelong. But it is absolutely not the case that thousands of mentally ill, criminally inclined, embittered ex-soldiers are being released into the 'community'. Those men and women who need help should be made aware of the resources that are available – and these resources should be available when they are required. Veterans deserve this, at the very least.

Perspectives

The UK has seen 440 servicemen and women killed in a ten-year period.[38] This is the equivalent of an entire battalion being taken out of the line: as we have only 30 or so of those in total, clearly in one respect this is a significant figure. On the other hand, compared to the casualties taken by British forces in the two world wars, the numbers are very low indeed. As one academic colleague pointed out to me, 600 men were killed on an *average* day in the First World War, and some days witnessed death tolls of many thousands.

In the Second World War, a single bomber station, RAF East Kirkby – just one of dozens of such bases – sustained 848 killed in less than three years. It was not uncommon for Bomber Command to lose hundreds of men in a single night of raids over Germany. For example, the raid on Nuremberg on the night of 30/31 March 1944 cost 545 aircrew – a hundred more than the total number of troops lost in Afghanistan over ten years.[39]

Losses of several hundred dead in a single day were not unusual for the Royal Navy, either – especially when a large ship like HMS *Glorious* or HMS *Hood* went down, each with the loss of well over 1,000 crew.

British army battalions often took savage casualties fighting the Germans, and it was not unheard of for entire companies of a hundred men to be replaced *several times over* during the campaigns in Italy,

France and Germany, with a few bewildered and very lucky survivors lasting throughout a campaign. There were no six-month tours with a two-week leave package for those soldiers, as there are for soldiers on operations today.

But these are invidious and historically inappropriate comparisons. In wars of choice, fought not by citizen-soldiers but by volunteer professionals, the levels of losses that are acceptable in wars of national survival are simply not to be contemplated. A more precise and instructive comparison would be with our previous so-called 'counterinsurgency' campaigns of the post-colonial era, when the army fought what amounted to a series of wars of imperial withdrawal. It is, incidentally, to these wars that today's military leaders look for their inspiration. When set against these, the Iraq and Afghanistan campaigns take on a considerably less favourable aspect:

- For the immediate post-war generation of soldiers, the defining campaign was a grim and squalid 'small war' that was destined to have global consequences: it resulted in the foundation of Israel in 1948. The Jewish insurgents (or 'terrorists', as they were called at the time) in Palestine killed 236 British soldiers between 1945 and 1947.
- The signature 'counterinsurgency' of the 1950s for the British was the Malaya campaign, which began in 1948 and ended in 1960. It was (and is) considered a success – with some justification. It cost the British army 340 killed.
- The Mau Mau insurgency in Kenya, which took place over roughly the same period, cost the British army 12 fatalities.
- Cyprus was rather less successful, and 371 soldiers were killed.
- In the 1960s, the Oman campaign, a very successful war that was fought, from the British perspective, largely by special forces and military intelligence officers, resulted in 24 killed.
- In the 'Confrontasi' against Indonesian-supported rebels in Borneo, the British sustained 126 deaths.

All these wars were fought with clearly understood objectives: to preserve British rule (as in Kenya or Cyprus); to assist in a smooth transition to local power (as in Malaya); or to aid friendly regimes following a genuine invitation from the local government (as in Oman or Borneo during the 'Confrontasi').

But what about campaigns closer to home? Some 252 British servicemen died in the Falklands War, and in the long, long Northern Ireland operation 763 members of the British armed forces lost their lives. Of course, these were not foreign wars, fought in countries that had nothing in common with 'home': they were fought to defend British territory (or territory credibly understood to be British) from aggression of one kind or another.

Between 2006 and the end of 2012, more soldiers died in the Afghan campaign than in any other 'unconventional' (i.e. counterinsurgency) campaign fought by Britain since the Boer War, which ended in 1902. Of all the foreign wars fought by UK forces since 1945, only the Korean War – an often very high-intensity conflict waged against the Chinese and North Korean armies – surpasses the latest Afghan war in terms of the number of casualties: 1,078 killed in action.

The recent Afghan campaign is the fourth war fought by British forces in Afghanistan. For over a hundred years, the British and Indian armies were constantly engaged in battles and skirmishes on the frontiers of what is now Pakistan and Afghanistan. The largest of these smaller campaigns was the Tirah Campaign of 1898, which resulted in about 400 British fatalities. There were, however, three larger engagements, which are now called 'Anglo-Afghan Wars'. The first was in 1842–43 and was marked (though not ended) by the famous Retreat from Kabul. The retreat left 690 *British* soldiers dead in less than a week; many more Indian troops lost their lives, as did even more civilians. The Second Afghan War, fought between 1878 and 1881, cost 10,000 British or Indian lives – mostly as a result of disease, although 700 British soldiers were killed at the iconic (for Afghans) Battle of Maiwand in 1880. The Third Afghan War, resulting from an Afghan incursion into what is now Pakistan in 1919, left 235 British troops dead.

Over the past decade, a distinctly sentimental approach has been taken to casualties, epitomized by the processions of the coffins of dead soldiers through the streets of Wootton Bassett attended by thousands of people, the vast majority of whom will never have met the soldiers they so visibly mourn. Indeed, very many will never have met any soldiers at all. If wars are to be fought, casualties are to be expected. The soldiers who are killed and wounded today are not victims – they are not the conscript ex-civilians of the First World War. They are professionals, willingly trained in the business of killing, and (by and large) well paid and well treated while they are soldiers. For the most part they love their jobs and love being deployed on operations. Servicemen are under no illusions as to the risks they sign up to. As the young, seriously wounded officer 'Peter' told me: 'I took my chances, but they didn't work out.'

The injured are real casualties, not the victims of inchoate and faceless forces. In looking so closely at the human costs of this war, the key point that must be borne in mind is not 'How terrible! Those poor soldiers . . .' Rather it must be a realistic and firm realization: 'We sent them, now we must take care of the consequences.'

But what about the consequences for those who had no choice in this war – the civilian residents of Helmand?

CHAPTER 3

Killing the Wrong People

We killed a lot of people . . . many of them might have been the wrong
people.[1]

Introduction

The British armed forces are a seriously formidable fighting organization. For 50 years, the services have been entirely professional – and it
shows. In terms of sheer fighting skill, the British people can be sure
that they will be very well defended indeed, should they ever be attacked
by an enemy army. Certainly the Taliban, despite their own formidable
tactics and fighting skills, have found that, in every engagement fought
on roughly equal numerical terms, they have come off significantly
worse than the highly tuned soldiers of the British armed forces, with
their access to extensive air cover and artillery support.

It can be very dangerous for anyone who gets between the soldiers
and their targets: that is the nature of any war, and particularly one
fought with high explosives and automatic weapons. The Taliban blame
all civilian casualties on the 'occupying forces', on the grounds that there
would be none if the British/US/Canadians were not there: they would

not have to destroy the lives of dozens of people in market squares throughout Afghanistan if there were not a corrupt, foreign-installed government. It is all the fault of the occupiers, they say. The truth is that the vast majority, usually far in excess of 75 per cent,[2] of the non-combatants who have lost their lives in this war have been killed, often deliberately, by the Taliban.

That needs to be kept in mind throughout this chapter. Neither British nor any other NATO troops ever deliberately kill civilians. When civilians are killed, the soldiers involved are invariably extremely upset – especially as they often see the aftermath. What follows is no reflection on the professionalism of our soldiers; rather it is an indictment of the kind of war they have been sent to fight, with unclear objectives and constantly changing rules of engagement. They are fighting against a truly formidable enemy – one that wages war under very different rules.

The difficulties of counting the dead

In any war, we are understandably focused on our own casualties and on how they are recorded. The same, of course, holds for the Afghans that we are in Afghanistan to protect (so the story goes). The question of civilian casualties in that country is highly emotive and controversial. Seldom does a week go by without some member or other of the Afghan government threatening the NATO mission with dire consequences, after yet another misguided weapon or night raid kills the wrong people. On one occasion, after such an incident in May 2012, President Karzai stated that civilian deaths threatened the NATO/Afghan pact.[3]

In Iraq, the 'Iraq Body Count' provides a generally accepted lower limit for how many people have died in violence in that country.[4] It is based on reliable media reports; but that clearly means that it can only count those whose deaths are *reported*. Since very many such deaths go unreported, its assessment is extremely conservative.

Ten years into the Afghan War, there is no agreed metric for calculating civilian death figures in Afghanistan. The various agencies, such as ISAF and the UN, use different techniques with highly variable degrees of objectivity. And different techniques inevitably produce divergent results. When it comes to the question of how many casualties among 'innocent civilians' are caused by NATO troops, matters go beyond mere issues of measurement and enter the world of politics. NATO's avowed role, after all, is 'protection of the people'.

These issues were examined scientifically in a 2011 article by John Bohannon in the well-respected US magazine *Science*.[5] In the article, he points out that the UN Assistance Mission in Afghanistan estimates the number of deaths caused by ISAF forces to be nearly three times greater than ISAF itself does. As we will see in particular cases below, the ISAF policy is only to count those casualties that can be confirmed by name. If NATO troops do not see the casualty, they will not count it. By contrast, the UN uses a far more sophisticated methodology, which disaggregates casualties according to province, cause and other key categories.

One of the difficulties for any agency involved in counting casualties in this war is defining who exactly is a 'civilian' – 'How do we know', ISAF might ask, 'that this man we killed in a raid on a house with his son was not a Taliban soldier?' The difficulty is compounded by the legal fact that, while not all civilians are Taliban, all Taliban are civilians, in that they are not members of a uniformed group. As a British officer interviewed by Bohannon honestly puts it: 'The vast percentage of the people we are fighting with are farmers – their day job is farmer; at night they fight us.'[6] In fairness, this creates appalling problems for ordinary soldiers.

The discrepancies between the various figures given by the agencies are, to a large degree, a result not only of differing methods of measurement, but also of completely different definitions: that clearly provides scope for (at best) misunderstandings. Similarly, accurate disaggregation of casualties by province or region is made far more difficult by the fact that the organizations doing the various counts have different regional subdivisions. Then there are further disputes over categorization of the injured: was an injury caused by direct fire or indirect fire? And who causes the injuries in, for example, shootouts? Clearly ISAF is not going to accept responsibility for casualties in a shootout if there is a *possibility* that the shot that killed or injured an individual might have been fired by the Taliban. Of course, even when it has been established that NATO fired the fatal shot, invariably the Taliban get the blame for 'hiding among civilians'. Incidentally, the same excuse is offered by the Taliban when they kill civilians in IED attacks: 'NATO hides behind civilians'.

This chapter concentrates on enumerating the casualties in one province – and primarily those casualties clearly caused by British forces. The approach taken will be conservative, as no one benefits from exaggeration. Lower estimates here will be based on a very conservative assessment of casualties drawn from ISAF figures and reliable media reports.

How civilians are killed

In July 2010, a now famous cache of classified documents was released in a joint effort by three major world newspapers and WikiLeaks. This collection included thousands of daily reports made by military units to their headquarters in the various wars being conducted by the United States and its allies. Those from Afghanistan became known as the 'Afghan War logs'. Many of these reports are postmodern anodyne accounts of horror, floating in an alphabet soup of military acronyms. This report, from 19 May 2009, is typical:

> TF NAWA 1 WG manning PB JAKER report that ANP with F Coy 2 RGR PMT received SAF from GR 41R PQ 2635 7288. FF returned fire with organic weapons. 1 × HARRIER GR9 on station ISO ground units.

To interpret: on the morning of 19 May, in the area of Nawa (in the so-called fertile 'Green Zone' of Helmand) a patrol of Afghan police

(ANP) set out with a British army Gurkha (RGR – Royal Gurkha Rifles) police mentoring team (PMT). These were part of the Welsh Guards (WG) battle group (BG). Shortly afterwards they came under small-arms fire (SAF) – rifles and machine guns. This attack was seen to come from a location that was identified to within an accuracy of 10 metres (the degree of precision offered by the eight-figure grid reference). The 'friendly forces' (FF) fired back with their own rifles and armaments (which may have included machine guns and anti-tank rockets). They were, it seems, unable to dispose of this annoying and possibly lethal threat on their own. Instead of withdrawing and leaving the insurgents to themselves, the officer in command decided to call in what soldiers call 'fast air' – Harrier jet bombers. The initial 'contact report' (any encounter with enemy action is called a 'contact') concludes by telling the headquarters that a Harrier jet is in the air around the gunfight in support of (ISO) the soldiers.

The shootout continued:

UPDATE 1153D*

The GR9 dropped 1 × GBU-12 onto EF FP resulting in a direct hit and no further INS activity was observed. 2 Mercian deployed in support of troops in contact, but no BDA was conducted. Nothing further to report. No casualties or damage reported.

At 191028D* CAS dropped 1 × GBU38 and INS SAF ceased.

So events have moved on. The jet the soldiers had called in was asked to drop a bomb at about 10.28 a.m. It was a laser-guided bomb (type GBU-12, which contains about 500 lbs of explosive). It hit the target (EF FP – enemy forces firing point) and the firing at the soldiers ceased; there was no further insurgent (INS) activity. The additional line given here ('At 191028D* . . .') is probably a supplemental from the Royal Air Force, telling us at what time the bomb (a GBU-38, as it turns out – a slightly different type from that originally reported) was dropped.

Afterwards a unit from another regiment – the Second Battalion the Mercian Regiment – was sent out to escort the Afghan police and their mentors back to their nearby base. The British soldiers conducted no after-action searches, and nor did they try to find out what the results of their gunfight and bombing had been (BDA – battle damage assessment). The Harrier pilot returned to his rather comfortable quarters, probably at Kandahar airbase – some ten minutes or so flying time away.

As always with such events, there will have been a debrief back at base, with the whole event deconstructed and lessons identified. Over lunch, there will have been the inevitable stories of who did what, as the adrenalin subsided. As the report says, at that stage there was really 'nothing further to report'.

This was not the end of the matter, though: there were further things to report. Later that day, the operations officer at the patrol base filled out the incident:

> An ANP foot patrol (with GBR PMT) was operating in NAWA when it was attacked with SAF and RPG by up to 30 INS using multiple compounds as Firing Points. The patrol was suppressed by INS fire and only able to engage one of the compounds effectively. IOT extract from the contact, FF requested CAS as mortars were not assessed [sic] appropriate and decided that a laser guided munition would minimise the chance of collateral damage. At 191028D* CAS dropped 1 × GBU38 and INS SAF ceased.

The number of insurgents was assessed at about thirty; they had had rocket-propelled grenades (RPG) and they had ambushed the soldiers and Afghan police from several positions. Combat air support (CAS) – jet bombers – was requested so that the troops could extricate themselves, and, bearing in mind the need to minimize 'collateral damage' (the possibility of civilians being killed), it was decided to drop a bomb. This evidently ended the matter and all thirty insurgents stopped firing – at this stage we must suppose that either they were killed or they left the scene. However, he adds . . .

At 1300D* 2 × AFG Civ came to PB JAKER informing FF that 8 × AFG Civ had been killed, a compound was destroyed and 2 × jerabs of wheat were burned. Compensation for relatives and the land owner has commenced and the investigation is ongoing.[7]

An hour and a half after the incident, which really must have occurred within earshot of the patrol base, two Afghan civilians appeared at the gate and informed the friendly forces that eight civilians had been killed. As we see, an investigation was begun. No information is available as to the result of this investigation. In a rather grim summary elsewhere in the report, figures are placed next to the various categories of casualties: friendly WIA (wounded in action), friendly KIA (killed in action), host nation WIA, host nation KIA, enemy WIA, enemy KIA and civilian WIA all attract a zero; against 'civilian KIA' the reporting officer has placed an '8'.

We know no more: whether they were children, women, old or young men was of no military reporting value.

It is easy to criticize soldiers in such high-stress environments. Those concerned were at risk of losing their lives in the heat, dirt and hostility of rural Afghanistan with only their friends between them and a horrible death. That must have been a time of desperation and panic. However, sympathetic as one must be to their plight, they were highly trained professionals. This was their job and they were very well prepared for it. Some of them – maybe all of them – had been through situations like this before. Their desperation and panic was as nothing compared to that of the people into whose lives they and their Taliban enemies had crashed that day. It is very difficult for us to imagine the fear that those eight people experienced that day, or the cacophony of deafening bangs, the shouting and screaming of children that was the last thing they heard.

This incident was only one of thousands that have occurred all over Afghanistan – and especially all over Helmand – in the last seven years. It did not make the news; and, because this report was classified as secret, the civilians who were (alleged to have been) killed never made it into any international assessment of civilian casualties. Instead, there will have been a fairly peremptory investigation, involving, perhaps, the army lawyer at the headquarters in Lashkar Gah. Clearly that is as far as the matter went.

No compensation was ever paid for the dead, and as far as the British army is concerned these casualties disappeared into history and would certainly never have been heard of again, had the matter not been reported in the *Guardian* as part of the WikiLeaks files. It was another tragic day in a tragic war, with what seem to have been appalling results.

Assessing and investigating our own dead

In late August 2007, the British army was fighting hard in Southern Afghanistan. In support, the Provincial Reconstruction Team (comprising a dozen or so British and other civilians) attempted, with limited success, to establish the basics of a state. I was one of those civilian officers. We lived alongside our military colleagues in the UK base at Lashkar Gah. Every few days (and sometimes more frequently) a small red sign would appear outside the main camp office: 'Operation Minimise is in force.' Everyone in the camp knew what that meant: somewhere in Britain a family was being informed of the death or maiming of a much-loved son, husband or father.[8]

After a few hours, it would usually become clear what had happened – perhaps a shooting here or a bomb attack there. On one particular day there had been five casualties, all from the Royal Anglian Regiment. Three had been killed – Private Aaron James McClure, Private Robert Graham Foster and Private John Thrumble – and two seriously injured. What made it especially memorable was that they had been killed by a bomb dropped from a NATO aircraft. After a day or so, we all knew that the bomb had been dropped by an American plane. I well remember the effort put into conducting the investigation into this tragedy. Clearly everything had to be done to ensure that this kind of thing could not be allowed to happen again.

A full inquiry was convened, with many witnesses summoned. I was not directly involved, but no one could be unaware of the seriousness with which it was conducted. The witnesses included one rather nervous US pilot, as well as every soldier involved in the incident. The hearings took three days. In due course, the inquiry concluded and the relevant lessons were, no doubt, learned. Procedures were changed and training in those procedures was implemented. A report was produced and, needless to say, was immediately classified.

Three years later, the incident was investigated in some detail during the civilian inquest into the deaths of the three young men. At its conclusion, the lawyer for the families said: 'There are lessons to be learnt by the MoD. There needs to be total transparency when incidents like this happen, the families need to have the truth and facts from day one.'[9]

The Ministry of Defence and its servants had conducted a meticulous inquiry into the death – by a terrible mistake – of three young men. And that is surely right. The inquiry made very clear to us not only the value placed on the lives of the soldiers killed, but also the processes and procedures that had led to their deaths. But such an inquiry is only available if you are British.

Air strikes in support of the military activities of NATO and particularly UK troops were and are very common in Afghanistan. Some of them clearly result in Taliban casualties; some of them are claimed to do so; and some kill only civilians.

No figures are kept on civilian casualties by the British – or for that matter by any international forces. Or at least none that we know of. While a count of British casualties is meticulously and publicly kept by the Ministry of Defence and by almost all credible news outlets, no such tally is conducted for the people who live in the houses, hamlets, villages and towns of the province invaded by the British in early 2006.

Accountability

In a famous speech that is regarded by some, including the veteran Labour politician Denis Healey, as the finest parliamentary speech of the twentieth century, Enoch Powell, soon to become controversial for other reasons, spoke of a massacre that had occurred in Kenya where 11 civilians had been killed:

> Nor can we ourselves pick and choose where and in what parts of the world we shall use this or that kind of standard. We cannot say, 'We will have African standards in Africa, Asian standards in Asia and perhaps British standards here at home.' We have not that choice to make. We must be consistent with ourselves everywhere.[10]

Many of the activities of the British campaign in Helmand have been based upon quantitative analysis. We know – or could easily determine – how many new wells have been dug, or what the response was to a call for a women's justice *shura* in the Nad Ali district. Particular tabs are kept on the education of children, especially girls. Anyone who wishes to know how many women police officers have been trained over the past year in the district of Gereshk, or what the PRT believes the level of support for the Afghan government to be will find the information available.[11] If your concern is the supposed number of hectares under opium cultivation, you are but a mouse click away from the answer. You will, however, search in vain for any enumeration of human beings killed by British forces.

The unpalatable but evident truth is that an Afghan life (or indeed many Afghan lives) is not worth one British life. The horrendous irony in all of this is that, as we have seen, one of the supposed tenets of the so-called 'counterinsurgency' tactic is 'protection of the people'. This requires that the 'people' of a country that an army occupies are treated with the dignity which the occupying soldiers rightly demand.

Assessing and investigating civilian deaths

On 23 June 2007, there was an air strike in support of British forces near the large Helmand town of Gereshk.[12] British forces had come under fire from two of what soldiers call 'compounds' (farmhouses) and they had ordered an air strike. Only after the bomb had been dropped did the British realize their mistake. It had hit its target and 20 or so insurgents had been killed. But no fewer than **25 civilians** were also killed in the explosion, including nine women, three babies and the mullah of the local mosque. There was little scope here for the commonly offered defence that everyone killed had been an 'insurgent'.

The journalist Ben Anderson reports what happened next. The colonel in charge of the regiment that had ordered the air strike went to the village concerned, offered the usual compensation and made a few comments to the villagers. He explained that he knew the Taliban had prevented the people from leaving the houses concerned, although he did not say how he knew. He told Anderson: 'We were duped. And frankly that rather hurts because we like to think we're a little bit cleverer.' He was asked whether he would change tactics. 'No. We just have to apply the tactics we've used in the past with a greater degree of certainty ... We need to be that bit more certain that there are no civilians in the area.'[13]

The colonel was not going to change tactics, just be a bit more careful. One wonders what would have happened if that had been the response to the parents and legal representatives of Privates McClure, Foster and Thrumble.

In his iconic book on the war in Helmand, *No Worse Enemy*, Ben Anderson describes a day with the Grenadier Guards, during which one young officer[14] came close to disaster during a 'contact' with the Taliban.[15] His unit had come under attack and he had asked for a bomb to be dropped on a house from which some of the firing appeared to be coming. But his request was refused – very fortunately, as an entire terrified family had taken refuge from the fighting in one room of it. Anderson is one of the very few journalists to have spent a significant time with the British army in combat. It is unlikely that he had witnessed anything unusual. Combat is chaos and most soldiers will understand and sympathise with that officer's predicament. When we and our enemies fight amongst civilians, such dilemmas are, unfortunately, inevitable.

When I served as a soldier in Iraq I very nearly shot a teenage boy during a patrol. The boy was aiming a toy rifle at us from a street corner. Fortunately, that morning we had been warned in briefings that there were realistic toy guns on the street and to be careful. There, as they say, but for the grace of God ...

One can recite story after story of civilian tragedy, but what does that tell us about how many we, the British, have killed? The answer is 'nothing'. One problem is the opacity of military reporting. The incident recorded in the WikiLeaks cables above was never reported in any 'open sources', as the British military call television, newspapers, etc. There was no press report of the incident related by Anderson, when 25 civilians were killed. And nor could I find any publicly available record of the baby, accidentally shot by a British soldier at a checkpoint, whose blood-covered body I had seen in Helmand.

Checkpoints: escalation of force

In an environment full of highly strung and extremely heavily armed young men, danger can appear even where there is no combat. The Danish-Afghan journalist and writer Nagieb Khaja has travelled extensively in Helmand and Kandahar provinces. Indeed he is from the region. In an interview in mid-2012, he told me: 'On a weekly basis when I was in Kandahar or Helmand in 2009 people were being killed at checkpoints. As with other casualties, these were reported in the local press but never in the international media, and I was in a position to know this as I was reading both at the time.'

He relates an incident that happened to him:

No one is sure what they are or are not allowed to do at checkpoints. One occasion a British soldier shot at me – something was going on along the road and the British had stopped the traffic. People had to wait. I couldn't see what was going on ahead, maybe there had been an accident, and got out to see; a soldier shot at me, presumably as a warning shot. No one told us why we were waiting, but everyone had somewhere else to be. I had to catch a plane, for example. You simply have to stop and wait. It is the same with convoys, which travel slowly and allow no one to pass. The only alternative to waiting on the road was to go through the districts, with the dangers of bandits, mines or Taliban. At the very best this is irritating to say the least. At worst it is very dangerous. These convoys are targets. People know that waiting behind a convoy when it is attacked is not a healthy place to be.

As he says: 'One of the worst day-to-day problems of a foreign presence is soldiers shooting [the local people] at checkpoints.'[16] Of course, from the perspective of the nervous young soldiers at a checkpoint, anyone who drives out of line is a potential suicide bomber (although common sense might indicate that someone who gets out of a car in a queue is more likely to want to find out what is going on than to be a suicide bomber, even in Helmand).

In fairness, the reader may object that the plural of 'anecdote' is not 'data'.[17] Equally, the plural of 'newspaper report' is not 'statistics'. But aside from newspaper reports and the anecdotes of Afghans and journalists, are there any reliable figures that might give us an idea of the number of civilian casualties inflicted by British troops? The answer unfortunately is 'no'. After ten years of fighting what has so often been claimed to be a war for hearts and minds, ISAF has made no effort to count the people it has seriously injured or killed. Though many military officers believe there should be a count, nothing has really been done to that end. However, there are ways of making an estimate.

Official compensation

The Ministry of Defence pays compensation to those Afghans who have the courage to apply and who manage to convince an MOD civil servant that their injuries or the death of their relatives were caused by UK forces. Needless to say, there is a process to go through in order to weed out those who do not qualify – those who might have been injured or killed while engaging in firefights with NATO forces, for example. As the ministry puts it:

> No amount of money can compensate for a family losing a loved one. The UK and other ISAF members will in certain circumstance make ex gratia payments to individuals affected by operations involving our national forces, but for which we have no legal liability. These payments do not affect the rights of civilians to make a formal claim for compensation. Providing restitution for civilians who have suffered in these circumstances is the right thing to do.[18]

It is not entirely clear where or how a Helmandi farmer might 'make a formal claim for compensation' beyond the ad hoc awards made by the military. Even after many years and several billions of dollars in assistance, the Afghan state has no legal system worth the name, and UK solicitors have no offices in the country. Nonetheless, to a degree the system does work for some.

The MOD says it settled 380 claims for death and personal injury from December 2005 to May 2012. The payments totalled £824,000.[19] Like the Armed Forces Compensation Scheme (AFCS), which pays compensation to service personnel injured in the course of their work, there is a tariff for injuries. It is, however, a great deal lower than the AFCS tariff, which is established by statutory instrument.[20] For example:

- Under the AFCS, total loss of sight results in a level 1 award (the most serious) and provides a wounded soldier with the current full award of £570,000; an Afghan would get $7,000 (about £6,000).[21]
- The same award applies for 'persistent vegetative state': an Afghan who is rendered unable to communicate or to function would get $7,000.
- For the loss of one eye, a soldier receives a level 8 award of £60,000;[22] an Afghan would get $1,000 (£750).
- A gunshot wound to a British soldier ('high velocity gunshot wound with complications which have required significant post-operative treatment'[23] – most gunshot wounds to the body do require this) is assessed as a level 7 award and attracts a payment of £90,000; an Afghan with a similar wound would receive at most $7,000, and probably far less.

It would be fair to say that the lives and limbs of Afghans are assessed in financial terms at between one-twentieth and one-hundredth of those of a British soldier.

Once again, it should be stressed here that these are for injuries caused by the British military machine to people it professes to be protecting. Needless to say, there is no compensation for psychiatric injury.

Dismal though the picture they paint may be, these numbers tell less than half the story. For death is also compensated. The UK pays between $5,000 and $8,000 for a dead adult; between $2,000 and $5,000 for a child; and (somewhat mysteriously) the tariff indicates that for 'dependants', $200 (sic) suffices.[24]

The numbers are instructive:

- For the financial year 2005–06 one death was compensated.[25]
- For the financial year 2006–07 one death was compensated.[26] No figures are available for May 2007 to December 2007.
- In the calendar year 2008 there were 33 pay-outs for death.[27]
- In 2009, the MOD paid compensation for the death of 105 civilians.[28]

- In 2010 there were 70 pay-outs for deaths, including of 18 women, plus payments for 46 injured; this is the only year where a full account of all claims is publicly available.[29]
- From May 2011 to May 2012 only 29 payments for death were made.[30]
- From May to December 2012, ten payments for deaths caused by the UK armed forces were made.[31]

This makes a total of 249 deaths for which compensation was paid.

The numbers of uninvolved civilians killed must greatly exceed these figures. Why is this? If compensation is on offer, surely people will jump at the opportunity to queue up at British and other ISAF bases for their hundreds or thousands of dollars in compensation? The discrepancy between the low claims and the much higher casualties is easily explained: the Taliban take a very dim view of those who enter foreign military bases for any reason, including to take money. Mohammed Salaam, who had suffered some damage to his house that was caused by British forces, told Jon Boone of the *Guardian*: 'the Taliban are still in the area and they told me they would kill me if I take the money'.[32] We saw above how, in the bloody first three years of the campaign, only two deaths received compensation pay-outs.

At this point, it must be said in fairness that the MOD does not claim that its figures tell the whole story. But as we will see, they come nowhere near it. To analyse how accurate the MOD figures are, we can look at a sample year and compare the deaths that are well evidenced in credible media with official figures for compensation paid.

The real story

2007

As we have seen, the figures available show that from early 2006 to early 2007, only one death was compensated.[33] Compensation was available, but few claims were made. How many people were actually killed in that period?

Ben Anderson describes in ferocious detail his several visits to British forces in late 2007, as well as later 'embeds' with US forces in Helmand. He tried to estimate the number of civilians killed in the early part of 2007:

> All I did back then was add up all reported deaths – reported in the press, by ISAF, reported by Afghans at shuras getting condolence payments and reported by the two different UK battalions I was with – in two months over one summer tour in 2007. I suspect the figure was much higher – I saw enough near misses and shuras dominated by condolence payments in my time there. At a shura with elders from families who had been hit in other air strikes, just two of the men attending that I interviewed had lost **47 family members** between them. About 20 elders attended this one shura alone – and a Police Commander *chairing* the meeting had also lost two brothers to an airstrike.[34]

It is not clear how many of these were killed by British forces, and there is no way of telling; but it surely must be a high proportion.

Anderson goes on to estimate the total number killed throughout 2007:

> I strongly suspect the actual number killed in 2007 is much higher than 250. I saw at least a dozen compounds flattened and no one was checking for civilians before they dropped bombs – you can't check without actually going in. And there were definitely bodies in some of those compounds, you could smell them a few days later, but no one checked if they were Taliban or civilians.[35]

The figure of 250 might include what was an appalling air strike in 2007. The small village of Hyderabad is about 80km from Lashkar Gah,

Had there been a good road (or indeed any road), it might have been possible to drive there from the provincial capital in an hour or two. But it took Aziz Tassal, an Afghan member of staff of the reputable Institute for War and Peace Reporting (IWPR), four days to get there to investigate reports of a hundred people killed in a NATO air strike. It remains unclear exactly what happened.

Villager Sher Jan told Tassal that on 27 June 2007 the Taliban had attacked a British convoy. (NATO/ISAF claimed they were American, but the distinction between one group of heavily armed Western men clad in brown and another is not always clear.) Aircraft were called in, and these started to attack the Taliban. People in the village then gathered up their possessions and loaded them onto tractors to escape the fighting. They formed a convoy: 'There were more than 150 people in this convoy of tractors. The planes came again and bombed the whole line. To the north of Hyderabad there were others trying to escape. They were bombed as well.'[36]

Anyone who has worked in places such as Kosovo will recognize the pattern, and at least understand the response. The NATO pilots will have been told that the convoy was composed of escaping Taliban (and some of the people probably were Taliban). It is not clear how many people were killed in the resulting inferno. The mayor of the district said that **45 civilians** had been killed, as well as 62 opposition fighters. NATO admitted to eight civilians and claimed 32 Taliban. I spoke to Tassal a month or so after his visit. He tended to the view that the true figure was very much closer to the mayor's than to NATO's.

Only a few weeks later, I saw for myself the difficulties, the deceit and the confusion on all sides regarding numbers. Every day the PRT would have a morning meeting, at which a soldier would report the various 'significant actions' of the previous day. One such occurred on Thursday, 2 August, in the village of Bughri, in the remote district of Baghran in Northern Helmand – many, many hours of rough driving from the closest town of Musa Qala. According to one version of events, dozens of people had gathered near a shrine for the weekly *mela*, or market, prior to the weekend (which in Muslim countries begins on Friday). A different version claims that a more sinister 'leadership gathering' was being held.

Three bombs struck, directed in this case by US special forces. The soldiers reported that great care had been taken to determine that every person there was Taliban. Afghan defence ministry officials stated that the destruction of this 'leadership gathering' had resulted in the death of the well-known Taliban leader Mullah Dadullah Mansour, among others. The claim was rather dented (to put it mildly) when, the following day, Mullah Dadullah spoke on the phone to Afghan journalists and was later seen with two other Taliban commanders said to have been at Bughri. Conclusive proof that he had not been killed in the air strike came when he was captured in a fight with Pakistani forces two years later.[37]

But hundreds of others were killed and injured in the three bomb strikes. Some made it to the rudimentary clinic at Musa Qala (at that time under the control of the Taliban), and some even reached the hospital at Kandahar. Dozens of the injured battled their pain and succeeded in getting to the hospital at Lashkar Gah.

'Many died on the way', said Abdul Karim, a resident of Baghran. 'One of my sons is in [Lashkar Gah] hospital. I don't think he will survive. Two of my sons are in Musa Qala and two others have been killed. Two of my cousins were killed and two others injured. It was a day of blackness, almost everyone had lost someone.'[38]

Those who made it to one of the hospitals in towns under government control (at that stage only Lashkar Gah) could offer the names of 17 victims. Therefore, by the reductive logic of ISAF, it was concluded that 17 people had been killed. Needless to say, as Tassal reported, Lashkar Gah was the furthest of several places to which the wounded had fled. There were many others who will not have made it to hospitals that were dozens of miles away, over appalling roads. None of them will have been counted in NATO figures.

At the meeting at which this 'incident' was reported, one very senior British officer bemoaned the fact that the Taliban had been able to 'get their message out' much faster than the ISAF bureaucracy allowed ISAF to do, and that consequently the ISAF message was not believed. Another reason why its message was not believed was that it was barely credible: all Helmandis know that Thursday afternoon is the time for the *mela*; many knew where the shrine of Shah Ibrahim Baba was located. Many would also have heard via their own sources of the disaster that had befallen the people of Bughri. Put simply, ISAF's subsequent claim, a day or so later, that only 17 civilians had been killed was far less believable than immediate Taliban claims, made on several local radio stations, of many hundreds dead.

Jean MacKenzie of IWPR, a rare Western journalist, has travelled extensively in Helmand training journalists, without heavily armed Western security guards. She researched this 'incident' with the assistance of some highly capable local investigative journalists. She is of the view that the real figure is probably well over **100 killed** and many more injured. Few if any were 'Taliban'. This number must be taken as a minimum.

The US special forces in this case did not set out to slaughter dozens or hundreds of civilians. They were acting on intelligence supplied, in all likelihood, by unreliable sources – perhaps paid, perhaps threatened, perhaps misunderstood. Needless to say, there was no investigation and no admission of any fault.

The number of civilians killed in 2007 in Helmand must, therefore, be in the hundreds. Let us recall: Ben Anderson reported an incident in June, when 25 civilians were killed; at a *shura* he met two men who had lost 47 family members; 45 civilians were killed in the Hyderabad air strike; and Jean MacKenzie believes well over 100 lost their lives in Baghran in August. As we will see below, at least two civilians were killed in November in a very sinister operation carried out in the town of Toube (UK area of responsibility). And in 2007, the family of one dead civilian received compensation. The total figure of evidenced civilian casualties for 2007 alone is at least **220**.

For subsequent years the situation is very opaque indeed.

2008

For 2008, the UK military admit to *at least* 33 civilian deaths. This figure is based on the number of those compensated. No journalists were permitted the kind of access that Ben Anderson had had the previous year, and so there is no firm evidence of other casualties. There was heavy fighting throughout 2008, and indeed in every year of NATO occupation.

The total figure of evidenced civilian casualties for 2008 is at least **33**.

2009

The British government acknowledges 105 deaths. This figure may or may not include the eight civilians killed in the incident described in the WikiLeaks report above (involving the Second Battalion of the Mercian Regiment). No other reports are available. To indicate how low a figure this is likely to be, in October 2009 alone Lashkar Gah hospital admitted 88 injured non-combatant civilians.

The total figure of evidenced civilian casualties for 2009 is at least **105**.

2010

This is the only year for which we have a disaggregated database of all claims made to the MOD. In this year the MOD paid compensation for 70 deaths. The picture that emerges is similar to that in 2007, with many more killings by NATO forces than would be indicated by the figures for compensation.

February of that year saw the start of Operation Moshtarak – a classic 'clear, hold and build' attempt in the district of Nad Ali. In that month alone, 12 civilians were killed in Nad Ali, where British forces were present in force.[39] No claims were made or paid for those deaths. In total, no fewer than 28 civilians were killed in the operation. In July, at least 39 civilian bodies were pulled from the wreckage of a farmhouse in the village of Ragi near Sangin, which had been bombed by NATO aircraft.[40]

In none of these incidents does compensation appear to have been paid for the deaths, and so they do not appear in the tally of civilian casualties.

At the very least, then, the total for 2010 includes the 28 killed in Operation Moshtarak plus the 39 at Ragi plus the 70 claims for deaths that were accepted as having been caused by UK forces. There were far more claims that were turned down. It may be that the US forces – by this time more numerous – were responsible for some of the deaths. While no compensation is payable if US forces may have been responsible, for Helmandis it hardly matters what NATO roundel appears on the aircraft that drops the bomb that eviscerates their families.

The reality of the intensity of fighting that year is perhaps far more vividly indicated by the fact that in a single month, October 2010, 158 civilian non-combatants were admitted to Lashkar Gah hospital with combat-related injuries. NATO admits of no deaths that month.

The total figure of evidenced civilian casualties for 2010 is at least **137**.

2011

On 25 March 2011, an RAF drone killed four civilians.[41] Two weeks later, on 6 April, two Helmandi women were killed in a road accident and a man was shot at the scene by British soldiers.[42] Fourteen civilians – most of them children – were killed in late May in an air attack.[43] Three months later, in August, in a similar attack, a woman and seven children lost their lives.[44] All these cases were reported in the press, but there is no record in MOD data of any of them having been compensated.[45]

Eight other deaths were compensated.[46]

The total figure of evidenced civilian casualties for 2011 is at least **37**.

2012

In early May, a family of six was killed in a NATO air strike;[47] on 3 July a boy was killed by an Apache helicopter;[48] and in October, three children were killed in an air strike in Nawa district of Helmand.[49] Compensation was paid by the UK forces for all of them.

The total figure of evidenced civilian casualties for 2012 caused by military action is at least **10**.

***

These figures, remember, are only for people killed by UK or NATO forces and whose deaths were reported by *credible* sources.

By adding up our figures, then, the well-evidenced total is at least **542** people killed by NATO forces in Helmand. This figure includes the 249 to which the UK admits and for which it has paid compensation. It should be stressed again that these numbers do not include any deaths caused by the cavalier use of British firepower in the reckless battles fought in 2006. The figure also does not include the dozens killed at checkpoints or those for whom we have no NATO evidence at all. As Nagieb Khaja has testified (see above), many – perhaps even the majority – of the civilian deaths caused by British forces and other NATO units at checkpoints go entirely unreported by the international press. And the same is true when a couple of people are killed in forgotten battles in obscure villages. Helmand is as remote and inaccessible to media coverage or monitoring as any part of Africa, and far more people have been killed by NATO (and by the Taliban) than has been reported. The evidence from the logs released by the Ministry of Defence also indicates many further deaths and injuries from road accidents.

Furthermore (and perhaps most importantly), there is no evidence available at all as to the number of people killed by other NATO countries, especially the US. Accordingly, it would not be unreasonable to estimate in excess of 1,000 people killed by NATO action, although such a figure would not be evidenced.

'I like to equate it to a football game . . .': body counts

The British army may be reluctant to record the number of civilians it kills, but it is rather keener to count the enemies it claims to have eliminated. Colonel Richard Kemp is a regular commentator on the UK media. For a short period in 2002, he was commander of UK forces in Afghanistan. He appeared at the UK House of Commons Defence Committee inquiry on Afghanistan on 3 November 2010. Although he had to leave the session early due to a more pressing appointment, one comment of his is worth quoting:

> I like to equate it to a football game. Britain play Germany at football and the Germans score three goals. The Britons . . . don't know the true score; they only know that we had a lot of goals scored against us . . . British people are, I think, very dispirited by hearing constant stories about British casualties and deaths. What they don't hear is how many casualties are being inflicted upon the Taliban, what damage is being done to the Taliban, and what gains are being made in military terms.[50]

The reader may take the view, shared by the chairman of the Defence Committee, that the age of body counts ended with the war in Vietnam, where (even disregarding the morality) their utility proved limited:

former US Marine Corps infantry officer Karl Marlantes, who served in Vietnam, has written that the idea of body counts there was 'disastrous and stupid', motivated by a patently wrong notion that wars against guerrillas are wars of attrition.[51] The British army, however, has swung from policy to policy on such matters: I remember sitting in on a briefing in Helmand by Brigadier Andrew Mackay (as he then was) at which he said that the next officer to mention a body count would be sent home: the practice was, he said, counterproductive. And yet the brigade that had previously been deployed had used it.

The habit of counting the number of enemies supposedly killed proved hard to break: in the following six-month rotation, when the next 'signature' operation (which would supposedly define that brigade's tour) involved the transportation of a turbine to the crucial Kajaki Dam in Northern Helmand British commanders estimated – and indeed trumpeted – that they had 'killed more than 200 insurgents – without any losses or injuries to Nato soldiers'.[52]

Death squads

Just before I left the UK mission in late November 2007, I heard rumours that 18 men had been killed in the village of Toube in the Southern Helmand district of Garmsir. Those rumours solidified in the months after I left the mission: the killings had been carried out at night, in the style of an execution, by US Marine Corps special forces outside the chain of command of ISAF. It had been a 'kill or capture' night raid of the kind that became far more prevalent later in the campaign. An account of it was given by a survivor, Abdul Manaan, who had been brought to Lashkar Gah hospital with a deep gash that had every appearance of being a slashing knife wound. According to Manaan, troops had been brought into Toube by helicopter. They had then swept through the village, killing at least 16 people in their homes. Three men, including Manaan, had been brought alive before the

foreign soldiers for interrogation. One by one, when they gave unsatis-
factory answers, they had had their throats cut. But Manaan had 'played
dead' and somehow survived.[53] Such stories will be familiar to those
who know of the interrogation techniques used in Vietnam.

Again, no investigation of these credible reports was carried out by
ISAF – or, more especially, by the British.[54] While there is no suggestion
that this particular alleged massacre was carried out by UK forces (it
was almost certainly a US Marine Corps special forces type 'recon'
unit),[55] it did occur in what the British army would call its 'area of
responsibility'. International law makes it clear that any organization
informed of allegations of war crimes is under an absolute duty to
investigate them. The British here patently failed in their duty under
European and international law.[56] Given the subservient relationship
that the UK military has to its US counterpart, it is highly unlikely that
the British would ever have taken action of a legal (or any other) nature
against the senior partner.

The mission in Toube was an example of the so-called 'kill-capture'
tactic, which has recently come to greater prominence as the latest
scheme to end the war. Based on similar operations in Iraq against Al
Qaeda, it has been taken up by NATO forces throughout Afghanistan.
It bears some resemblance to Operation Phoenix – the US's so-called
'black' operation in Vietnam to neutralize the political leadership of the
Viet Cong – involving as it does the large-scale deployment of special
forces in missions against 'high-value targets' (though this term is used
somewhat flexibly).

A remarkable piece of work carried out by Alex Strick van Linschoten
and Felix Kuehn has uncovered the number of 'Taliban' operators alleg-
edly killed or captured in these operations.[57] Helmand is the province
with far and away the greatest number of 'kills' – well over 900 – along
with over 1,000 'captures'. Given that many (indeed very probably most)
of those captured will be released, it would appear that these missions
are focused far more on the 'kill' than on the 'capture'.

In September 2012, an officer closely involved in such operations told me that, while on their own terms they were successful (which is to say they achieved their immediate objectives of killing or capture), no one had adequately explained to the operators in these missions how they related to any overall plan or strategy in the long term.[58]

Even after the British leave Helmand and it reverts to its former status as a mini narco-state, these 'kill-capture' missions will almost certainly continue to provide work for many human rights lawyers and their agents in the UK and Afghanistan.

The wounded

It is even harder to determine the number of wounded and injured civilians. But the picture painted by the information we do have is grim indeed. For every dead soldier, roughly seven soldiers are wounded badly enough to require hospital attention (see chapter 2). We can be certain that many thousands of Helmandis who have the benefit of neither body armour nor first-rate and speedy medical care have been rendered disabled by NATO action. Add to these the thousands injured in IED attacks by the Taliban.

Our own wounded, as we have seen, receive the utmost care. Considerable efforts are also made by NATO soldiers to ensure that Afghan wounded or injured are treated in British or other NATO hospitals, where they receive first-class care (no distinction being drawn between Afghan and NATO casualties). On occasion, even Taliban fighters are treated. But unfortunately not all – indeed not even the majority of – Afghan wounded benefit from such care. For the rest, there are only two alternatives: either they can attempt to access the very limited Afghan medical institutions (which all too often are every bit as corrupt and inefficient as the rest of Afghan officialdom), or there is self-help.

In what is one of the two or three poorest countries in the world, this is a dreadful prospect. While Western efforts have resulted in slightly better medical coverage in some provinces, generally speaking for most people medical facilities are at least as bad or worse than they were before this war, and supplies of medicine are disrupted by the prevailing nationwide insecurity. Prior to the current phase of Afghanistan's long war, the Taliban never interfered with medical supplies.[59]

Some hospitals are well run and well supplied, however. The Lashkar Gah hospital, just 2km from the British PRT, is run very effectively by an Italian NGO called Emergency. In the single month of October 2010, 158 civilians were admitted to it as casualties of the fighting – a 77 per cent increase over the previous October, when 'only' 89 war-wounded were admitted.[60] This figure alone implies thousands of casualties over the eight years of sometimes extremely heavy fighting since the British entered the province in 2006. A doctor at the nearby Bost hospital, which deals with longer-term care and is run by another heroic NGO Médecins Sans Frontières, placed the suffering in context:

> There is no such thing as a nice war wound . . . Even the simplest weapon has devastating medical consequences. But the biggest danger is for Afghans travelling any distance to get here. The biggest problem is them arriving late in terms of their disease. So a two hour peace-time journey could take two or three days as they go around the checkpoints, with the result that the disease has progressed much more seriously to life threatening in some cases . . . We hear lots about how dangerous it is for doctors, but the biggest danger is for the poor farmer with the sick child.[61]

No figures are available for the number of children or adults seriously disabled by the fighting. But of one thing we can be absolutely certain: if the situation of a war-wounded soldier is bad, the lot of a disabled Afghan is infinitely worse. For in a subsistence society such as Helmand, a person who does not produce in some way is a person who is useless. And a useless mouth is not a priority for food or any other essential item.

No care is available outside the family; indeed, all too often precious little is available within it, so desperately poor are the families themselves. Many of these unfortunate Helmandis will have been disabled by Taliban bombs. Several, however, will have had their lives shattered by misplaced shells, bombs or bullets loosed by British weaponry.

Refugees

The horrific damage done to Helmandis does not stop with the wounded and dead. In trying to escape the horrors of death and mutilation, many people have had to flee Helmand. One category of suffering that has been ignored is that of the refugee. And yet in war, that is almost always the most numerous.

In late 2007, I was part of the civilian element of the Provincial Reconstruction Team. In theory (and only in theory), the British mission was supposed to be civilian led. To preserve this fiction, civilians were often invited to planning meetings for military operations, and one afternoon I was asked along to just such a briefing. I do not remember what the name was of the village that was to be the target (the 'objective'). But I do remember a map overlaid by the usual cat's cradle of arrows and lines and a jumble of acronyms and jargon. The upshot was that the next day the village was to have a couple of hundred British troops, with a similar number of Afghan police and soldiers in their wake, sweep through in search of the 'enemy'. The 'enemy' would, it was presumed, fight back.

After the briefing, questions were invited. I asked whether any thought had been given to the inevitable refugees that would be displaced from their homes by the fighting (or indeed by the mere possibility of fighting, occasioned by the British presence). This elicited nonplussed expressions from around the table: 'They'll probably go to the desert or find some family. Next question.' The attitude was that this was not the army's problem.

Abdul Zia has been living for six years in the dirt-poor camp of Nasaji Baghrami, set in a sea of mud, excrement and pathetic tarpaulins. It is located in Kabul's particularly dirty and unpleasant fifth police district, and about 20,000 people live there. Rebecca Stewart is a journalist who has worked in Afghanistan for several years and is no stranger to squalor. But even she calls Nasaji Baghrami 'as close to hell as any place on Earth'.

There was a time when life for Mr Zia was much better: he used to have a small farm and seven children. That farm was in the Lashkar Gah district of Helmand. But then one day in 2006, shortly after the British entry into Helmand, for no reason that he can fathom his house was hit by either a missile or a bomb from a NATO aircraft. Whatever it was, it killed six of his children. He was not compensated.

Rebecca Stewart, along with ITN colleague Emma Murphy, visited Nasaji Baghrami in the winter of 2011. Two more children had come into the Zia family, but both had died. The most recent, Shah Gul, froze to death at the age of four months in the savage Kabul winter: 'We huddled around to try to keep her warm.' But to no avail. That winter at least 40 children froze to death in just the Nasaji Baghrami camp, itself one of hundreds filled with refugees from the fighting all over the country. Most of Nasaji Baghrami's 20,000 people are from Helmand and are refugees as a direct result of the fighting initiated in the province by the British army in 2006. We will never know, even roughly, how many refugees there are, because the Afghan government does not acknowledge them to be refugees – or, in the correct international parlance, 'internally displaced persons'. Instead, the desperately poor inhabitants of Nasaji Baghrami and the camps like it are classed as internal economic migrants. They therefore do not qualify for assistance from the UN Refugee Agency or other international bodies. According to Afghan law, the camps are 'informal settlements' and international organizations are barred from providing help. According to Amnesty International, in the first half of 2011 alone, some 91,000

Afghans fled their homes. According to Horia Musadeq, an Amnesty International researcher: 'This is a largely hidden human rights crisis.'[62]

While the British army does not consider the refugee issue to be its problem, and while it may not look like its problem now, the plight of these people – the poorest of the poor in Afghanistan – may well come back to bite the British. One man in Nasaji Baghrami told Stewart and her crew: 'I don't care about going to paradise. If I had a knife I would cut off the head of the British who made me leave Helmand.'[63] We may forget these people; they are unlikely to forget us.

Protecting the people

In 2008, Human Rights Watch, a tenacious and brave NGO, inquired of ISAF what procedures had been put in place to investigate incidents of 'collateral damage'. This is the reply:

> In the summer of 2007, NATO-ISAF reviewed its tactics, techniques and procedures. We committed ourselves to undertake rigorous and constant investigations of incidents involving possible civilian casualties. In particular, the Commander of ISAF mandated that the greatest possible use be made of precision systems and that, when taking fire from an Afghan house, on-scene commanders satisfy themselves that every effort had been made to confirm that the Afghan facility did not shelter innocent civilians. In addition, SACEUR [Supreme Allied Commander Europe] mandated that enhanced and timely After Action Reviews identify lessons learned and that there be a strong system of reporting from investigations when deemed necessary.[64]

Any methodology for the recording of civilian casualties would work best if placed on an international footing, agreed at the very least between military forces and international missions such as the UN.

Initial steps have been taken on the long and very tortuous process in the UN and elsewhere.[65] Experience worldwide has shown that this is entirely practicable, it can be done and it works.[66] There is absolutely no sign of any real effort on the part of any major military power in Afghanistan to take those efforts seriously enough to propose protocols or international standards on the recording of civilian casualties.

Openness in recording civilian casualties is not simply a moral or legal question. It would have operational benefits to the forces prosecuting wars like that in Helmand. First, the impression is created of a 'shared humanity' – all casualties have validity, demonstrating that an occupying army respects locals enough to deal with them honestly. Second, recording could provide an evidentiary basis for substantiating claims, for example, about the effectiveness of measures taken to reduce casualties. Third, accurate recording of civilian casualties could be used as a measure of effectiveness of operations to 'protect' civilians from violence on the part of insurgents, as well as on the part of the occupying army.[67]

Perspectives

Former British soldier and veteran of the Afghan campaign James Jeffrey points out the deterioration of language that attends warfare: 'in Afghanistan, the linguistic corruption that always attends war meant we'd refer to "hot spots", "multiple pax on the ground" and "prosecuting a target", or "maximising the kill chain".[68] Jeffrey points out that targets are not considered as people: they are items on a battlefield. Perhaps it was always so. Nonetheless, there can be no doubt that he is right when he says that the traditional role of armies as protectors of civilians has been almost completely eroded. He quotes Hannah Arendt as saying that the role of armies has changed over the last century from 'that of protector into that of a belated and essentially futile avenger'.[69] Nowhere is this more true than in the wars of 9/11, which have been fought with no coherent strategy or clear political objective.

Wars in the twenty-first century, like those of the twentieth, almost always cause more casualties among civilians than among the armed protagonists. The figures given above surely corroborate this for one province of Afghanistan, Helmand. The number of civilian casualties, who caused them and even who was a civilian will be debated for years. This occurs after any 'war among the people'.

Let us remember one thing. Before the British entered (or blundered into) Helmand, the province was, as we saw in chapter 1, reasonably peaceful and (by Afghan standards) stable, with a small and fairly insignificant Taliban presence. As the campaign draws to a conclusion, nearly a thousand allied troops have been killed and thousands of others have been maimed. More than 3,000 civilians have been killed, most of them by Taliban bombs, but at the very least 500 of them by British forces – and many hundreds more by US forces, which since 2009 have outnumbered British troops in the province. Countless thousands more (literally countless, as no one has counted them or ever will) have been rendered disabled. And then there are the thousands – also uncounted – who have been killed fighting for the Taliban, most of them (as is regularly acknowledged by NATO) local men.

But that is not all. Perhaps tens of thousands of 'internally displaced' people eke out an existence in squalid camps in Kabul and elsewhere. Before 2006 they were on the poverty line; today they are well below it. And still thousands more Helmandi men have been captured by British and other forces and have spent time in a prison camp. All this in just eight years.

The province has a population of about 1.5 million, roughly the same as Northern Ireland. Thirty years of fighting in Northern Ireland resulted in fewer than 3,000 deaths on all sides (plus thousands of injured, all of whom received excellent medical care). There were no squalid refugee camps in London crammed with thousands of Ulstermen and women. Indeed, there were no refugees at all from Northern Ireland. Jets did not patrol the skies; ordinary people did not fear that a bomb might land on them at any moment; no artillery was ever used; and no anti-tank missiles were ever fired. Nonetheless, Northern Ireland will take decades to recover from its trauma.

Not one of the Helmandi civilians ripped apart by a bomb, buried in rubble, shot (whether deliberately or accidentally) or otherwise horribly killed presented a risk to the UK or the US. And nor did any of the thousands of Helmandi, other Afghan and Pakistani 'Taliban' killed by the foreign troops. Of all the thousands of civilians and combatants, *not a single* Al Qaeda operative or 'international terrorist' who could conceivably have threatened the United Kingdom is recorded as having been killed by NATO forces in Helmand.

Whatever the reasons for the British entry into Helmand – whether they were genuine (a desire to 'stabilize' and 'reconstruct') or disingenuous (the need to 'use or lose' infantry battalions) – the results have been catastrophic for all those killed or maimed and for their surviving relatives.

Of course, the human cost of the campaign in Helmand is only part of the equation. Before turning to any benefit that might have accrued, there are two further elements in this squalid calculation that we must examine. The first is the financial cost – the money spent that would not otherwise have been spent. The second is the rather less quantifiable (but no less real) social, diplomatic and strategic price that has been paid. Let us begin by examining how much money Britain's latest Afghan adventure has cost.

PART II
THE FINANCIAL COST

CHAPTER 4

Military Costs

Six staff nurses for a year or a gunfight in the southern Afghan deserts?

Sixty years ago, President Dwight Eisenhower made the unequivocal point that the money for military operations did not grow on trees:

> Every gun that is made, every warship launched, every rocket fired signifies, in the final sense, a theft from those who hunger and are not fed, those who are cold and are not clothed. This world in arms is not spending money alone. It is spending the sweat of its laborers, the genius of its scientists, the hopes of its children. The cost of one modern heavy bomber is this: a modern brick school in more than 30 cities. It is two electric power plants, each serving a town of 60,000 population. It is two fine, fully equipped hospitals. It is some 50 miles of concrete highway. We pay for a single fighter plane with a half million bushels of wheat. We pay for a single destroyer with new homes that could have housed more than 8,000 people . . . is there no other way the world may live?[1]

War never comes cheap. Take, for example, the 'contact report' we looked at in chapter 3, when a unit of British soldiers was attacked by a group of Taliban. In the report we are told that the unit 'returned fire with organic weapons' – i.e. the weapons the soldiers were carrying with them. We are not told what weapons these were, but they would have included machine guns and grenade launchers, as well as the personal automatic rifles of the soldiers. Most patrols of 20 men or so (a platoon) will carry a few Javelin anti-tank missiles, and it is likely that at least one was fired. Why? Because the Taliban have tanks? Well, as an anti-tank missile, designed to pierce armour, Javelin also has the potential to penetrate walls and other obstacles behind which Taliban fighters commonly lurk.

Once it was recognized that these 'organic' weapons had not had the desired effect, 'fast air' was called in – jet fighter-bombers. These are always 'on station' while soldiers are on patrol (which is to say all the time), poised to deliver their weapons. In this case, the aircraft was a Harrier and the ordnance (or weapon) used was a Brimstone laser-guided bomb. This was one of thousands of small battles fought by the British army in Helmand. It resulted, as we saw, in the death of eight civilians. But how much did it cost?

The bullets fired are small beer: about 30 pence each. With 20 men firing automatic weapons for two hours, and with each man carrying between 180 and 500 bullets, some two or three thousand rounds may have been loosed off, but still that will only have cost around £1,000.

Moving up the scale and escalating the force used, let us assume that a Javelin missile was indeed fired: that will have cost the taxpayer £70,000. Soldiers will talk of 'firing a Porsche', as a Javelin missile costs the same as a new Porsche 911.[2] Sometimes more than one is used, but we will assume here that a single missile was fired.

But the escalation did not stop there. A Harrier jet (at least £8,000 per hour)[3] dropped a Brimstone laser-guided bomb, costing £77,000.[4] Assuming that the Harrier was on station for two hours, this 'contact' will have cost the British taxpayer a total of at least £164,000. This is enough money to employ six fully qualified mid-career nurses for a year.[5] It comes over and above the huge sums required to get the soldiers to Central Asia and to feed, fuel and cool them while they are there (see below). Literally no expense is spared. But unfortunately, as we will see, by no means every expense is accounted for.

Does the Ministry of Defence know how much it is spending on the war?

In 2010, in its evidence for the House of Commons Defence Committee's report 'Operations in Afghanistan', the Ministry of Defence claimed that, 'given the Department's purpose and how it is funded, it is not possible to identify which elements of the core Defence budget are being spent in Afghanistan'.[6]

The members of the committee were not prepared to accept this mandarin-speak, however:

> . . . we do not accept that it is not possible for the MoD to estimate the full costs of operations in Afghanistan. Whilst we recognise that the MoD cannot calculate accurately the full cost of operations, we nevertheless ask the MoD to provide us with a broad estimate of the total costs of operations in Afghanistan.[7]

No such estimate, broad or otherwise, was forthcoming. In its reply to the Defence Committee, the MOD simply restated its position: 'It is not possible to provide a meaningful estimate – however broad – of the "total" cost of operations in Afghanistan.'[8]

The MOD is unable to tell us the *full* expenditure on operations.

One might be forgiven for believing that the MOD is (to borrow from a former cabinet secretary) being literally economical with the truth. But there is an alternative interpretation: that the ministry simply does not know and has no means of finding out. The National Audit Office's 2011 report on the accounts of the ministry stated that 'the Department is still not able to provide enough evidence to support the accounting for over £5.3 billion worth of military equipment'.[9] As a result of that and other deficiencies, the comptroller and auditor general 'qualified' the accounts, essentially refusing to sign them off.

Against the background of a somewhat chaotic Ministry of Defence, it is very difficult indeed to discover the real total cost of any campaign. 'No one is being dishonest', a military officer with extensive experience of the confused financial world of the MOD told me. 'It's just that, since we haven't settled on a system of accounting for kit that everyone accepts, it is very hard to establish the cost of anything. We just don't know what things really cost.'[10] The strange and rather disturbing truth is that, within defence, it seems no one knows. Attempting to work out from government figures the true costs of a single year's campaigning has proved a difficult and probably futile task.

As Neil Davies, former chief economist at the Ministry of Defence, points out, extracting money from the Treasury involves negotiation, and the people at the Treasury are ferocious negotiators: 'In the MOD, the Treasury is the real enemy. The Taliban are temporary adversaries, like the Russians.' The Treasury will accept no requirement that cannot absolutely be proved to be additional to what otherwise would have been spent, had the war in Afghanistan not occurred. This is why calculations of the cost of the war are always phrased as 'additional costs' – the NACMO (Net Additional Costs of Military Operations). The numbers seen in the figures presented to Parliament are, accordingly:

the narrowest basis of costs ... Getting the Treasury to fork out money is very difficult. They look to try to strike everything out. Their underpinning assumption is that you would have those forces and pay for all the forces that might be needed. Only things that can be demonstrated as essential and unavoidable are included in the 'additional costs' figure. The Treasury are not necessarily interested in an objective assessment. The numbers that come out of their challenges will be very robust. *But, consequently, they are a very low figure.*[11]

When trying to work out any form of costs, one needs to bear in mind that all agencies are, for their own reasons, in the business of trying to minimize costs. As we have seen, the procedure is that the Ministry of Defence asks the Treasury to pay those costs that are over and above what would otherwise be spent on defence. There is a reasonable rationale behind this. It is the job of the Ministry of Defence to provide *capability to fight*. It is the Treasury's job to pay for the *use* of that capability in pursuance of national policy. To that extent, as Neil Davies puts it, there is a counterfactual element to this: calculating what might be additional to normal requirements involves making an assessment of what *would have been spent* on maintaining that capability had there been no war in Afghanistan.[12] It is in the Ministry of Defence's interests to minimize that figure, and it is in the Treasury's interests to maximize it, so that it ends up paying less.

Professor Keith Hartley of York University considers the 'additional costs' to be a helpful metric, as it enables calculation of the purely military costs of the operations (rather than confusing those costs with the rest of the budget, much of which would be spent anyway). In other words, we can see how much is being spent that would not otherwise be spent, rather than all the costs of the operation.[13]

But not all the costs of the operation are included in the assessments. 'Total cost' is a sum of very many different assessments. And as the officer quoted above said, there is no agreed way of assessing the real cost of many items of kit or how much it costs to use them. Assessment on the basis of 'additional costs' may be fair, but it is not complete.

So what does the MOD say the war has cost?

The MOD estimates that in 2009–10 it cost £3.82 billion to keep the operation in Afghanistan going; in 2010–11, it was in the region of £3.75 billion. The Ministry of Defence helpfully states that this approximated to over £397,000 per soldier per year with a further £61,000 for new equipment *per soldier*.[14] In 2011–12 the total was slightly lower still, at just under £3.46 billion with a per soldier cost of £364,000.[15] A further £60,000 was spent per soldier on new equipment in 2011–12.[16]

In April 2012, the Labour MP David Winnick asked a parliamentary question about the estimated cost of UK operations in Afghanistan to date. In reply, Defence Secretary Philip Hammond said: 'We estimate that, as at 31 March 2012, the *net additional cost* of military operations in Afghanistan since 2001 has been some £17 billion.'[17] (The House of Commons Library later estimated it at **£17.3 billion**.)[18] This figure – which, it must be recalled is for *military costs alone*, as one might expect with the Ministry of Defence – is only part of the story.

Since 2006, it has cost, on a conservative estimate, about £15 million *per day* to maintain the UK's military presence in Helmand. That is the annual income of the Army Benevolent Fund or, if you prefer, enough to run 15 average local primary schools for an entire year. As one soldier wag put it to me as we queued to buy home-made cakes to support a primary school's roof fund 'the day the MOD starts cake sales outside its HQ to buy aircraft we'll never use is the day I start complaining about a reduction in our defence budget'.

This is not by any means the whole story.

What is not included in MOD estimates?

A whole raft of other costs that are supposedly already accounted for in the defence budget is not mentioned or included in the calculations. Things stated by the MOD to be excluded from NACMO claims to the

Treasury include 'overheads associated with the procurement process'.[19] Anyone with the slightest acquaintance with procurement and the vast costs associated with it might consider this rather a large exclusion. Significantly, the salaries of service personnel deployed to Afghanistan are not included. The MOD states that 'this figure [salaries] does not represent a true cost of operations in Afghanistan, as the MoD incurs the cost regardless of the operation' – not quite true, as the size of the army is certainly greater than it would have been had the Helmand operation not taken place.

Without this extended operation, many of those 'use them or lose them' battalions would have been disbanded much sooner than they have been. The costs of those soldiers should arguably be assessed as 'additional costs', although persuading the Treasury to include them would surely be a fruitless task. As we saw in chapter 1, one of the reasons the army was so keen to proceed from Iraq to Afghanistan was self-interest or self-preservation. The figure given to the Defence Committee also 'excludes the military personnel based in the UK and elsewhere who support Operation HERRICK either directly or indirectly'. Again, this is a rather large exemption, as a vast amount of effort is expended in the UK on supporting the operation.

'Getting on for £6 billion a year'

A rather more beefy estimate of the *total* cost of operations (which, as we have seen, the MOD itself is unable to supply) comes from a rather well-placed source. In his evidence to the Foreign Affairs Committee in November 2010 (so around the same time as the Defence Committee was taking evidence for its fourth report), a former ambassador to Afghanistan, Sir Sherard Cowper-Coles, stated that we were spending 'getting on for £6 billion of taxpayers' money a year' on the war.[20] Clearly this figure was not a mere figment of this highly regarded and exceedingly experienced diplomat's imagination. The British ambassador is, by virtue of his role as the Queen's representative, the leading British official in a country. Quite apart from his ceremonial role, the British ambassador in Afghanistan is required to have day-to-day oversight of all British activities in the country. In other words, he is in a position to know the real total cost of what is being done.

Where does all this money go?

It is, as Tony Blair put it, 'an extraordinary piece of desert'.[21] Or as Major General Jeff Mason has said: 'You couldn't select a worse place to fight as a logistician. Land-locked, significantly far from a port, a country [with facilities] not even the third world regards as infrastructure . . . overall distance and the environment really affect what we do there.'[22]

This is Camp Bastion, named not after a famous fort or battle, but after the large canvas bag, reinforced by steel mesh and filled with rubble, that surrounds all military bases in places such as this – the HESCO Bastion. Bathos rather than heroism.

It is an impressive place by any standards. Camp Bastion is now the largest British base constructed since the end of the Second World War, a fact that places the Afghan War in something like its proper historical perspective. In early 2013 it was home to 20,000 (at times far more) British and US soldiers, and its scale is little short of breath-taking. There is a perimeter fence of 40km, so that in terms of area the base is about the same size as the Berkshire town of Reading.[23] There is the constant chatter of helicopters flying to or from the air base, which is equipped to take some of the largest military transport aircraft. Bastion has one of the busiest airports in the world, with several hundred aircraft landing and taking off each day, most of them helicopters. The central warehouse is said to be the largest building in Afghanistan. Some elements are surreal in their normality: should you crave a snack, as many soldiers do, you are spoiled for choice – there are as many fast food outlets as might be found in a medium-sized shopping mall.

It is a town that, in places, is frenetic. Workshops are constantly busy servicing and repairing vehicles damaged by enemy action or simply worn out by the dirt roads of the province. Convoys crawl through the base on their way to or from remote outposts (the drivers and escorts have one of the most dangerous of all jobs – many convoys come under some form of attack). Meanwhile, in huge air-conditioned tents, hundreds of staff officers and soldiers tap away day and night on computers. In summer, the heat assails you as soon as you leave the tents and cool prefab buildings.

Outside, the hum of the air-conditioning units is replaced with the drone of the diesel generators. From the time you land to the time you leave, this din is constant. All these devices need fuel, and that fuel needs to be paid for – and not from petty cash. In an interview with national public radio, Brigadier General Steven Anderson, former chief logistics officer to General Petraeus, revealed the annual cost to the US *of air conditioning alone* in Afghanistan (and Iraq, to be fair): 'When you consider the cost to deliver the fuel to some of the most isolated places in the world – escorting, command and control, medevac support – when you throw all that infrastructure in, we're talking over $20 billion.'[24]

Most of this huge desert camp has been paid for by British taxpayers. It has been brought in, piece by piece, mostly by road, from the UK. The cost of maintaining this town in the middle of a Central Asian desert must be borne by those same taxpayers. Let us start to build up a picture of the expense by looking at what is involved.

Logistics

Any army, wherever it is deployed, depends totally on the supply of absolutely everything – missiles to toilet rolls – working properly. Traditionally in warfare, the supply of *matériel* was the responsibility of the armed forces. Indeed, very significant branches of all the services are dedicated to this task. In the army, for example, it is the job of the Royal Logistics Corps; the navy has an entire fleet of civilian-manned ships known as the Royal Fleet Auxiliary; the Royal Marines, the most combat-effective and efficiently organized of all, has the army's Commando Logistic Regiment attached to it. The junior service, the RAF, runs a very capable and extremely expensive organization, which operates a so-called 'airbridge' to Helmand.

There are, at any one time, on average around 9,500 British soldiers serving in the remote southern Afghan province of Helmand. The main task of the 'airbridge' is to transport these troops and their baggage to and from Afghanistan (though not, as we shall see, equipment). To support these 'airbridge' commitments, the RAF has acquired a fleet of eight C-17 Globemasters – vast, majestic aircraft that are capable of carrying hundreds of troops each. These are in addition to the 38 or so propeller-driven C-130 Hercules aircraft, the workhorse of the transport fleet. Moreover, every month the Ministry of Defence makes use of dozens of flights on civilian charter aircraft. Indeed over half of all passenger movements are made with charter aircraft. For 2011–12 the cost of running these flights was £198 million.[25]

In other words, the RAF essentially runs the equivalent of a large airline simply to send out and bring back home what amounts to the population of a small town twice a year, and to assist in supplying them while they are away. Needless to say, this does not come cheap. So how much does it cost to send one soldier on a return flight to Afghanistan? The full figure is in the region of '£1,680 per return trip calculated on a full-costs basis that includes cost elements that are incurred whether or not an aircraft actually flies'.[26] In fact, each of the 9,500 or so soldiers deployed to Afghanistan is flown out there not once but *twice*, as he or she comes back to the UK about halfway through a six-month tour on leave, and is then, of course, flown out to Afghanistan again. Each soldier therefore makes two return journeys every six months. And there are two full rotations every year. Therefore the full cost is £3,360 for each soldier every year. By way of comparison, a return ticket from London to Kabul retails at between £650 and £900 (depending on the airline) – roughly half of what the same journey costs the RAF. It must also be borne in mind that the amount quoted by the MOD does not begin to approach the full cost, as it claims: it does not count the expense of running the various military airports, the security or the other running costs that are factored into commercial airline prices.

Of course, a key difference between the Royal Air Force and a large airline is that the airline knows *to the last penny* what it costs to run its aircraft and to pay for the associated services. It will make strenuous efforts to mitigate costs and to increase efficiency. It must also turn a profit. Many soldiers could pinpoint another important difference: you can generally rely on commercial airlines to get you to your destination within a day of the schedule.[27]

Huge amounts of supplies are flown to Afghanistan, although most of it goes by land. Much of the gear transported by air is carried in charter aircraft. Indeed, as we have seen, the Ministry of Defence knows the cost of every charter flight, since airline charter companies bill it for every journey. But how much does it cost per hour to run one of the RAF's huge C-17 transport aircraft or the four-engined C-130 Hercules? Unfortunately, no one knows.[28] One officer called financial costs a 'basic management metric' on which the various commands are trying to get a grip. 'We have a way to go', he said. As we will see, the financial costs of almost any aspect of this operation (save for those that involve commercial companies) are a mystery.

Convoys

Once equipment and supplies arrive at the main NATO bases, much of it – fuel, food and ammunition – needs to be distributed to the hundreds of NATO patrol bases throughout the country. That is a job for the army itself, and for probably the only group of men who may truly be described as unsung heroes – the truck drivers and escorts of these supply convoys. No swashbuckling books have been written about the drivers of the Royal Logistic Corps.

However, first it needs to get to those main bases, and those who get it there are generally not soldiers. There is a vast private security industry in Afghanistan. Its workers do the tasks that the NATO military forces will not or cannot do – tasks ranging from the personal protection of VIPs to guarding the gates of embassies. It is fair to say that, as a result of the activities of certain (largely US) companies such as Blackwater (a company that has changed its name twice),[29] these security men have a very bad reputation in Afghanistan on account of their cavalier attitude to Afghan drivers and, on occasion, pedestrians. At least 10 of the 40 companies operating in Afghanistan and some 3,000 of the estimated 30,000 security employees in the country are British.[30] UK companies have rarely been involved in the kind of scandal that besets their US equivalents, but nevertheless one of President Karzai's more popular initiatives has been an attempt to ban all foreign security companies.

However, many of the operators employ people of great dedication and professionalism in a dangerous and unforgiving environment. NATO does not have the resources available to supply its bases by road. Many soldiers do not realize that a sizeable proportion of their supplies (about a quarter)[31] does not come in on the huge aircraft that land at Helmand. Before the Pakistanis imposed a moratorium on convoys taking NATO supplies through their territory, *matériel* would be taken from ships which had docked at the Pakistani port of Karachi, some two weeks drive from Helmand. Now they come via Central Asia. Either way, they need to travel very many miles through Taliban-controlled territory.

There is more to security than providing guards. Many security companies that bring supplies in to NATO forces, including UK forces, pay the Taliban for protection. The author and journalist Nadene Ghouri told me that at least one international security company employs what are essentially Taliban liaison officers: these men strike deals with local Taliban commanders along the route of a convoy, paying what is in effect protection money in exchange for safe passage. 'Everyone wins', she told me. 'The Taliban get to pay off and keep the loyalty of local chiefs, the security company fulfils its contract and NATO get their supplies.' Arguably the only losers are the taxpayers of the countries who pay the security companies – although even they get the *matériel* they have paid for through the Taliban 'badlands'. The irony of NATO paying the Taliban to get its supplies surely has more than a little of the Catch 22 about it.

An insight into the ordeals facing those private companies that work to bring supplies to the military bases and do not pay off the Taliban comes from a private security officer 'John', a British ex-special forces soldier.[32] He provides security, finds recruits and supervises the guards for the logistics convoys that transport essential supplies by road into Afghanistan. The convoys are manned largely by Afghan employees of private security companies. As he says: 'These convoys are being ambushed on a regular basis because they are big, slow-moving targets, the security personnel are not allowed heavy weapons, and there is no air cover to protect them.'

Peter Lee, a former armed forces chaplain and now a lecturer at the Royal Air Force College, submitted a Freedom of Information request about this issue. He asked the Ministry of Defence for a range of information relating to British supply convoys in Afghanistan. Questions included: 'How many times have convoys come under attack between 2006 and 2011? How many fatalities and woundings have resulted from those attacks?'

After 20 days I was informed that the MoD wanted to use its right to take a further 20 days to consider my request. When the eventual reply came, I was encouraged to learn that the MoD 'holds information relevant to these questions'. The response continued: 'There is a public interest in understanding the robustness of NATO overland logistic supply routes, the impact of insurgent attacks on NATO supply lines and the threats faced by UK and other personnel protecting logistic convoys in Afghanistan' ... Then came the 'but'. My request was turned down because releasing the information into the public domain 'would potentially provide hostile elements with a much greater understanding of the impact, at the operational level, of insurgent action on NATO convoys'.[33]

As Peter Lee pointed out in an article in the *Daily Mail*: 'If there is one group of people who know exactly what impact they are having on NATO operations it is the anti-government fighters who risk their lives to lay roadside bombs and ambush convoys. There are so few roads in and out of Afghanistan that the task of gathering information on truck convoys is the Afghan equivalent of train-spotting at your local railway station.'[34]

Petrol

None of this comes cheap. American officials have been somewhat more open about the scale of the costs attached to supplying this kind of operation. Some indication of British costs can be gleaned from what the United States pays to get a gallon of fuel from its source to where it is used.

The US Department of Defense pays $2.78 for each gallon of JP-8 fuel, the standard gasoline grade for US vehicles and helicopters.[35] This, it must be said, is the cost at source – at the refinery. This gallon of fuel must be transported to one of the patrol bases in Helmand where the US marines have been fighting since they bailed the British army out with their 'surge' in 2009. As we saw above, to get there, it must be driven into Afghanistan usually from the port of Karachi in Pakistan, in convoys that face lethal dangers, changing carriers on the way, before it arrives and is stored at a major base, such as Camp Bastion.

Our gallon of fuel then needs to be transported by one of those military supply convoys, over perhaps two or three days of appalling roads. It may be that there are no roads at all, in which case the fuel will need to be taken by helicopter. Needless to say, all of this requires a great deal of personnel, effort – and, of course, more fuel.

In 2009, the US Department of Defense Comptroller's Department – a kind of overseer of activities – reported to the House (Congressional) Appropriations Defense Sub-committee that a gallon of fuel costing $2.78 at the pump (as it were) will cost about $400 (*sic*) by the time it gets to a forward patrol base.[36] Similar costs will apply, of course, to fuel for British troops. It must all be paid for. Needless to say, no information is publicly available as to the cost of fuel for British operations or the amount consumed.

'Urgent Operational Requirements'

When senior officers deliver, as they regularly have done, 'urgent operational requirements' (UORs) – i.e. requests for new and better kit – it is usually taken to mean extra equipment ordered when it becomes apparent that the equipment they have is insufficient. In a single year (2011–12), the army asked for, and got, £415 million worth of new equipment that was 'urgently required'.[37] The 2011–12 MOD accounts reveal that the campaign in Afghanistan has given rise to no less than £5.6 billion worth of UORs.[38] As we saw above for 2011–12 *alone*, just over £60,000 was spent *per soldier* on additional equipment costs.[39] The costs were similar for the previous year.

If the MOD is to be believed, nearly a quarter of the total cost of the operation has been incurred after senior officers have asked for equipment. Allegations by senior officers – often vented by leaks to the press – that the army has been betrayed by parsimonious politicians are simply inaccurate. As one senior officer told me: 'They had the kit they asked for. Sometimes they did not ask for enough or the right equipment at the right time, and politicians got the blame when these officers came back and asked for more.'[40] Commanders asked and commanders received.

New vehicles

A large proportion of the £5.6 billion of these requests concerned vehicles and other equipment bought in an attempt to increase the levels of protection afforded to soldiers due to the ever-increasing IED threat. The state of the vehicles being used by soldiers in Afghanistan was, as was well reported in the British press, a scandal. Everyone who served in that country or in Iraq before 2009 has stories about this. When I served in Iraq in 2003–04, the teams I commanded drove around the city of Basra in white four-wheel-drive cars – the kind one sees in many supermarket car parks, except that ours were very much bottom of the range. When I made representations to our commanders in Baghdad, I was told to get on with it; everyone had the same problem. Eventually it became too stupidly dangerous to drive these cars and they were confined to camp. We felt much safer in the infamous Land Rover Snatches we had. But soon these also became too dangerous to drive outside the camp.

Things were far worse in Afghanistan, as combat there was usually more intense than in Iraq. I remember seeing a Land Rover patrol vehicle parked outside the offices of the Provincial Reconstruction Team. It was festooned – as were most of these vehicles – with machine guns, giving it something of the Second World War 'Long Range Desert Group' swagger that soldiers like. No number of machine guns was going to protect this vehicle from an explosive device of any power at all, because the vehicle's driver and crew were entirely open to the elements. Only a couple of rather pathetic-looking pieces of what looked like scrap metal bolted to the side of the driver's and the commander's doors offered any kind of protection. Indeed, two soldiers and an interpreter were killed in such a vehicle during my short time in Helmand.

The Ministry of Defence responded to the great increase in casualties with a flurry of orders to various vehicle companies: 'In 2009, the Department will begin to deploy to Afghanistan a total of 564 new protected vehicles and augment the existing proven vehicle fleets, approved at a cost of around £800 million. These include Jackal, Mastiff, Ridgeback, Panther and Tactical Support Vehicles Wolfhound, Husky and Coyote.'[41] The procurement process for these vehicles has been marked by inefficiency and waste.[42]

Much of the vast quantity of equipment bought for the campaign will be left in Afghanistan. After the British army leaves the bases of Southern Afghanistan in 2014, many of the vehicles are to be left with the Afghan army. As one senior officer has said: 'There is obviously good reason in making sure they have the right kit, but this is huge money we are gifting to them at a time when the British Army is skint. We are seeing soldiers made redundant, assets being sold off all over the place, capability of our frontline units reduced and yet we are giving all this away.'[43]

There is another aspect to this: to whom are we going to give all this expensively acquired, high-end, high-tech equipment? For the Afghan army will not be staying long in Helmand once the British leave. With only 3 per cent of its number ethnically southern Pashtun, the Afghan army is almost as foreign to Helmand as the British army. A very senior British official related to me an Afghan army officer's smiling reply when asked by a British minister how long his army would stay once British and other NATO forces left Helmand: 'As long as it takes to pack up.'[44] With a little encouragement and some support from remaining UK and US troops, it may stay longer than that. But not much longer. One wonders how many of those well-built, prestige vehicles will end up in the hands of the various militias that governed Helmand before the British arrived and that (very many serious commentators believe) will govern there again. One of those groups, of course, we call the Taliban.

Hidden extras

New aircraft

Urgent operational requirements are included in the NACMO estimates. But many other large outlays are not. These comprise the costs that the MOD finds it impossible to account for. Do we know what some of those costs may be?

In 2000, the MOD leased four huge Boeing C-17 aircraft for the Royal Air Force for seven years. The whole deal was worth nearly £800 million.[45] Even to those at home in the stratospherically expensive world of defence spending, the renting of aircraft for the same amount of money as it would take to buy them (they retail at under £200 million) seemed a good deal for the lessors, though rather less so for the RAF.

In 2006, the decision was taken not to extend the lease, but to buy the aircraft outright. Over the next six years, as the requirements of the vast operation in Afghanistan became apparent, four more were bought. The eighth (and last) was purchased in 2012: the more than £200 million for it was found, the MOD claimed, out of 'money saved'.[46] It is not clear where money was 'saved'. But it is clear why the purchase of this 'absolutely brilliant workhorse' was made – to get the troops back: 'The C-17 has shown its worth in Afghanistan ensuring that our troops are given the fastest, most efficient passage home.'[47] As well they might be: a single C-17 mission to Afghanistan costs about $250,000.[48]

'Buying equipment off-the-shelf allows us to quickly deliver equipment that our troops need on operations at best value prices for the taxpayer', claimed Defence Secretary Philip Hammond.[49] Not such good value, says a defence industry trade website: apparently, at

$317 million, the MOD was charged rather more than the usual price paid by US users ($260–270 million).[50] Though in fairness, the RAF specifications would be different from those of the US Air Force, which also, of course, has the advantage of buying in bulk.[51]

The MOD tells us that these aircraft can also evacuate civilians, in much the same way as a chartered Boeing 747, or the ex-Soviet An-124 chartered by China to evacuate its nationals from Libya. The C-17 has not yet been used to evacuate any British citizens. When such evacuations are required, one of our 70 or so propeller-driven C-130 Hercules heavy transport aircraft is generally used.

So, of the eight aircraft purchased, only four would have been required, had it not been for the Afghan campaign (and to a lesser extent Iraq). We therefore have (at least) four more huge transport aircraft than we would otherwise require, costing well in excess of **£800 million**.[52] These aircraft were not paid for by the UORs: they came out of the MOD's budget. They are not included in the NACMO assessments.

A similar tale surrounds the procurement of a fleet of new Chinook helicopters, whose thumping rotors provide the soundtrack for Afghanistan in much the same way as their smaller cousin, the Bell Huey, gave its sound to Vietnam. The 46 of these huge flying buses that the RAF had were too few to provide adequate and consistent coverage for UK forces. So the decision was taken to buy 14 new aircraft. Needless to say, these helicopters do not come cheap: the total cost will be **£1 billion**.[53] Most of them will not be available until well after the British troops have largely left Afghanistan. With big reductions in army personnel imminent and (it is to be hoped) no major deployments like Iraq or Afghanistan on the horizon, it is difficult to see why the UK armed forces need far more aircraft of this type than any other European nation. Equally, if it were not for the huge deployment to Helmand and the attendant scandals concerning a lack of helicopter support, the aircraft would not even have been considered at this time of financial stringency. They must accordingly be regarded as a cost of the campaign.

A larger army than we needed

A strong argument can be made – and is made here – that the size of the British army has been kept artificially inflated on account of the commitments in Afghanistan. Indeed a strong argument can be made that one reason for such a large commitment to Southern Afghanistan (far larger than the commitment of any other European nation) was to retain the size of the army. As the army's head, General Richard Dannatt, reportedly said of the dozens of infantry battalions, 'It's use them or lose them' (see chapter 1).

In 2012, the army lost many of them anyway. In recognition that commitments will fall dramatically once major military operations cease in 2015, the decision was taken to cut the regular army by about 20 per cent – from a force of 102,000 to one of 82,000 (augmented by 30,000 deployable reservists, who are far cheaper than regular soldiers) by 2020. Seventeen army units will disappear or be amalgamated.[54] Many argue that the British army does not need to be even that big: including trained deployable reserves, the 2020 plan will leave the army about the same size as it was during much of the nineteenth century. Indeed, in 1883, at the height of empire, just after the Second Afghan War and the Zulu War, the army numbered just 124,000.[55] In 2020, the British army will have no overseas bases. There are those who consider that, even then, the army will be too large for the UK's defence requirements.

The Helmand operation has forced us to maintain an army that is too large for our needs. Needless to say, had the 'use them or lose them' moment not arrived in 2005 and had the vast Helmand operation not happened, these cuts could have taken place long ago. So how much was spent that otherwise would not have been spent?

The notional cost of a single soldier in 2011 is a remarkable £219,528 per annum.[56] This is a distorted figure, as it is derived by simply dividing the defence budget by the number of servicemen. Given that the defence budget includes vast high-end procurement items, as well as large numbers of civil servants (many of whom are also being cut), this is not really a helpful figure in establishing how much will be saved by cutting 20,000 servicemen.

The so-called 'capitation cost' (the notional annual cost of salary, benefits, pensions and upkeep) of a private soldier – the lowest rank – was about £31,000 in 2009. For an officer of the rank of major, it was over £100,000. The MOD no longer calculates capitation costs.[57] If we take an average of £30,000 for each serviceman cut (clearly on the low side), we are looking at a saving of £600 million. It should be pointed out that this is an extremely conservative estimate, as capitation does not include costs such as the purchase and maintenance of equipment that the soldier will use.[58]

It is impossible to say with any certainty how long we have had an army that is larger than would otherwise be needed, since that requires a counterfactual assessment. Few would deny that the defence cuts would have come at least four years earlier if Helmand had not dominated the army's existence, and indeed the activities of all the armed forces. In fact, such cuts were looming – hence the 'use them or lose them' moment. So we have had an army that has been overinflated by 20 per cent for at least five years. At a minimum of £600 million each year, that totals **£3 billion** – at the very least.

Return and reset

'Reset' is the process of restoring military units to a reasonable degree of readiness after deployment. It involves repair of kit and replacement of damaged or missing equipment. It also involves retraining and the costs associated with resting units. It is an accrued cost that (like the accrued cost of casualties) has not been budgeted for. Leading defence analyst Francis Tusa calculated the cost of resetting the British army's vehicle stock to be in the region of £1.5 billion to £2 billion, on the optimistic basis that 75 per cent would be returned to the UK.[59] He ran these numbers past a two-star general responsible for organizing and costing these matters. Apparently the general initially thought that Tusa has received leaked figures!

Very many of the vehicles used by the UK army in Afghanistan are now unserviceable for use in the UK. Indeed, very many were designed and built exclusively for Afghanistan. Many of them will be left behind for the Afghan army or (more likely) will fall into the hands of others. The cost of returning the kit that the army intends to keep will be huge – Tusa puts it at up to £600 million. As of late 2012, no official estimate had been forthcoming about the realistic costs of the return of kit and *matériel*. It is, says the government, a matter that is subject to sensitive 'commercial in confidence considerations'.[60] It will involve moving 16,000 containers across Central Asia and Russia, with a rate of loss (from theft and damage) estimated to be in the region of 50 per cent. Each of the containers will cost between £10,000 and £30,000 to return home.[61] Even these prices may soar, as Britain will be competing for very limited space on suitable commercial aircraft, trains and trucks. In other words, chaos is always a possibility. Of course, much of the kit and *matériel* is not suitable for transport by container – not least the large quantities of sensitive and hazardous military equipment.

And what will happen to the huge base at Camp Bastion? 'We will try to sell the relevant facilities to the US marines and other US military, and wave goodbye on the last aircraft we have out of there. Of course, that assumes that we manage to get all our ducks in a row and start our withdrawal in time, so that we finish first.'[62]

There can be little doubt that the cost of return and reset will be not less than **£2 billion**.

What did the war in Helmand cost the Taliban?

As we saw in chapter 4, the gunfight or 'contact' that we examined would have cost the UK about £164,000. What did it cost our enemies? First of all, there *may* have been several casualties. No one is sure how many, as the Taliban are adept at hiding (or on occasion exaggerating) their casualties when it suits them to forestall further air strikes. But however many casualties there were, there are many more young men willing – indeed occasionally desperate – to die in order to drive out of their country those they see as invaders.

But what about the financial cost to the Taliban of their attacks? The most common weapon used by the Taliban is the improvised explosive device. The raw materials are often available at no cost from the Soviet anti-tank mines that still dot the countryside. For the other components of IEDs, they would have to pay in the region of $5–15. The maker of the IED usually gets something like $5.[63] The Taliban and those supporting them have planted thousands of such devices, very many of which are found and defused by the British or American 'Barma' teams that sweep ahead of every patrol. Let us assume that the 'enemy' has planted 100,000 such devices in Helmand – a very liberal figure. We are looking at an investment of, at most, $2 million.

Then there is the cost to the Taliban of paying their troops. (This is a highly controversial subject, but it does seem that some *aslee* Taliban fighters are paid.) In 2011, in one of its many schemes to try to stop the insurgency, ISAF was paying fighters £100 a month.[64] This figure was based on intelligence received concerning the pay of Taliban fighters. No one (certainly no one in Western intelligence) knows how many men the Taliban have under arms. Many of them are simply farmers who take up arms to fight the invader whenever they can. Gilles Dorronsoro, arguably the West's leading expert on the Taliban, states:

Most of the fighters do not join the Taliban for money. They join because the Afghan government is unjust, corrupt, or simply not there. They also join because the Americans have bombed their houses or shown disrespect for their values. For young people, joining the Taliban is a way to earn social status. The Taliban may give fighters money, for example, if they want to marry. And some part-time fighters may fight for money, though in my experience, that's becoming increasingly rare.[65]

Most will not be paid. It is highly unlikely that there are at any one time more than a few hundred paid fighters in Helmand. The US estimates a nationwide figure of 25,000, but Dorronsoro is sceptical about this, as so many Taliban are part-timers. Let us assume a figure for Helmand of 1,000 paid fighters – almost certainly a huge overestimate. The cost to the Taliban of paying 1,000 men $100 a month (again a high figure) is $1.2 million per annum. Over the eight years of the conflict in Helmand (2006–14), that gives a total of about $9.6 million.

Add to that their investment in IEDs ($2 million at most), throw in another $10 million for extras, such as the purchase of rifles (which most Afghans possess anyway) and ammunition, and we are looking at a grand total of Taliban spending of no more than $22 million. This equates to about £16 million. This is truly asymmetric warfare.

Summing up

In his evidence to the House of Commons Defence Committee, defence analyst Francis Tusa summed up some of the problems we have looked at in this chapter:

It goes to budgets, and so on. Unfortunately, in areas like that, the MoD is frequently a stranger to anything close to the truth or accuracy, which then hinders the core MoD mission. They are spending far too much time cooking the books and they do not end up running the Ministry effectively, which applies to civil servants and the military in equal number.[66]

Most British troops will be gone from Afghanistan by the end of 2014. Yet a significant presence will remain after that date. Britain has committed itself, for example, to setting up an 'Afghan Sandhurst' to train the officer cadre of the Afghan armed forces.[67] That will need staffing, as will the inevitable special forces teams that will continue to range the country in search of wrongdoers. Clearly none of this will be done on a shoestring.

No indication is available from the Ministry of Defence as to what it estimates to be the next two years' expenditure. No clue is forthcoming from the MOD's business plan, in which Afghanistan, despite being one of the purported priorities of 'defence', gains but two passing mentions – and Helmand none at all.[68] By the end of 2012, the British presence was down from 9,500 to about 9,000 troops. Further drawdowns will take place later in 2013–14. The financial year 2012–13 is likely to show a reduction from the £3.46 billion of 2011–12, but the figure will certainly not be lower than **£3 billion**. The remaining two years of the mission – from 2013 to the end of 2015 – will see an end to the large-scale deployment of British soldiers. Thus the figure should fall well below £3 billion for 2013–14 and even further in the final financial year of the mission. Nevertheless, the final two years of the mission will not produce a bill of less than **£4 billion**.

Summary of costs

Admitted total to April 2012	£17.3 billion
Costs of financial year 2012–13	£3 billion
Estimated costs for 2013–15	£4 billion
Costs of purchase of additional aircraft	£1.8 billion
Costs of maintaining a larger army	£3 billion
Return and reset	£2 billion
Total	**£31.1 billion**

These, of course, are only those costs that are relatively easily calculable. The figures do not include the cost of 'provisions' (including fuel and food) for the tens of thousands of troops stationed in Afghanistan. Though in fairness, soldiers need food wherever they are. Nor do they include separate initiatives like the 'Sandhurst in the Sand', planned for the period after the NATO withdrawal. As we will see, the civilian effort has a separate budget.

Other, even less easily quantifiable costs will increase the bill of the Helmand campaign considerably. We now turn to the costs related to the thousands of casualties sustained in the campaign.

CHAPTER 5

Financial Element of Death and Injury

The costs to the nation of all those dead and injured soldiers extend beyond the pain, suffering and worry of bereavement. There is a financial element to death and disability, too. This needs to be paid by the state in one form or another, and must be taken into account.

Value of a life

It is said that a cynic knows the price of everything but the value of nothing. But statisticians know both. When a person is killed, the loss is not only to the family, friends and immediate community: there is also a loss to society at large. The person will no longer contribute to his or her country, will no longer work and give of his or her skills. In the film *Unforgiven*, the character played by Clint Eastwood says, without irony or humour: 'It's a hell of a thing, killing a man. Take away all he's got and all he's ever gonna have.' You also take something away from the state. As with anything else, all governments place a value on life that is expressed in financial terms.

In the United States, the value placed on the life of a person killed or very seriously injured (also lost as a net contributor) is called the 'value of a statistical life' (VSL). In the UK it is sometimes termed the 'value of preventing a fatality' (VPF). Economists have developed VSL for very sound actuarial and policy reasons: it is used to determine whether the potential cost of a new law or regulation covering road safety is worth the lives saved. For government – for perfectly understandable and logical reasons – the phrase 'life is beyond value' is specious. Clearly, some risk has to be accepted for the smooth running of society and a limit must be placed on 'risk aversion'. Our roads would certainly be a great deal safer if all vehicles were mechanically limited to a speed of 30 miles per hour, and many lives would be saved. But the cost to the state of the resulting slow-moving economy would be far too great.

As of 2011, the VSL of a life in the US, as assessed by the Environmental Protection Agency (which is responsible for much of what in the UK we would call 'health and safety', as well as for key matters such as air pollution) is in the region of $9.1 million. Other agencies put the VSL rather lower, but this is the assessment that is generally used as the reference standard.[1]

In the UK, our lives are worth rather less. The Department of Transport's latest official VPF is about £1.585 million in 2009 figures;[2] this should be updated with inflation to give a 2013 figure of about £1.68 million.

It should be made very clear here that this figure has no bearing on the way decisions are reached about going to war. At no point do generals or politicians make a cost/benefit assessment of a military campaign with reference to the VPF. The decision to go to war is made far more quickly than any decision to change a transport regulation. Some would argue that the decision to go to war is made with far less consideration of all the consequences . . . Be that as it may, the notional financial value of a life plays no part in military decision-making.

We have lost in the region of 440 dead soldiers, sailors, marines and airmen in the Afghan War. The financial loss to society is around **£1 billion**. Yet surely the argument could easily be made that any notional value of a military life should not be based on an average of all UK citizens. Most people who have worked with serving or former soldiers will attest that these men and women bring far more to a company or organization (or indeed to the country as a whole) than the average man or woman. At the very least, many of them are extremely well trained and skilled. They tend to be reliable, hard-working and positive in their outlook. As such, a case can easily be made that their loss at a young and vigorous age is all the greater.

The injured

The reader will not be surprised to learn that, as with other costs of the campaign, 'there is no specific budget set aside for the ongoing care of soldiers wounded or sustaining psychiatric injury'.[3] Like most other expenses, this will be covered by the 'net additional costs of military operations'.

But the cost of this will continue to rise. The dead are gone, leaving their families with the permanent pain of bereavement; but the injured are still with us. In 2010, the Armed Forces Compensation Scheme was set up in the wake of a report by Admiral Lord Boyce, former chief of the defence staff.[4] It is intended to assist those who have been injured as a result of service with the armed forces since April 2005 (which covers almost all of those injured in Afghanistan, but curiously does not assist many soldiers injured in Iraq).

It is a reasonably straightforward system in theory: lump-sum awards are calculated by reference to a scale of severity, ranging from £1,200 (level 15) to £570,000 (level 1). The point at which any given injury or set of injuries registers on the scale is defined by an extensive and sobering list in the statutory instrument setting up the scheme.[5] Roughly two-thirds of applicants are successful. Over 15,000 payments have been made so far, and each year the number of awards rises by about 2,000.[6] These sums for disabled veterans roughly correspond to those under the civilian Disability Living Allowance scheme, with payments 'at least' equivalent.[7]

Not all the payments are made to soldiers who have deployed on operations: some go to servicemen and women who are injured in the course of their duties. But by mid-2012, nearly £103 million had been paid out for injuries sustained in Afghanistan.[8] In an answer to a parliamentary question in 2009, the then minister for veterans, Kevan Jones, gave the following assessment: 'the scheme has future liabilities estimated at £352.4 million[9] in respect of service related injuries already sustained but unclaimed at 31 March 2009 and the future value of the Guaranteed Income Payments'.[10] As of early 2013, no further assessments have been made.[11]

Clearly the value of 'future liabilities' will have increased considerably since 2009: indeed it will have more than doubled, along with UK casualties sustained. And the liabilities will continue to accrue. While the rate of injury and death has fallen since the appalling year of 2009, the number of claimants continues to rise. An eventual baseline figure of **£1 billion** for Afghanistan is surely reasonable, assuming no great increase in casualties or the rate of claims and with the emphasis on *baseline*. This is only the beginning. That compensation covers damage already sustained. It does not pay for ongoing care.

Ongoing care of veterans

The compensation that has been and will be paid to injured servicemen will amount to hundreds of millions of pounds. Again, this is a small sum in the grand scheme of military expenditure. Even the projected outlay of £1 billion is less than the purchase price of a single Daring Class missile destroyer and a year's running costs. Yet even the hundreds of millions of pounds that will be paid in compensation to the British victims of the war are dwarfed by the costs that will be incurred – particularly by the National Health Service – in relation to ongoing care. This is where we get into really serious money (though even this commitment is as nothing compared to the outlay on military kit and equipment, and on support for the vast organization in Afghanistan itself).

At the front line, the care given to wounded soldiers is second to none. When I joined the British forces in the late 1980s, our combat medics were sent to places such as South Africa, so that they could train and gain daily practice on the victims of gun crime there. Nowadays no British service combat medic need go outside the service to gain such experience. The British-led hospital in Camp Bastion is the world leader in trauma medicine, and its discoveries have brought benefits far beyond Afghanistan. For example, when I deployed to Libya as a stabilization officer in 2012, I had in my medical pack several packets of a compound made from the shells of crabs, which the doctors in Helmand had found to be excellent in staunching the flow of blood from wounds by congealing it. It is now commonly available. Very many other, more high-tech innovations have ensured that once a soldier is brought by the superb medical evacuation teams to the equally excellent hospital at Bastion, they are highly likely to survive.

However, the problems begin when injured soldiers return to the UK – which all of them long to do, to be near their families and their homes. The recent history of care given to wounded soldiers in the UK outside the military system is not a happy one. Traditionally, all servicemen were cared for in service environments. Right up until the 1990s, there was a network of military hospitals staffed by military personnel, doctors and nurses. But a series of defence cuts eventually reduced this constellation of hospitals to one – the Royal Naval Hospital at Haslar near Portsmouth. Finally, in 2007, that hospital also closed. By then it was the norm for wounded soldiers to be cared for in civilian wards, alongside other injured people.

There is a temptation for civilians to believe that one injury is very much like another: that a leg broken when an armoured vehicle rolls over is very like a leg broken in a fall from a ladder. But the impact on a seriously injured soldier of going from an environment where everyone has at least the army in common to one where he has almost nothing in common with the people coughing and wheezing around him is not to be underestimated. And needless to say, very many injuries were not broken bones, but gunshot wounds or injuries from explosions.

There were also many instances of other patients or visitors abusing or insulting the wounded men. In other words, a basic requirement of any hospital ward – security – was no longer present. This need for injured servicemen to feel secure resulted in the setting up of a dedicated ward at Selly Oak Hospital in Birmingham.

'You can't build people a life on the cheap'

Care for soldiers does not stop when they are discharged from hospital with their Armed Forces Compensation Scheme payments. After Selly Oak, seriously injured soldiers go to the rehabilitation facility at Headley Court in Surrey, another world-class institution. Even after treatment there, very many require continuing – indeed lifelong – assistance and treatment. The ongoing cost of care for injured veterans is unknown and has not been assessed in detail or budgeted for. But an initial idea of how much this figure might be can be gleaned from the fact that the Royal British Legion spends £1.4 million *per week* on what it calls 'wrap-around services' to supplement the care given by the NHS to injured veterans.[12]

The National Audit Office produced a report in 2010 entitled *Treating Injury and Illness Arising on Military Operations*.[13] It contains a rich variety of graphs and tables. One of the most interesting is the one indicating the number of admissions to the hospital in Camp Bastion for illnesses not related directly to combat. For Afghanistan is a very unhealthy place and every week more than 7 per cent of deployed personnel suffer from some form of illness.[14] Clearly, much of this is common-or-garden 'diarrhoea and vomiting', which (though it certainly does not feel common-or-garden at the time) usually has no effects lasting beyond the end of the tour. But some conditions are more serious and require evacuation home. Of the 7,000 or so field-hospital admissions, no fewer than 4,000 are for non-battle injuries.[15] The figures show that almost all of these were eventually evacuated to the UK.[16]

Some of those illnesses will pass. Others, such as the ever-lurking prospect of mental illness, will be present throughout the veteran's life. As we saw in chapter 2, it is highly likely that thousands of veterans of Iraq and Afghanistan will present with PTSD.

US statistics quoted by Joseph Stiglitz and Linda Bilmes in their *Three Trillion Dollar War* indicate that 35 per cent of Iraq veterans have presented to the hospitals of the Department of Veterans Affairs with medical conditions.[17] Clearly it is very difficult to separate conditions that might have arisen in any event from those that derive from operational service. However, it is surely fair to say that the stress of operations, the acutely unhealthy environment, and indeed the recent and more mundane stress of unemployment or redundancy will take their toll. And that toll will only get greater as the years go by. Stiglitz and Bilmes examined US figures and found that the Department of Veterans Affairs is providing medical care to 48 per cent of veterans of the Kuwait War, for example. They also discovered that the *average* annual cost of treating veterans in the system is $3,500.

Let us assume that only 25 per cent of UK Afghan War veterans (about 45,000) seek out medical care and that this costs on average £12,000 for five years (a rough conversion from the US dollar figure). This alone produces a cost of £540 million. Some veterans – notably the 600 or so seriously or very seriously injured – will require treatment costing hundreds of thousands of pounds. It should be recalled here that the largest award made by the Armed Forces Compensation Scheme is £570,000. Yet in the civilian world, awards are very commonly in the millions of pounds and are not just to compensate the person for the pain and injury, but also to ensure that the victim receives care for as long as he or she lives. Just over half a million pounds for the most seriously injured under the AFCS will not even begin to cover a veteran's lifelong needs.

To place this in context, a soldier of my acquaintance who had his head crushed when a concrete bunker was brought down on him by a mortar bomb and who is now unable to communicate in any way will get, in all likelihood, £570,000 from the AFCS. Had the same soldier been injured in a car accident caused by negligence, the award would be somewhere in the region of £4 million.[18] Such cases are by no means unusual in the civilian world: many barristers quite regularly deal with cases involving million-pound settlements from insurance companies. The bulk of such awards comprises the 'care element'.

As well as suffering brain damage as a result of an IED explosion, 'Peter', the soldier we met in chapter 2 who had been so shabbily treated by the MOD, may well at some time in the future require extensive and expensive surgery to remove bullets lodged in his body. There are many hundreds like him. Peter received the full award from the AFCS and, as we saw, may be considered relatively lucky in one respect: he has a strong personal support network and is very well educated. But very few have those assets. 'You can't rebuild life on the cheap,' he says, 'and the AFCS, with its limits, is very much life on the cheap, especially for those very seriously injured.'[19]

All cases differ, but in the case of a head injury, a properly cared-for individual should receive long-term brain-injury case management, which might include expert psychiatric nurses and full-time care workers. It would not take long for £570,000 to be used up in care costs. After that, it would probably be into an NHS hospital, as it is highly unlikely that the victim's parents could cope. Or they might call on one of the service-related charities (we look at their role below).

Then there are the wounds that cannot be seen. Those with mental health problems will certainly require treatment for many years to come, and as we have seen, a number of them will only present in 10–15 years' time. The cost of their treatment – sometimes over many decades – will certainly exceed **£1 billion.**

These figures, it must be stressed again, are only a robust baseline. They make assumptions that could fall far short of the mark (certainly they are well shy of the estimates made for US veterans). The final cost of ongoing care will be many times greater.

What provision has the UK government made for funding future care?

The following question for the Ministry of Defence and the answer to it were published in *Hansard* for 16 April 2012:[20]

> Mr Umunna: To ask the Secretary of State for Defence what recent assessment he has made of the long-term outcomes for disabled and traumatised veterans; and if he will make a statement.
>
> Mr Robathan: The Government continue to monitor closely the arrangements for veterans whose physical and mental injuries are such that they will need long-term support and assistance. The Ministry of Defence works with other Government Departments, devolved Administrations and voluntary sector organisations to ensure that the needs and circumstances of these veterans are known, with the aim of improving their access to services and to assist with their transition to civilian life.
>
> The Armed Forces Covenant underlines our commitment to ensuring that all the service community, including family members and ex-service personnel, receive the support and recognition which they deserve. This includes work undertaken by the Department of Health to inform GPs about the potential health problems that veterans may face and a programme run by the Department for Communities and Local Government to ensure that local authorities give eligible veterans priority in housing.

Anyone familiar with political language would be able easily to translate that into plain English: 'Assessments continue, but no action is planned and we refer you to the Armed Forces Covenant.'

This corroborates an answer I received to a Freedom of Information request to the Ministry of Defence about how much has been budgeted for the ongoing care of veterans. The answer was: 'There is no specific budget set aside for the ongoing care of soldiers wounded [in action].'[21] To a very great extent, the cost of caring for our veterans will fall on charities. A separate Freedom of Information request to the Department of Health elicited the information that £7.2 million had been set aside for 'mental health services for veterans'. Much of this will go towards recruiting dedicated mental health nurses.[22] Some £15 million has been set aside for 'the provision of prosthetics for veterans who have lost a limb as a result of their service'.[23] This funding runs through to 2015. Given that prosthetic limbs alone cost up to £30,000 each,[24] before we even consider ongoing care, it is highly unlikely that the sums will be anything like adequate.

Hidden costs

Charities

As we have seen, since so little work has been carried out by the British government on the expense of caring for our veterans, almost all the costs are hidden, in the sense that they have not been formally assessed or accounted for. Some costs, however, will not fall to government at all. This is because other agencies will do the work which (in the US, for example) is often carried out by government.

In June 2011, the charity Help for Heroes celebrated having raised £100 million.[25] Given that it had been in existence for only three and a half years, this was a remarkable achievement. Help for Heroes has stepped into the gap left by government in its funding of care and rehabilitation facilities nationwide. Or take another example: everybody in the UK is familiar with the fund-raising work of the Royal British Legion, which, since it was founded in 1919, has assisted the veterans of our wars through its annual 'Poppy Appeal'.

A great deal of money is given to military charities, and they provide a wide range of facilities for former service personnel. The Royal British Legion, for example, offers bereavement counselling, financial loans, respite care, care for the old, and information on returning to civilian life.[26] Meanwhile Help for Heroes focuses on the provision of care for those wounded in Britain's recent conflicts and operates a constellation of rehabilitation and recovery centres throughout the country, as well as offering direct support in the form of grants and other practical assistance.[27]

Vast amounts of money are set aside for the care of veterans in the United States, where much of this work is not devolved to charity, but is the statutory duty of a major government department – the Department of Veterans Affairs.[28] The VA (as it is commonly known) offers a huge range of services, ranging from dedicated hospitals for veterans, through considerable educational assistance, to home loans. A budget in excess of $112 billion means there is great scope for action.[29] The care afforded to our own veterans by the taxpayer is emaciated in comparison, and such budgets as there are tend to be fragmented and ad hoc in nature, dealing with specific issues. There is no significant separate budget within the Ministry of Defence, Department of Health or any other department for the care of veterans. The Service Personnel and Veterans Agency deals with such matters as pensions and medals, but enjoys nothing like the remit of the US Department for Veterans Affairs.[30]

A strong argument may be made that it is wrong to draw comparisons with the US. After all, relative to the UK, it has poor health provision for those without significant means or insurance cover, and it has no National Health Service. Furthermore there are a remarkable 22.7 million people in the US who are veterans of one or other of the armed services,[31] whereas the total number of UK veterans is perhaps 3 million, including former members of cadet forces.[32]

No figures are available as to how many ex-servicemen access the veterans' charities, but it would be very surprising if it proved to be more than a very small percentage of those who have served or who might be eligible for help, for servicemen are very (sometimes overly) self-reliant. According to Hugh Milroy, chief executive of the leading homeless veterans' charity Veterans Aid: 'If you are a former soldier in crisis, and you know where to go, you are likely to get help . . . But the huge bulk have no idea of how to get help.'[33]

He points out that, in fact, service charities are well funded compared to many other areas of the charitable sector. He contrasts the fairly large financial resources available to those veterans who do know where to go for help with the relatively small sums dedicated to conditions that affect huge numbers of people in the community at large.[34] As an example, he takes Alzheimer's disease – a condition that affects hundreds of thousands directly, with devastating consequences, and millions more indirectly. The income for Alzheimer's Society, the main charity, was £71 million in 2011–12.[35] The second-largest charity, Alzheimer's Research, raised £8 million.[36] Others have income of perhaps £1 million. It might be argued that, relative to the number of potential beneficiaries, service charities are well funded compared to such charities as Alzheimer's Society.

Nonetheless, in the case of the service charities, their often large incomes and endowments will certainly be required. It will not take many cases involving care needs that stretch into the millions of pounds for the resources of Help for Heroes and other charities to be depleted. As we saw above, in the civilian world of personal injury litigation, compensation (the bulk of which comprises the so-called 'care component') very often runs into several millions of pounds. How many of those awarded the maximum amount by the AFCS will find themselves needing to call upon the services of Help for Heroes and charities like it for their needs far into the future? I would suggest – very, very many.

As matters stand, in the middle of a war where the soldiers (if not the war itself) enjoy the support of many people, charities such as Help for Heroes are able to meet expenses that, in any just society, should be covered by the state. The truth is, though, that there should be no need for such charities: the care and rehabilitation of those who have suffered at the behest of the state should be up to the state and be funded by the state – not by the charitable sector, where competition for money is fierce. 'Peter', who has himself been assisted by Help for Heroes, takes a robust view: 'Help for Heroes and charities like it are fig leaves for a government that wants to pass on the costs to an unaccountable charitable sector.' Compared to other charitable fields, service charities are doing well. But this may not always be the case, for the real needs arise long after the campaign has ended.

Hugh Milroy, chief executive of Veterans Aid, has a picture on his office wall. The original was painted by the prominent Victorian artist Sir Luke Fildes and is titled *Applicants for Admission to a Casual Ward*. It depicts the homeless and destitute queuing outside a workhouse for a night's accommodation in the late 1870s. From left to right, the queue contains, in decreasing order of respectability and perceived worthiness, a middle-class mother with a child, some out-of-work labourers, a large family (perhaps immigrants) and some other staples of the lower reaches of Victorian society. But unmistakable at the far right – the only figure with his back to the viewer – is a red-coated soldier begging for money from the already poor.

Milroy makes the point, strongly expressed by Kipling in his famous poem 'Tommy', that today's hero is tomorrow's drain on society. Our obligations to the physically or mentally disabled will not end with the war. As 'Peter' puts it: 'I will be like this for decades, long after anyone remembers the war.' The frenetic fund-raising for veterans' charities in this time of conflict perhaps unconsciously reflects the reality that there will come a time when helping injured servicemen is not so fashionable. Who then will operate the helplines for ex-soldiers who are getting older and more vulnerable to serious physical and mental health problems? Will a state, strapped for cash and unwilling even now to budget for long-term care for veterans stump up the billions needed to provide the care that most would regard as proper?

Quality of life

As Britain's leading academic expert on defence costs, Professor Keith Hartley, says: 'When you come to injuries you have a real problem.'[37] He points out that it is perfectly possible to place a value on a serious injury – indeed this is done every day in the courts. There is a well-established scale for such injuries and precedents for compensation for any injury, however horrific. And there are very many horrific injuries to be considered when it comes to this or any other war. Valuations for the purpose of compensation in the courts comprise what are called 'general damages' (which is what might be called 'pure compensation'). There seems little reason not to put the same value on soldiers' injuries as is commonly applied in civilian contexts. But clearly such sums will never be paid to soldiers.

The world of statistics employs the so-called 'Quality Adjusted Life Year' or QALY.[38] A notional value is placed on the quality of an individual's life, so that an assessment can be made and a figure be put on the loss of quality of life. For example, a young man of 20 reduced to borderline function by injuries (nearly as bad as death) would be assessed as having lost total quality of life. In the bed next to 'Peter' in Birmingham was a young man aged 20 who, as a consequence of an IED, was in a persistent vegetative state. He would undoubtedly be assessed as having lost all quality of life. The figure used now is in the region of £40,000 per QALY.[39] In the case of this young man, that figure would be multiplied by 50 to reflect his life expectancy. That would yield a total (in 2012 values) of £2 million. 'This is an entirely appropriate measure to include in overall costs of the war', says Neil Davies, former chief economist at the Ministry of Defence.[40]

Clearly, estimating such costs is difficult. But it is not impossible. In order to arrive at a figure in the US context, Stiglitz and Bilmes used a global figure of 20 per cent as the average loss of 'quality of life' for all those wounded in recent military campaigns. For the more than 2,500 injured in Afghanistan, this would represent a conservative figure, since over 500 are listed as 'very seriously' or 'seriously' injured. As we saw above, the Ministry of Defence has given no indication of how badly injured the other 2,000 are. Taking Stiglitz and Bilmes' global average and assuming a highly conservative average of 40 years' life expectancy, we arrive at a figure for what the courts call 'pain, suffering and loss of amenity' of **£800 million**.[41]

Summing up

Summary (all figures are minimum baseline figures)

Statistical value of lives lost	£1 billion
Armed Forces Compensation Scheme	£1 billion (for casualties sustained in Afghanistan)
Ongoing cost of treatment of veterans	£1 billion (unbudgeted)
Loss of quality of life	£800 million (unbudgeted)
Total	**£3.8 billion**

None of the above figures include the social cost of there being thousands of mentally and physically injured veterans or their impact on society at large.[42] Much of this cost will be underwritten by the charitable sector, whose liabilities are also not assessed in these figures. Help for Heroes alone, which deals predominantly with the casualties from Iraq and Afghanistan, raises over £50 million a year and has already disbursed well over £150 million.[43] For the charitable sector, liabilities are likely to increase for many years to come. There is no doubt that the continuing costs of taking care of the wounded will far exceed 1 billion. The *baseline figure* for the financial cost of our casualties will certainly exceed £4 billion.

CHAPTER 6

Developing Afghanistan

In the early nineteenth century, one of the British Empire's impressive political agents (essentially administrators) operating in what is now the North West Frontier Province of Pakistan said this:

> There is nothing more to be dreaded or guarded against, I think, in our endeavour ... than the overweening confidence with which Europeans are too often accustomed to regard the excellence of their own institutions and the anxiety that they display to introduce them in new and untried soils ... The people of these countries are far from ripe for the introduction of our highly refined system of government or of society, and we are liable to meet with more opposition in the attempts to disturb what we find existing than from the exercise of our physical force.[1]

The vast costs of the military effort are by no means the whole story. In parallel to the military effort, the UK has poured money into its civilian activities. Britain's largest embassy is, of course, in Washington DC, reflecting the key importance that the UK attaches to its alliance with the world's superpower. But its second largest is not in Paris, Brussels, Berlin or Beijing, but in Kabul.

The Kabul embassy

The neighbourhood of Wazir Akbar Khan is the Knightsbridge of Kabul. It is (by Kabul standards) secure, being surrounded by rings of checkpoints and patrols. Here the palaces of Afghanistan's narco-lords overlook the well-tended lawns of Western embassies. The largest of these is the small town that is the US embassy, with its apartment blocks, gyms, bars and restaurants. Twenty minutes' walk away, down largely empty suburban roads, are to be found the walls and block-houses of the British embassy, the second-largest mission in Kabul. Unless you have some very definite business, you will not be allowed in (or indeed near) it. If, however, you can get through the searches and negotiate the questioning through bullet-proof glass, you will discover that there are worse places to be in Kabul.

Some 300 British diplomats and staff live here (not including the extensive, largely ex-Gurkha guard force that mans the machine-gun towers and roams the perimeters). Led by the ambassador, the diplomats make daily trips to various Afghan government ministries to press the British case. The consular staff deals with the very many visa applications to the UK, as well as with the occasional UK citizen in distress. The British Council looks after cultural matters. And there is the stalwart of any British mission – the defence attaché and his team, which here is very large indeed (some say that MI6 might also have a considerable presence). While the trade and industry salesmen may not be as numerous as in other missions, the dozens of DFID staff occupy an entire section of the embassy. Then there are the British private military contractors, mostly former servicemen, who guard the vehicle convoys out of the embassy and provide every single staff member who leaves the compound with a team of bodyguards.

Kabul is a hardship posting. Anyone posted there will have far more choice when it comes to his or her next posting than most people in the diplomatic service – a so-called 'silver ticket'. If you have done your time in Kabul, the chances are slim of being sent to another unpleasant posting (such as West Africa) and high of landing one of the plum postings to North America, Canberra, Paris or Rome. By the standards of most people in the country, though, life is not particularly hard. Living conditions, though Spartan by diplomatic standards, are positively sybaritic by military or NGO norms, and everyone has his own 'pod' – essentially a container-sized apartment. It is not all work and hardship: there is a very well-stocked and well-patronized bar.

Yet no one need endure the pressure for too long. Every six weeks everybody gets a so-called 'breather break'. Until recently, that meant a trip to Dubai and a business-class flight on to London, but things have changed and nowadays staff have to slum it in economy class. The cost of running this rather large embassy is in the region of £35 million per annum (2011–12 figures), made up of £29,739,716 from the Foreign Office itself and £6,420,894 from other departments such as the Home Office, for detached staff and attendant costs.[2]

Clearly this sum does not include the work of MI6, which in theory (but scarcely at all in practice) is part of the Foreign Office. No figures are available on its funding in Afghanistan, nor on the funding of the Government Communications Headquarters (GCHQ – the crucial signals intelligence department), which operates extensively in the country.

But this is only the beginning.

DFID in Afghanistan

The Department for International Development is the UK government ministry that deals with aid to developing countries. The very large DFID team in Kabul supervises a vast range of projects and programmes. By statute, DFID is mandated to focus on the priority of poverty reduction. It is consequently not permitted to spend its money in direct pursuance of the UK's national interest. This comes as a surprise to many people, even in government (and especially in the Ministry of

Defence), who believe that this is entirely the function of a British government department like DFID. Therefore, the bulk of DFID's projects are not located where the British military has been fighting its campaigns, in Helmand.

In 2010, the UK announced a 40 per cent increase in its commitments to aid to Afghanistan. But what is not fully grasped is that 'At least 50 percent of our annual budget to Afghanistan will go directly to the government.'[3] This money is administered by a body called the Afghanistan Reconstruction Trust Fund (ARTF), which itself is overseen by the World Bank. Only about 20 per cent of UK money goes direct to Helmand to build roads (at over £1 million per kilometre)[4] and other infrastructure – or at least that is what it is supposed to be for.

DFID focuses on what is called 'institution building' – helping governments to provide better services. This means that a certain degree of trust is placed in governments: after all (the thinking goes), if they were not trustworthy we should not be giving them money . . .

Corruption and accountability

Anyone reading about DFID's arrangements with the Afghan government might be forgiven for assuming that Afghanistan has a functioning government that is capable of handling large sums of money with some semblance of probity.

Transparency International is a highly respected international NGO that provides what is regarded as the benchmark index for corruption – the Corruption Perceptions Index. This index ranks countries according to how their public sector is perceived in terms of probity, and it draws information from many sources. Ten years of 'anti-corruption' activities and constant mentoring have achieved the remarkable result of taking Afghanistan from a position as Transparency International's forty-second most corrupt country in the world to a very serious contender for the title of 'most corrupt country in the world': of the 183 countries ranked in 2011, Afghanistan lies at number 180. Albania (95), Ethiopia (120) or Azerbaijan (143) are all countries where your money would be comparatively safe![5] Afghanistan's government and public services are more corrupt than every other country in the world with three exceptions: Myanmar (which ties with Afghanistan), North Korea and Somalia, which has no working national government at all. The survey is based on consulting local people (who, after all, know best) and analysing their views. They do need to be consulted, however, and being quizzed by Western researchers is unhealthy in places like Myanmar and North Korea.

Very few UK taxpayers would be content if they thought that hundreds of millions of pounds a year were being given straight to the governments of Eritrea (134) or Haiti (175). Yet every year that is exactly what is happening in Afghanistan, which has a more corrupt government than either of those two countries. It is for this government in Afghanistan, then, that British soldiers have been dying.

It is claimed that there is a rigorous system of checks and balances and that DFID is committed to transparency. DFID claims to be leading by example: every donation to the Afghan government is entered on the 'publicly accessible database' run by the Afghan Ministry of Finance. This database is simply a recitation of amounts given to the government by various international donors; no attempt at disaggregation or assessment is made. It contains only a small fraction of the annual £178 million of UK donations (known as 'bilateral aid') to Afghan government authorities.

DFID's overall performance in Afghanistan recently came under rather closer scrutiny than that offered by the Afghan government. In a 2012 report, the Independent Commission for Aid Impact concluded that DFID's programmes were 'not performing well':[6] 'neither DFID nor its partners and managing agents have estimated methodically the extent of leakage [sic] in Afghanistan . . . DFID is not proactive enough in detecting fraud and corruption.'[7] Anyone with the slightest experience of living and working 'outside the wire' in Afghanistan will attest to this 'leakage' – though people in Kabul speak not of 'leakage', but of wholesale fraud, theft and corruption. It is clear that DFID has been as much a victim of what even the secretary of state for international development has called 'endemic' corruption as any resident of the country.[8] One respected former security officer with extensive experience in Afghanistan put matters this way: 'The only Afghan lives I've seen transformed by western aid agencies are warlords who've used siphoned funds to build mansions, amass huge overseas property portfolios and arm private militias.'[9]

In fairness to DFID, in a country like Afghanistan it is almost impossible to verify what is really being done with the money, for the very simple reason that it is too dangerous to send Western assessors to project locations. At best, local assessors are subcontracted, and the results of their researches are all too often incomplete or inaccurate. It is, of course, impossible to monitor their work.

Helmand

If Helmand were a country, it would be the fifth-largest recipient of US aid in the world.[10] The UK also provides a great deal of money to the development effort there – as we saw above, it receives about 20 per cent of DFID money. The declared purpose of the military mission in Helmand (and nationally) was to provide security for 'development' to take place. Killing thousands of Taliban was all very well, but surely there ought to have been a political purpose behind it?

The original idea was that the huge military investment in the province would produce 'ink-spots' of safety, within which the Afghan government could begin to build its institutions and legitimacy. The plan was that those ink-spots would expand into the places around them, as people realized the benefits of having the Afghan government there to help. This would then 'secure' Helmand. Security and living standards would improve and Helmand could be a shining example for Afghanistan's

33 other provinces. That in turn would ensure that the country could develop and be well governed, and would no longer provide the 'safe havens' that were thought to threaten the UK and its interests.

The idea of 'ink-spots' was a theory developed for the British effort in Malaya in the 1950s. It was the crowning achievement of the idea of 'counterinsurgency' and the British army has been trading on it ever since. Unfortunately for the British effort, the key differences between Malaya and Helmand had escaped the theorists. The most important of these was that unlike Malaya, which clearly had a functioning government, Afghanistan did not – or at least not in any form that might attract the allegiance of Helmandis. In other words, there was very little ink to place in those spots.

Even when this came to be realized, the theorists were not unduly troubled: they would build a government – cultivate one from the almost non-existent roots in the less than fertile political soil of Helmand. It was the perceived imperative of trying to create a legitimate government that drove the civilian effort alongside, or at least in the same place as, the military's efforts. As we will see in chapter 7, the campaign showed that many Afghans did not associate their government with any form of good governance.

The British civilian effort has not approached the vast British military commitment, either in terms of personnel deployed or in terms of money spent. After all, it was simply impossible to go outside any of the British forts without extensive security; and this did not come cheap. There was simply no point in deploying large numbers of civilian advisors if it was too dangerous to use them. But without visible development, security failed to improve, and indeed deteriorated. From the army's perspective, the civilians were failing to step up to the plate and do their bit. As the months dragged into years, the campaign began to ossify into a primarily military campaign, led by and for the benefit of the army.

Of course, this is not what had been planned. The idea was that, as in Malaya, the campaign would be led by the political and civilian effort.

As in Malaya and elsewhere, it should be the civilian leadership that called the shots, as it were. In the early days, this simply did not happen.

The story of the Oxford books

In 2007, I deployed as a well-paid consultant to the Helmand mission. While there, I visited the teacher training school in Lashkar Gah with a Danish colleague. This was the only institution of further learning for hundreds of miles. However, it had no library, save for a few worm-eaten books in what appeared to be a storeroom. 'We need some books. Can you help us?' asked the principal. I got in touch with some Oxford University colleges, which managed to collect thousands of just-out-of-date textbooks that would otherwise have been sold on. At the request of the principal, these had to be vetted for content that might offend the rather strict Islamic tastes of the staff, but there were still several thousand fairly current scientific and engineering textbooks.

The plan was that the books were to be presented to the teacher training college when BBC Oxford came to do a piece on Oxford people in Helmand. They were to be picked up from the colleges by an Oxford Territorial Army unit and would go on the same aircraft as the journalists, travel with them on helicopters and be presented at the college. All the logistics were staffed and organized. The principal of the college was extremely pleased: he would have a library and the fact that most of the books were in English would only help the students with their language. Oxford University was pleased because it was helping another institution in clear distress. The BBC was pleased because it had a ready-made story. Most importantly of all, the army was pleased because – well, because this made it look good. It seemed everyone was going to gain.

But things went awry. Because of a helicopter shortage, the BBC trip had to be postponed. This removed the need for the books to come to Helmand at all – after all, where was the publicity value now? Then a general at the army's headquarters wondered what people would think if they found out that *books* of all things were being transported on RAF aircraft (instead, presumably, of weapons). The books never were picked up from the colleges. They were, I understand, eventually given away to charity shops. The point of the story is that the mission in Helmand was led not by civilian interests, but by the army's priorities (which at that stage did not include education).

The Provincial Reconstruction Team

As the years wore on, there was a shift in attitude and several huge projects did get under way to develop Afghan governance. It took many years, but eventually a plan was agreed on civilian reconstruction 'structured around seven themes: Politics and Reconciliation; Governance; Rule of Law (Justice, Police and Prisons); Security; Economic and Social Development; Counter Narcotics; and Strategic Communications'.[11] These were led from the PRT HQ in the city of Lashkar Gah. In chapter 4 we briefly visited the huge base at Camp Bastion, in the Helmandi desert. Although much smaller, the PRT was intended as the beating heart of reconstruction in the province.

Each major NATO country has at least one PRT in its allotted province. Between 2002 and 2005, American special forces based themselves happily and generally peacefully at a base near or on the outskirts of the capital of Helmand, Lashkar Gah. Their base was the compound of the PRT in the town itself. Until 2006, the Helmand PRT was run by the US. It stood, and indeed continues to stand, on the edge of the city cemetery.

Until 2006, protected by a company of Spanish-speaking US National Guard, the personnel of the PRT rarely ventured out to bother anyone, and no one – Taliban or otherwise – had ventured to bother them. Very few casualties had been sustained by US forces in the years prior to the British entry. When the British arrived in force in 2006, they based their military headquarters here. The idea was that, since it was going to be a reconstruction mission, military and civilian efforts should be in one place, under one local command or management structure. This mirrored a much smaller set-up that had worked, although with very little civilian input, during the British efforts in Northern Afghanistan in 2002–05. It was also a model that had sometimes worked in Iraq.

By 2012, at the height of the mission, there were about 120 civilian staff in the PRT itself from Britain, the US, Denmark and Estonia, including several advisors on justice, governance, democratization, policing, education and a myriad other topics. All of them are foreigners, with often only the haziest notion of what goes on outside the wire.

When speaking to people who have worked in the PRT, it is striking how the focus of the conversation so quickly turns to life in the compound and its petty rivalries and friendships, rather than life outside. There is a very good reason for this: most civilians in the PRT rarely, if ever, venture outside the wire. When they do, it is in the company of heavily armed private security guards and a convoy of armoured vehicles. All conversations with Afghans outside the wire take place in the presence of armed bodyguards from private security companies. These bodyguards are themselves constrained by a certain understandable paranoia. On very many occasions, meetings I was having with Afghan officials in their offices were cut short by body-guards insisting that the time had come to go. It was simply too dangerous to stay longer.

Here it might be useful to look briefly at the reality of life in a PRT through another civilian's eyes. In an article written in the *Guardian* in September 2011, my successor as justice advisor for the Helmand PRT gave an account of daily life:

Everyone was a long way from their different day jobs, slotting into multinational, civil-military teams, putting their skills to work in a wholly novel environment. And yet for the 12 months of our tours, we lived similar existences to one another and the soldiers around us: the morning run around the helipad before the heat began in earnest;

breakfast in the mess tent; the trips downtown for meetings to train, mentor and advise, always travelling in a convoy of armoured vehicles; the afternoon video conferences with Kabul and London to discuss progress and challenges; the evening emails home, followed by sweet oblivion in a shipping container.[12]

Clearly this is a very different life indeed from that led by the Helmandis. It amounts, in fact, to living in a garrison fort, where every single aspect of life – from social habits to language – is different from that outside the walls. Culturally, too, there is a major gulf in perspective. 'Mentoring and advice' is given following transport in an armoured convoy to and from the meeting, which itself is preceded by a military-style security briefing.

There is another aspect of this cultural rift between internationals and 'locals'. In his bestselling history of the US campaign in Helmand, *Little America*, US journalist Rajiv Chandrasekaran recalls seeing a British senior female official appear to instruct the provincial governor: '"She'd try to direct him and tell him what to do in front of other Pashtun males," said one US diplomat who observed her interactions. "It crossed a line".'[13] This was indeed an astonishing *faux pas* in intensely conservative Southern Afghanistan, where the mores of the DFID headquarters in London's Palace Street do not apply. For anyone with the very slightest acquaintance with Afghan life, it will appear to be quite remarkably undiplomatic.

Cultural problems also existed, of course, between civilians and soldiers. Even at the outset, the civilian approach was satirized by soldiers with savvy as attempting to create 'Helmandshire'. The civilian compound in the PRT in Lashkar Gah is known by soldiers as 'Lash Vegas', due to the perceived (and indeed actual) relative luxury enjoyed by its residents. Some civilians adapt better than others to the predominantly military environment. Parties are not uncommon among the civilians in the PRT: the 'Pimps and Hoes' party in early 2010 did not impress either the neighbouring British soldiers or the US marines, who were not invited.[14]

Far more important divisions were apparent. There can be few cultural chasms as great as that between Western liberals and conservative Pashtuns over the issue of gender. Naina Patel recalls one seminar organized to train judges:

A heated debate erupted between an elderly Pashtun judge and a persistent young man from the national human rights commission. 'Why were women in prison for running away from home?' the young man asked. It was not a crime that appeared in the penal code. 'Sharia,' answered the judge from under his imposing turban, with a glance that told the young man not to ask any more. A worried training coordinator, concerned at the way this exchange was going, decided to call a tea break while we discussed with the trainer how to respond. Understanding the importance of clarifying the issue, the trainer spent the remainder of the afternoon with both the code and religious text, explaining where one began and the other ended, and the centrality to both of asking why the woman had run away – adultery was clearly problematic, abuse was a very different matter. And custom, he made clear, had no basis in law.[15]

However one reads this, the distinct impression remains that the 'persistent young man' may not quite have gained the traction with the 'elderly Pashtun judge' that is desired by the PRT and its staff.

Consultants

Much of the work on the ground is done not by direct employees of the UK government, but by people who are paid daily rates as 'consultants'. The cost of these consultants is vast, making up a huge proportion of many of the project budgets. In a single year, DFID is said to have spent more than £500 million worldwide on consultant experts.[16] Helmand has provided many such programmes.

Take, for example, the 'District Delivery Programme' (a programme being a series of projects). Its supposed objective is to 'improve the relation between Afghan citizens and the Afghan state in districts which have recently been made secure. This is to be achieved through the improved delivery of basic services, such as security, justice, health, education or water.'[17] The programme budget is £18,407,486 (£1.4 million of which was to come from Denmark).[18] It began on 1 March 2011 and is due to end on 31 March 2014. 'Appraisal and design' cost £120,000.

By early 2013, just under £5 million had been spent. Over £1 million had been spent on the 'central support team', and a further £100,000 on paying a 'district co-ordinator' for one year. As we will see, pay makes up only a fraction of the overall cost of employing a consultant.

This 'district co-ordinator' is unlikely to have a salary as such. Rather there will be a daily rate of somewhere between £500 and £1,000, depending on what DFID is prepared to pay for a given individual. The honest consultant will invoice only for days worked, which do not usually include Fridays. Furthermore, he will have to take two weeks' leave every six weeks, for which he will not be paid. It is rare for a consultant in Helmand to clear more than £100,000 a year before tax. Living conditions can be Spartan, but most consultants live comfortably on military bases, and always far more comfortably than soldiers.

Many consultants never venture outside the relative safety of the PRT, and no one leaves it without armoured vehicles and a security team, provided not by the soldiers on the base but by a 'private security company', composed largely of ex-soldiers, each of whom is paid a daily rate sometimes not much lower than the consultants. The costs of this team will take up a considerable portion of the total budget for the project.

Costs for consultants (also known in the aid world as 'technical assistance') are far higher in Afghanistan than in other developing countries because of the appalling security situation. The cost of security, transport and putting the consultants up in their 'pods' (see above) constitutes what is known as 'life-support'. This raises the actual annual cost to the taxpayer of each consultant in Afghanistan to about £500,000. It is worth mentioning that a great many people, several hundred, could be employed in Helmand for the price of a single consultant plus security team and 'life-support'. There, the equivalent of $100 a month is a good, living wage.

A consultant has no 'capitation costs' – that is, no pension or fringe benefits. He or she will get the basic 'life-support' and an insurance policy in case of injury – and that is about all.

The District Delivery Programme budget has set aside a further £218,000 for 'monitoring and evaluation'. This is likely to fund a contract to one of the burgeoning private companies that have grown up around the Afghan international development world. The company selected to conduct this 'monitoring and evaluation exercise' will be paid a commission fee to hire another consultant to review such matters as 'value for money'.

The job of the consultant is undertaken far from home, and very commonly this has negative consequences for family life. And in the event of injury or death, consultants are at the mercy of private insurance policies. In those circumstances, some may agree that the job of consultant is not always necessarily overpaid. Then there is the element of personal security: for some (though by no means all) the job carries serious risks.

What kind of people are these consultants? The first key thing to note is that they are of course 'experts'. No one who has worked in the international community, or in any form of aid work overseas, will be unfamiliar with the cult of the 'expert'. In English law, the term 'expert' used traditionally to be applied to the person in a courtroom who knew more than anyone else about the subject in question. Nowadays an expert is generally someone who is widely respected for his knowledge of a topic. Unhappily, this is not always the case in the world of international development assistance. There, a consultant 'expert' is someone who declares himself (or herself) to be one and who can convince those doing the selecting of his credentials.

Since those who have to determine 'expert' status are rarely truly 'expert' in anything at all, this can be quite simple. As a result, the international development world is full of people claiming to be 'international police and law enforcement experts', but who had previously never done a day's work abroad. Indeed, some of them have hardly worked in their own country in the capacity in which they are employed overseas.

The ever-expanding field of 'experts' in 'justice and rule of law' – a very broad church indeed – is filled with men and women who have rarely (if ever) set foot in a courtroom or counselled a client in the often squalid world of the criminal courts.

In his 2011 critique of Western efforts in Afghanistan, Rory Stewart compares the background of the current crop of 'experts' with that of the men who assisted in the governance of the British Empire – men who spent years preparing to serve for decades in the same place. Clearly there is neither the will nor the resources for this kind of deployment now.

Stewart points out that such staff as are sent to Afghanistan now are 'experts in fields that hardly existed as recently as the 1950s, and which are hardly household names today: governance, gender, conflict resolution, civil society and public administration. They are not experts in gender or governance in Afghanistan: they were experts in gender and governance in the abstract.'[19] To that list could be added the fields of 'justice sector reform' and 'human rights' – areas in which I am considered an 'expert'.

What does all this money and expertise actually do?

Afghanistan is said to be 'the UK's top foreign policy priority' and it is, of course, the subject of an extensive development plan:

The plan marks an intensifying of DFID's effort on the ground and will focus on three key areas:

- Improving security and political stability;
- Stimulating the economy;
- Helping the Afghan Government deliver basic services.[20]

The largest of all programmes in Afghanistan into which DFID pays is the Afghanistan Reconstruction Trust Fund (see above). The latest phase of contributions to this fund started in 2009 and is likely to end in 2014; over £360 million (*sic*) will be paid out. The ARTF apparently has little to do with poverty reduction – supposedly DFID's main statutory role:[21] its 'principal sector' is 'public finance management' – or, put more simply, giving money to the Afghan government so that it can be seen to work (or to use the phraseology of the project's 'business case', to 'meet the operating budget's financing gap').[22] As the business case explains: 'The ARTF was established in 2002 as a multi-donor trust fund to support reconstruction needs in Afghanistan.'[23] Between 2002 and 2009 the UK contributed £490 million to this fund, so the total from 2002 to 2014 is in the region of £850 million.

As we saw above, most of this money will be given to the Afghan government for it to use in accordance with its own priorities and budgets:

The UK will not specify the individual projects for which its funds should be used, and will instead entrust the ARTF Management Committee to make allocation decisions based on guidance from the ARTF Steering Committee, of which DFID is a member . . . agriculture and rural development sectors will be the main beneficiary (40 percent of total DFID funding), followed by education (26 percent) and governance, justice and human rights (12 percent).

Other supported sectors will be economic governance, private sector development, infrastructure, natural resources, and health.[24]

DFID officials would point out that this is not a simple gift, but is closely audited.

The second-largest Afghan-wide project is Supporting Employment and Enterprise Development. Its budget is £36 million and it ends in June 2013. This is more in tune with what most people believe DFID does or should do: it is intended to help small and medium enterprises. Particular mention is made of support for women's businesses. The bulk of the budget, however, is dedicated to what is called 'procurement of services', which means the employment of consultant 'experts' to advise government (though in fairness, a similar amount has been set aside for an Afghan business innovation fund).[25]

Other projects with budgets in excess of £20 million include:

- the Afghanistan Infrastructure Trust Fund (at just over £35 million);[26]
- the National Solidarity Programme, which aims 'To lay the foundations for a strengthening of community level governance, and support community-managed sub-projects comprising reconstruction and development that improve the access of rural communities to social and productive infrastructure and services' (£31 million);[27]
- the Microfinance Investment Support Programme (£30 million);[28]
- the Strengthening Tax Administration project (£23 million up to 2011).[29]

The Strengthening Civil Society in Afghanistan project (which we look at briefly below) has cost £19 million. There are ten more projects that cost over £10 million each – again, some of them seem to put the alleviation of suffering centre stage, such as 'Support to demining' (£11 million) and 'Support to Afghanistan food appeal 2009' (£14 million). A further 39 projects weigh in at between £1 million and £10 million.[30]

A look at a national project

So most of the investment by the UK in Afghanistan has been in the
form of funding for 'programmes' or projects, each of which is run by a
coordinator or advisor, who might have more than one project to run.
Ideally, each project should have a defined and clear objective. But some
objectives are clearer than others. Take, for example, the Strengthening
Civil Society in Afghanistan project.[31]

The project is concerned with a series of objectives. There does not
seem to be an *overriding* objective or aim, but the lack of such direction
is not unusual in this context. Rather a series of 'impacts' is envisaged.
One 'impact' is stated to be 'improved governance in Afghanistan
through greater accountability & responsiveness to citizens' – a novel
concept to be sure in the Afghan government, but no doubt a worthy
aim.[32] We know that this and the other 'impacts' have been achieved by
examining certain 'indicators' (each impact has at least one), such as
'the extent to which Afghan population has confidence in public
administration and government ministries'[33] or the 'number of men &
women supported to have choice & control over their own development
& to hold decision-makers to account' (a number that should increase
from 27,000 to 265,000). Such 'indicators' will be examined in '5
thematic areas & 4 cross cutting themes'.

Impacts are achieved through 'activities'. The extensive list of activities includes 'Analyse stakeholder mapping findings to identify strengths,
weaknesses, opportunities & threats facing CSOs & engage with civil
society to address key issues through the grant programme' and
'Develop, introduce and implement transparent & accessible arrangements for core & project grants with effective feedback loops.'

Needless to say, most or all of the activities will be led by 'expert'
foreign consultants. Most will take the form of training seminars held
in draughty hotels in Kabul or, security permitting, elsewhere. The
activities will target what is called 'civil society'. This is one of those

phrases that can apply to a plethora of disparate organizations and ideas. In the British context, it would include the 'voluntary sector', sports teams and clubs, special interest media, human rights pressure groups and minority interest groups. It might also apply, depending on the context, to political groups. David Cameron's media advisors might call it something like the 'big society', and it is perceived as essential to the development of an accountable government. Needless to say, in Afghanistan only those interest groups that meet the requirements of the deputed representatives of the British government need apply for grants from such projects. Very few organizations promoting 'traditional Islamic values' have been or will be funded, even though Afghanistan is a solidly and immovably conservative Muslim society. Those who control the disbursement of funds for 'civil society' will have little sympathy for 'civil society groups' whose views are not in harmony with metropolitan British ideals.

The next question is how empowering NGOs – the 'third sector' as it is now called in the UK – can assist in the overriding objectives of improving Afghans' trust in their government. The overall idea is that these groups will 'hold the government to account' and thereby encourage it to improve its services. With a government as corrupt as Afghanistan's, this may be over-optimistic.

The Inter-Departmental Conflict Pool in Afghanistan

The money from DFID is not all the civilian funding that has been poured into Afghanistan. Up to 2009, the so-called 'Global Conflict Prevention Pool' spent about £20 million a year in the country. Since 2009, the Foreign Office has administered a fund called the 'Inter-Departmental Conflict Pool', which is jointly funded by the Foreign Office, the MOD and DFID. Needless to say, it is pointless scrutinizing the MOD's figures to try to identify its contribution, which should be in the region of a third.

To those working with the British government in the field of justice or security, this programme (like its predecessor) is generally regarded as a catch-all potential source of money.

At the more strategic level there are funds to support ad hoc peace-keeping activities and the interdepartmental Stabilisation Unit, which is responsible for recruiting and deploying the consultants we encountered above. But at the 'field' level, if you have a good idea but cannot get funding from DFID because it does not meet the department's mandate, application to the Conflict Pool may well be the answer. It is a very efficiently run scheme that can get money quickly to wherever it is deemed necessary, be it for a training course run by British trainers for Czech soldiers who are soon to be deployed in Afghanistan[34] or a conference for Helmandi police in Kabul. Since the fund was set up, Afghanistan has absorbed about 40 per cent of it – £75 million in 2010–11[35] and £68.5 million in 2011–12.[36] Spending in Afghanistan will remain at this level until the UK draws down its commitment in 2015, by which time the fund will have disbursed at least £300 million in Afghanistan.

So how much has all this cost?

In fairness to the various civilian agencies, calculating the overall cost of assistance to the Afghan government is not at all easy. The problem is that many programmes overlap. As with previous assessments, it is surely right to err on the conservative side and to take DFID's word as to what has been spent so far and what is planned. These figures keep changing, of course, and DFID does make an effort to keep them up to date. I will therefore capture the data for early 2013, in the certain knowledge that the figure will have grown considerably by the time this book is published. The DFID website keeps tabs on how much is being spent, and as far as I can see it strives to provide estimates and does not seek to minimize them.

As the reader will by now appreciate, the world of project management and aid delivery is every bit as complex as the financial side of
deploying thousands of soldiers. Yet DFID has managed to estimate
with some degree of precision (which is not necessarily the same as
accurately) how much it has spent. The figures presented annually and
quoted above are consistent, whatever source is consulted. Yet the work
of DFID is complex and not easily costed. DFID thus differs greatly
from the geographically close Ministry of Defence, whose obfuscation
we encountered in previous chapters. One wonders why DFID's cousins
'across the park' cannot be as precise or open.

The figures up to early January 2013 were as follows:[37]

- Spending on government and civil society – by far the largest cate-
  gory, including large subventions to the Afghan government –
  amounted to £596,528,391.
- Other social infrastructure and services had cost £33,713,426.
- Assistance to the banking and financial services sector had absorbed
  £33,494,579.
- Assistance to agriculture totalled £40,462,611.
- Some £52,198,262 had been paid out for transport and storage.
- 'Other' categories of work claimed £193,356,534.

The total actually spent on projects run by DFID up to early 2013 was
thus just under **£950 million**. This sum includes the big-ticket projects
mentioned above, such as the Afghanistan Reconstruction Trust Fund.
It is worth checking the DFID site, as the number is constantly updated
– and is therefore constantly increasing.

What, though, of the final years of the campaign, the years up to
2015? Here again DFID comes up trumps, showing the Ministry of
Defence that it is possible to budget for the future. The ongoing DFID
budget is £178 million per year from 2011 to 2015, again including all
the projects mentioned above.[38] Future spending through to 2015 will

total at least **£534 million**. It may well be, of course, that some of this money will not be spent; conversely it may be that more than this is spent. Certainly this level of spending is likely to continue into the foreseeable future.

It should, however, be noted that these figures are for 'projects': they do not include the cost of deploying and paying for the hundreds of DFID staff (i.e. not the consultants) who work on them. It is therefore safe to say that by 2015, DFID will have spent well over **£1.5 billion** in Afghanistan.[39] Only about a fifth of that is disbursed in Helmand.[40] This figure does not include the cost of DFID 'core staff' (i.e. not consultants), as they are employed in any event: if they were not in Afghanistan, they would be employed elsewhere.

Summing up

Summary of costs

DFID expenditure to early 2013	£950 million[41]
Future DFID spending to 2015	£534 million
Conflict Pool to 2015	£300 million
FCO spending to 2015	£300 million[42]
Total	**c. £2.1 million**

Once again, it must be stressed that these are minimum figures, based on the government's own assessments.

PART III

AND FOR WHAT?

CHAPTER 7

And For What? – Afghanistan

Everything would have been fine if Helmand were an island.[1]

Civilians in Afghanistan always told me the same story. They told the stories of a lack of construction. 'We hear about all this assistance, but all we see are tanks and soldiers.'[2]

What benefit has the war brought to Afghanistan?

Professor Paul Collier of Oxford University, author of *The Bottom Billion*, is arguably the world's leading expert on development economics. He has summed up what he sees as the West's quixotic approach to Afghanistan as a whole thus:

The fantasy that we have been pursuing as an international donor community is that what these countries need is an election ... and that we can then rapidly let go ... [In Afghanistan] we massively overloaded the agenda. What was going to happen in post-conflict Afghanistan? It was going to fix our drugs problem, for a start, and it

was going to achieve gender equality. Basically, it was going to become
Denmark in two years. This was preposterous.[3]

After thirteen years, tens of billions of dollars in international development assistance from that 'donor community', and at least $900
billion of military expenditure by the 'international community',[4]
how is Afghanistan faring? A good and widely accepted assessment is
that made by the United Nations in its human development index.
The findings are summarized in useful factsheets, which are available
for almost every country on earth. Afghanistan's makes for a tragic
read.[5] In 2009 the country was ranked overall at 181 (out of 182
countries) in human development terms, with only the famine-
stricken country of Niger below it. In terms of poverty, it was the
poorest country out of the 135 for which accurate figures were
available. It came bottom of the lists for access to safe water and enrol-
ment in all levels of education, and second to bottom for adult literacy.
The World Health Organization reports that one in every four children
dies before the age of five, the third highest infant mortality rate in the
world.[6] Those who do survive can expect to live for 43.6 years, making
Afghans' life expectancy the lowest in the world. About 42 per cent of
the population live on less than $1 a day, an often quoted benchmark
for poverty.[7]

By any standard, this represents an epic and catastrophic failure of
the international effort. Had a strategic view been taken on any single
one of those figures, the resources available could have brought about a
significant improvement. This situation is the result of three decades of
war; and with that war set to continue, fought now mostly by Afghans
again, matters are unlikely to improve much, if at all. A new generation
of young men has been brought up to war. Journalist Jonathan
Steele has been a regular visitor to the country since the 1970s. He saw
the country fight a savage war during the Soviet occupation and

observed it fall into total disarray afterwards: 'We have lost another generation to war.'[8]

Results of British efforts in Afghanistan

Helmand is, of course, the centre of the British military and civilian effort in Afghanistan. It is significant not so much for its role in the Afghan insurgency (which is probably commensurate with the province's size and location), but for its function in illustrating the industrial-scale militarization of counterinsurgency in the country. The discourse over the last few years has revolved around 'clear, hold, build', 'degrading the Taliban's command structure', and (although this phrase is largely a thing of the past) 'ink-spots of development'. All these ideas stem from military planners overlaying the experiences of Malaya and Northern Ireland on Helmand.

There is one thing that any Ministry of Defence official is happy to tell you: the military effort in Helmand has succeeded in pushing insurgents out of certain areas of Helmand. This is only to a very limited degree, but it is the case. Military wisdom would seem to imply that the insurgents then simply disappear. In evidence to the parliamentary Defence Committee's inquiry into 'Securing the Future of Afghanistan', former British military intelligence officer David James said:

> Our current strategy of trying to defeat the insurgency in the south is like smashing a military fist into the insurgent jelly. The harder we pound the more the jelly spreads into areas previously unaffected. Whilst it may take us millions of dollars and thousands of troops to retake an area like Marjah, a dozen Taliban can ride into a village in the north of the country on motorbikes and bring the villagers under their control in a matter of minutes. There was almost no insurgency in the north before NATO went to secure the south.[9]

But there certainly is now. David James moved with his family to Badakhshan, a formerly very safe and firmly anti-Taliban province in the far north east of the country, and knows what he is talking about. He was forced to move out again as militant Islamists, pushed out of areas where NATO was heavily present, began to take control.

One Norwegian officer who served in the north of the country in recent years told me that 'as time went on, the Taliban became stronger and stronger, and this in an area where even before 2001 they had absolutely no influence'.[10]

The West has focused its effort almost entirely on military means, and this has had certain consequences. The executive director of the charity War on Want believes that 'Western intervention has managed to produce a country which, even after the 20 years of civil war which preceded it, is even more militarized and fractured than it was before. We have seen Afghanistan become such a militarized society. So much of its resources are being channelled towards militarization'.[11]

The 'comprehensive approach'

As we saw in chapter 1, it all seemed so simple in the early days of the Afghan operation, in 2001. Those who were there at the time say there was a feeling in the country of a bright new dawn. For Afghans, at last it seemed as though their nightmare had ended. Ambitions were, perhaps understandably, high. But that was before the accession to power of the 'democratically elected government', composed largely of gangsters and warlords who had preyed on the country before the Taliban took over.

The tool selected to achieve the desired transformation of Helmand from an insignificant backwater, badly ruled but relatively rich, was the 'comprehensive approach' to 'stabilization'. The basic idea was that military and civilian authorities would work together closely, with the military providing the security that was essential to the work of the civilians. The idea was to 'clear' areas, so that 'stabilization' could be carried out by the Provincial Reconstruction Team. Kate Fearon, one of my successors as a civilian advisor on justice, writes in her book *City of Soldiers*, about her time in Helmand: 'the work we are engaged in is "hot stabilisation", which is, as far as I can see, a pre-development phase of development that draws on Merilee Grindle's concept of "good enough" governance and places it in a COIN [i.e. counterinsurgency] context.'[12] Most Helmandis were unfamiliar with the work of Merilee Grindle; but they certainly did not believe that the service provided by the kleptocratic government, installed and supported by the British at great expense (in casualties and money), was 'good enough' for anything.

The 'comprehensive approach' was to be state-building in action. Much of it was intended to promote the 'democratic model',[13] which might be compared to 'government in a box' (to use the later words of the then ISAF commander, General Stanley McChrystal). In practical terms, this meant that when Western forces took (or more accurately, temporarily removed Taliban elements from) a town ('clear' and 'hold'), there would be a tranche of government officials, supported and advised by foreign experts (chapter 6), ready to move in and take over the running of government ('build'). In turn, the idea went, 'governance' would be established and Helmand would no longer be a safe haven for terrorists and Taliban. As we saw above, prior to foreign intrusion Helmand was not a safe haven for terrorists. Nonetheless this was the latest avatar of 'counterinsurgency', the military cousin of 'hot stabilization'.

A key element of 'hot stabilization' was recruiting the right Afghan staff to be the officials in this all-new government. The degree to which it has been an uphill struggle to recruit such staff might be illustrated by a story told by a successor of mine as justice advisor, Naina Patel in the *Guardian*:

Farid, a mild-mannered criminal prosecutor from Kabul, was one of
several assigned to a district – in his case, Sangin – to 'take justice to
the people'. He hailed from the Tajik middle-class elite, and I doubt
very much whether, when he was completing his studies at Kabul
university, he imagined he would be living in a shipping container on
a forward operating base, patrolling alongside troops and dodging
bullets while trying to explain to people what a prosecutor was and
why they should report crime to him, let alone why witnesses should
attend court. Shortly after he arrived, he was gone. Farid became the
third prosecutor to leave Sangin in a year.

It was the chief prosecutor, during one of his monologues over tea,
who pointed out the folly of expecting to retain prosecutors in such
difficult environments on a salary of $60 (£38) a month – a quarter of
what the average policeman received – or if they did stay, expecting
them to be honest. Lawyers like myself were paid hazard allowances
to deploy to places such as Helmand; why did we expect Afghan
lawyers to deploy on far less, he asked, smiling.[14]

What might have lain in store for Farid, had he stayed, is illustrated by
the case of Mohammed Azam, the chief prosecutor of Gereshk district
in Helmand, who was shot dead in August 2011.[15] Other government
prosecutors in Helmand are said to work with the express consent of the
Taliban. For example, Jonathan Steele, in his *Ghosts of Afghanistan*,
reports that the district prosecutor of Marjah (a heavily advertised
success of the US-led surge in 2010, when General McChrystal claimed
to have installed 'government in a box') is 'believed to have obtained
clearance from the Taliban before taking up his appointment'.[16] A wise
precaution in the circumstances, one might feel.

Intimidation and co-option by the Taliban, coupled with institutional
corruption and overlaid with a continuing campaign against foreign
and Afghan government forces – that is a toxic cocktail that is fatal
to any form of 'hot stabilization'. A focus on the visible results of

'development', rather than on more intangible things (such as professional training) can be equally harmful.

Does 'hearts and minds' mean schools and clinics?

One of the more rewarding aspects of military life, and one carried out with superb professionalism, was the regular construction of schools and clinics for the people of Helmand. The military idea behind these facilities was that they might assist in 'winning hearts and minds'. Of course, as Northern Ireland showed, 'hearts and minds' are not won by building hospitals, schools and roads, with which Northern Ireland was lavishly furnished. Rather, what people really need is a satisfactory political settlement, providing security for all.

If one insists on going down the 'schools and hospitals' road, the buildings must be staffed, so that they can function. A constant problem in a place like Helmand is that it is very difficult to find trained teachers, nurses and medical assistants. As a result, there has been what has delicately been called 'overbuilding'. As the British ambassador to Afghanistan, Sir Richard Stagg, says:

> With the best of intentions, between the period of 2003–2008 we developed a very expansive view of how we could help Afghanistan, and many countries invested a lot in that mission. We focused on the physical and visible rather than the human capital which would manage the country in the longer term.
>
> The challenge for Afghanistan now is not a lack of roads and school buildings. It is a lack of capacity in its governmental structures in particular to run the country.[17]

One might be inclined to point out diplomatically that the challenge for Afghanistan has *always* been a lack of government capacity. In September 2012, the British finally called a halt to the building of schools and clinics: no staff could be found or trained for the new establishments in Helmand.

The British would have done well to have looked to the example of the Soviets. During their occupation of the country from 1979 to 1989, they took many tens of thousands of doctors, lawyers, soldiers, police, prison officials and other key staff back to the Soviet Union, often for several years. One result was that almost every professional and official in Afghanistan spoke Russian (actually still the case). The British might also then have understood the importance of taking the long view, as the Soviets did, and of providing proper, extended training to those whom they expected to run the country.

In summer 2012, I attended a seminar at the House of Commons, at which a number of experts were present. Also there was a junior member of the British government. He struggled to find justification for the war, but in conversation after the event he claimed: 'Everything would have been fine if Helmand were an island. If it all goes wrong it will be because of Kandahar.' An interesting and unusual perspective. Unfortunately for him – and for all of us who have fought or worked there – Helmand is not an island.

In their eight years in Helmand, the British have succeeded (with very considerable American help) in establishing a ramshackle group of officials – which might be considered the basis of 'government' – in three of the province's 14 districts. These officials are of decidedly varying quality and probity, but that is how it is throughout the country. However, there must be very serious doubt as to whether this 'government' is anything more than temporary, pending the withdrawal of foreign troops. A former UK ambassador to Afghanistan, Sir Sherard Cowper-Coles, relates how, in 2009, the foreign secretary visited Afghanistan and invited two Afghan ministers for dinner in Helmand:

David Miliband asked our guests innocently enough, how long they expected the Afghan central government authorities, civilian and

military, to stay on in Lashkar Gah after Western Forces left . . .
'Twenty four hours' came the reply. In just three words, the whole
object and purpose of our presence were being called into
question.[18]

Cowper-Coles takes the view that, without a sound political foundation
of the kind that might allow some form of central government to
survive in Helmand, there is no future for *almost anything* that is
achieved there. There is another factor, though, that has been like
a virus running through all British and international efforts in
Afghanistan – and especially Helmand.

Opium

Richard Holbrooke, President Obama's special envoy for Afghanistan
and Pakistan, stated, 'Breaking the narco-state in Afghanistan is essential, or all else will fail.'[19] He was right: all the military assistance, the
bankrolling of the police and military, the building of courts and such
establishment of 'government' as has occurred will be for nothing.

By far the most important single factor in Helmand's economy is
opium.[20] And that goes for the country, too: according to the US
Council on Foreign Relations, opium accounts for over 50 per cent of
Afghanistan's Gross Domestic Product.[21] It produces about 85 per cent
of the world's heroin – a 'near monopoly', as the UN puts it.[22] Poppy has
bankrolled the Taliban to the tune of hundreds of millions of dollars,
and one estimate suggests that they rake in up to $125 million a year
from its cultivation.[23] Of course, their share is as nothing compared
with the vast wealth being amassed by Afghanistan's many narco-lords,
who bank billions of dollars a year in places such as Dubai.

Opium has been grown in the country for centuries, but it was in the
1970s, with the decline in production in the so-called 'Golden Triangle'
of South East Asia, that cultivation really took off in Afghanistan. The

Soviet invasion provided even more of an impetus and opportunity for farmers to increase their cash flow. In turn, this linked those farmers into far larger networks: 'The criminal networks that have sprung up around the drugs trade provide farmers with seeds, fertiliser and cash loans; in short they offer an alternative welfare system.'[24]

Opium and the Taliban

This steady increase in production continued for several years after the Taliban took over in 1994. But ultimately they proved the most successful of all abolitionists: by 2001 they had virtually eradicated opium production. Indeed their success was recognized by the US government with a large cash gift:

> The sudden turnaround by the Taliban . . . opens the way for American aid to the Afghan farmers who have stopped planting poppies . . . Secretary of State Colin L. Powell announced a $43 million grant to Afghanistan in additional emergency aid to cope with the effects of a prolonged drought . . . The Afghans are desperate for international help, but describe their opposition to drug cultivation purely in religious terms . . . [A US counternarcotics official] said that in the southern provinces of Kandahar and Helmand, where the Taliban's hold is strongest, farmers said they would rather starve than return to poppy cultivation – and some of them will, experts say.[25]

Not all were so ready to take at face value the 'religious' aspect of Mullah Omar's somewhat belated enthusiasm for poppy eradication: many argue that the real reason was that overproduction in previous years had caused oversupply, to the extent that the price had fallen to unprofitable levels. In this regard, it is interesting to note that Mullah Omar banned only the cultivation of the crop, and not its export. Opinion in Helmand itself is divided as to whether the ban was due to religious scruples or was for rather more worldly reasons. It is probably right to say that there were elements of both.[26] Whatever, the important point is that the Taliban managed to bring about eradication.

Helmand, opium and the British

Thus, by the time of the Western intervention in 2001, very little opium was being grown in Afghanistan. But when the US and the British arrived, the Taliban departed, taking with them their draconian means of enforcement, and opium came to be seen as a potentially serious problem for the future. At the Bonn Conference, which sketched out Afghanistan's political future and the role of the international effort in that future, Britain volunteered for the task of 'lead nation' on counter-narcotics. This task took on even greater relevance when the British army, along with a few civilians, occupied Helmand in 2006.

By 2007, the Taliban was long gone, one of President Karzai's cronies had been in control for five years, there had been a year of chaotic British 'stabilisation' – and Helmand could make the astonishing claim that over 50 per cent of the world's opium was grown there.[27]

It makes good commercial sense for Helmandis to grow opium. Since the days of the Helmand River Authority, Helmand has been the most fertile of all Afghanistan's provinces. A hectare of wheat is worth £475, while the same area under opium might be worth up to £6,500. Furthermore, opium requires far less in the way of scarce irrigation resources.[28] In a highly insecure environment such as Helmand, farmers are also well aware that if they grow wheat they will need to be able to get the crop to market in good time. If they are to make any profit at all, the roads will have to be clear of predatory groups of bandits or policemen (all too often the same thing). Whereas those who run the opium trade – tribal satraps, government officials or Taliban commanders – tolerate no disruption of the trade from anyone, and certainly not from ragtag groups of poorly trained police.

Needless to say, for a cut, the Taliban are happy to arrange free passage. But they exert their influence in other ways, too. In early 2009 they led attacks on a government eradication project near the town of Nad Ali.[29] In the battle for some form of allegiance from an often sceptical citizenry, it serves their interests very well to be seen as protectors of livelihoods. And it does them no harm financially.

Against these forces were ranged the 'counternarcotics experts' of the British government. Technically, as justice advisor at the time, I was funded from the counternarcotics budget. One of my priorities was to support the development of certain newly created agencies, among them the Counter-Narcotics Police of Afghanistan. On several occasions, we were informed of large seizures by this organization – not, unfortunately, of opium itself, but of so-called 'precursors', the chemicals required to turn opium into heroin.

I had one particularly memorable conversation with one of the prosecutors we dealt with, a jovial and extremely bright – one might even say wily – man who, like so many of his generation, had been trained in Russia. At one point he interjected: 'Some people think you are fighting a war against the farmers here because you cannot control your young people at home. Of course, I would never think such a thing, but I have heard it said . . .'

At the time, he was the only prosecutor dealing with possession and supply of opium and other drugs. At our previous meeting I had expressed the hope that he would bring along all the cases he had that dealt with narcotics. Now he drew out a small sheaf of handwritten pages: 'Here are the files you asked for. Possession of zero point five grams of marijuana . . . Ah, here is a serious one: supplying half a kilo of opium.' He had seven cases in all, none of which would trouble any of the accused with more than a few months in prison – assuming they were so unfortunate as to be unable to find the money to grease the palms of the various officials who had the power to keep them out of jail.

Out in the 'Green Zone' – the strip of land running along the Helmand River, where the opium was being grown – different dilemmas were being confronted. British soldiers found themselves in a quandary as to what to do when they found large quantities of opium (as they regularly did in their search for weapons). On one typical occasion, a patrol found a ton of opium in a storeroom near Sangin. The soldiers' unit had spent much of its tour trying to convince the farmers in the area that the troops were there for the farmers' protection and benefit. The bale of opium represented the year's harvest, and therefore a year's income for the village. To confiscate this would compromise what the soldiers believed was a 'hearts and minds' mission. It is surely testament to their discipline that, instead of quietly shutting the door to the outhouse with the baled opium and wishing the farmer who owned it good day (thereby preserving their hard-won relationships with the villagers), they reported it up the chain of command and asked what they should do.

Needless to say, the order was given to confiscate the opium. With it – as the inhabitants of the village made abundantly clear while the soldiers were removing the offending substance – went many months' painstaking work of listening and building relationships. As a British officer heavily involved in counternarcotics put it to me: 'We caused so many areas to be destabilized that had not been destabilized before.'[30]

The same officer told me that he was never quite sure why some opium fields were cut down and others left. He was working on what the US and UK governments call a policy of 'forced, non-negotiated, targeted poppy eradication in Afghanistan, to be carried out exclusively by force-protected ground teams employing manual eradication methods.'[31] The soldier's question of who was doing the 'targeting' and why some farmers were targeted and others were not was addressed by my friend, the narcotics prosecutor. He knew one of the government ministers well. The minister had jovially told him that he had taken a senior police officer on a helicopter ride to give orders as to how he wanted his part of the opium eradication plan to work. As they flew over Helmand and Kandahar, certain areas were pointed out and marked for eradication. These were areas owned by landlords who had not paid their dues to the minister. Perhaps next year they would understand better where their interests lay.

There have been some positive initiatives. In the Helmand Food Zone run by the British PRT, concerted efforts are made to persuade farmers to abandon the poppy by supplying them with subsidized high-grade wheat and fertilizer. Some of these projects have met with significant success, albeit in a relatively small area,[32] though one problem has been that wheat seed donated to 'the authorities' is sold on by them at whatever price the market will bear to anyone who can afford it.

How successful was the counternarcotics effort in Helmand?

The British campaign from 2006 in Helmand has had very little positive effect. Indeed, it has had no effect at all in terms of reducing overall production. The province today produces 49 per cent of the country's opium,[33] up from about 40 per cent in 2006 (when 69,234 hectares were under cultivation). In 2007–08 there was a huge increase to over 100,000 hectares: at that time the province produced an astonishing 62 per cent of the country's opium. There was then a drop to a low of 63,307 hectares in 2011. The number of hectares under cultivation has recently increased to over 75,176 at the end of 2012 – an increase of 19 per cent in one year.[34] It very much looks as if, barring blight, this is an upward trend, despite a high level (3,600 hectares) of 'eradication', where poppies are cut down. As we saw above, the system of selecting areas for eradication can be very corrupt indeed. It is all too often used as a punishment, rather than as a genuine tool in counternarcotics.

From time to time there have been falls in opium production or 'yield', and this has led to occasional boasting by the advocates of the 'counternarcotics' campaign. But these declines are usually a result of blight, as in 2011–12. Sometimes the reduction is driven by market forces: occasionally a glut following a bumper harvest one year may render it far more profitable for a poor farmer to grow wheat the next (though, as mentioned above, he may have to buy the seeds from the district 'authorities' to which the British or Americans had donated them). Once the market corrects itself, opium is planted again. Any sensible farmer seeking ways to feed his family would do the same. As one British officer put it to me: 'If I grow half a field of wheat and half of opium, my sixth child will survive the winter. It's not a difficult calculation.'[35]

It is highly likely that production will return to its former level, for the simple reason that there are many incentives for it to do so.[36] The vested interests of those senior Afghan government officials who made millions from opium will ensure that there is no meaningful or lasting decline in the trade. There is simply too much money to be made in such a poor society and no real incentives to stop growing the poppy. As one farmer told a journalist in 2012: 'The poppy is always good, you can sell it at any time. It is like gold, you can sell it whenever and get cash.'[37] As we saw above, if the Taliban, for reasons of their own, decided that cultivation was to cease, it ceased. But those days are gone now, and the Taliban are quite content to allow continuing opium production. It may well be that when new arrangements are made after the withdrawal of British and American troops, the Taliban will again take the view that opium production should cease.

The problem of addiction is not, as my prosecutor friend believed, confined to young people abroad. Any visitor to Afghanistan, particularly its poorer regions, will attest that this is a huge problem within Afghanistan. As a spokesman for the Afghan Ministry of Counternarcotics admits, 'Afghanistan never had a history of drug addiction 30 years ago. But today we have one million addicts.'[38]

The overall picture is not at all rosy. From having virtually no opium cultivation in 2001, Afghanistan is today far and away the biggest producer in the world. According to the United Nations, in 2011 Afghanistan had 63 per cent of the 193,000 hectares in the world planted with opium.[39] This is bad news for law enforcement worldwide.

Nigel Inkster sums up where we are now:

> Drug seizures, while rising, still account for less than 5% of opium produced. As a general rule, the United Nations estimates, law-enforcement agencies need to interdict about 70% of supplies to make the drugs trade less financially attractive to traffickers and dealers. In any circumstances, this is an extremely challenging objective. In the large swathes of Afghanistan where the central government and security forces wield no control, it is completely unrealistic. Meanwhile, no major trafficker has yet successfully been prosecuted due to a widespread culture of impunity.[40]

For this is not simply a problem of a single country – or indeed a single province – being the source of most of the world's heroin. With its interlocking gangs of criminals, oligarchs, landowners, politicians and terrorists, the trade gives rise to, and provides the impetus for, a vast shadow state run by tribal mafias, where anything resembling real government is subsumed by the vast corruption of opium. The 'narco-khans' have an interest in maintaining a very weak state. This – more than poverty, more than war and most certainly more than the Taliban – has made and maintained Afghanistan as the third most corrupt country in the world.

Nowhere has the failure of the international efforts to combat drugs been starker than in Helmand. Any soldier who has done any time at all on patrol in Helmand will recall the fields of purple flowers stretching as far as the eye can see. Those fields of poppy are likely to remain long after the last British soldier has left.

I was told by a very senior army officer that it was Tony Blair's dream of taking on the opium problem at its source that brought the British to

Helmand in the first place: that was why the British 'chose' the province. On the face of it, the thinking was cogent and the purpose laudable: after all, far more British citizens have been killed by heroin than by the Taliban. But the operation needed to be conducted efficiently and pragmatically.

Of course, if we were to consider purely British national interests, then, on the heroin issue at least, a strong case could be made that the Taliban would have served those interests far better than the ramshackle, corrupt kleptocracy that is the Karzai government.

Women

During their stay in Afghanistan, the Soviets were intent on improving the rights and conditions of women. While there was little attempt to impose such foreign ideas as gender equality on areas outside the capital, in Kabul itself the role of women was significantly improved. Universities were built, including the impressive Kabul Polytechnic University, which was destroyed almost as soon as the Russian military left the country. Factories were established and cultural centres set up. All are now in ruins. While it was not safe for European Soviets to walk the streets and markets of Kabul, there was certainly nothing like the sense of apprehension that exists in today's Kabul, with its regular battles with Taliban insurgents, suicide bombers and car bombs. That time was also a golden period for the women of Kabul (if not for the women living in areas held by the mujahedin). The Soviets encouraged their education and employment, and the city had a relatively modern feel about it.

When the Soviets left, some opportunities remained for women to develop. Fawzia Koofi is a prominent Afghan politician and deputy speaker of the Afghan parliament. In her book *The Favored Daughter* she describes life in Kabul during and after the Soviet occupation.[41] Even in the chaos of the immediate post-Soviet period, she managed to gain an education and qualify as a teacher of English. Opportunities such as these ceased entirely, of course, when the Taliban came to power, but previously around 70 per cent of teachers, 50 per cent of government workers and 40 per cent of doctors were female, according to some estimates. These figures were largely a legacy of the Soviet occupation.

Since the beginning of the most recent phase of the Afghan War there has been a single very strong thread. The protection and promotion of the rights of women has been front and centre of the justifications for extensive Western state- and society-building efforts in the country. The tone was set in the very early days of the intervention, and was epitomized by the words of First Lady Laura Bush in November 2001: 'Only the terrorists and the Taliban forbid education to women. Only the terrorists and the Taliban threaten to pull out women's fingernails for wearing nail polish.'[42] Cherie Blair meanwhile urged the women of Afghanistan to throw off the *burqa*: 'The women of Afghanistan still have a spirit that belies their unfair, downtrodden image. We need to help them free that spirit and give them their voice back, so they can create the better Afghanistan we all want to see.'[43]

At least in Kabul and the main cities there was, for a year or two, a sense that things might be changing. But after 2003 that feeling began to wane. By 2006, with a strongly resurgent Taliban encouraged by the clear distraction of Western forces, it was very clear to Afghans that matters were at best getting no better, and at worst were slipping rapidly downhill.

Women, the Taliban and Pashtun culture

The cover of the 9 August 2010 issue of *Time* magazine featured the portrait of Bibi Aisha with the headline: 'What happens if we leave Afghanistan'. The photo shows the 18-year-old Afghan girl's face, disfigured by having had her nose cut off. This picture won the 2010 World Press Photo organization's 'photo of the year'.

The clear implication of the headline and the associated article was that the Taliban had been responsible for this mutilation and that more of the same could be expected if Western forces left the country. While the editorial accompanying the article insisted that the photograph, which hit the international headlines because of its shock factor, was not being published to support or oppose the presence of international forces, the implication in the article was crystal clear: for Afghanistan's women, an early withdrawal of international forces could be disastrous. Setting aside the fairly obvious point that this happened on the international forces' watch, in fact the whole episode was an instance of what might, in the West, be called 'extreme domestic violence'. The story merits retelling, as it highlights both the Western misunderstanding of traditional Afghan justice and the uncritical nature of much of what passes for comment outside the country.

Bibi Aisha comes from Uruzgan, a province bordering Kandahar and Helmand and the home province of Mullah Omar, the founder and commander of the Taliban. Aisha had fled from her in-laws' house on account of abuse. She had been caught by her husband, who decided to punish her in order to teach other young women a lesson. He cut off her ears and nose and left her bleeding on the hillside. The only link with the Taliban was that the man was a local commander. This was as far as the *Time* article took the account.

There was, however, much more to it than that. The story reflects far more on traditional Afghan justice than it does on Taliban justice, summary and intensely cruel though that can be. Aisha had been awarded to her husband's family when she was 12, under a system called *baad*. *Baad* is a key element of *pashtunwali*, the code of the Pashtun, which treats girls and women as commodities to be traded, given and received. They are, for instance, offered as compensation for injury or death inflicted by one group or tribe on another. This is what had happened in Aisha's case. Her uncle had murdered one of her future husband's relatives. As part of the 'blood debt' settlement, she and her sister had been handed over. When she attained puberty, she was formally married, clearly against her will.

As the investigation unfolded, it became clear that Aisha's husband had acted not as a Taliban official, but as a Pashtun male. As the head of the Uruzgan branch of the Afghanistan Independent Human Rights Commission put it: 'We have found out that the Taliban were not behind this. This was a case of family violence, not the Taliban.'[44] Sharia law, under which the Taliban operate, forbids *baad*. So this was not a case of 'What happens if we leave Afghanistan'; it was what was happening in the here and now, and the Taliban were, at best, a bit-part player.

Among some forward-thinking senior British and other ISAF officers, there is an acute awareness of the key political, economic and moral importance of the rights of women. 'Even if we win the military campaign,' one senior British officer told me, 'if we lose women's rights, if we allow Karzai to bargain away the gains in this field that have been made, our success will not matter.'[45]

It is not only traditional rural attitudes that undermine the dignity of Afghan women: the Karzai government is also playing its part. In 2009, for example, it upheld a law that allowed men of Islam's Shi'a branch to force their wives to have sex, that granted guardianship of children exclusively to men, that required women to get permission from their husbands to work and that 'effectively allows a rapist to avoid prosecution by paying blood money'.[46] It was described, justifiably, as 'barbaric' by Human Rights Watch. This was all part of a deal, said that organization, to secure Karzai's re-election in the presidential election in August of that year (which anyway turned out to be partially rigged).

Then in 2012, Karzai endorsed a series of regulations, a 'code of conduct' drafted in collusion with Islamic clerics. Thus a woman is not to travel without a male guardian and should not mingle with men in such places as schools or markets. Beating one's wife is permitted, so long as there is no Islamic reason not to do so.[47]

Clearly these rules would meet with the approval of the Taliban, and it seems that this was indeed the purpose. The move was seen as part of a process of reaching out to the Taliban in advance of what, it is hoped, will be a form of peace negotiations. Women's rights, it seems, like so much else in Afghanistan, are up for negotiation.

Karl Marlantes, in his thought-provoking book *What it is Like to Go to War*, makes the observation that if you go into a prison in the West and ask the inmates whether it is wrong to steal, burgle houses or murder, all will agree that it is indeed wrong to do these things. There is by no means the same degree of unanimity in Afghanistan as to whether it is wrong to cut off a woman's ears and nose for offending against tribal honour.[48] Marlantes is making a profoundly important point: the values we have been proclaiming and fighting for, and telling our troops they are fighting for, are not the values of many of the people among whom we are fighting. The attempt to impose Western-style government and legal systems on a country that has no real inclination to adopt either – and to do it in a matter of a decade or so – was always doomed to failure.

What do Afghans think?

What are Afghans' beliefs as to why foreigners are in their country? There must be a reason. Are the foreigners occupying and fighting in the country simply because they want something from it? Why else would they come so far? And if they are here purely for their own benefit, then clearly they must be fought . . .

A senior former military 'media operations' officer made the striking observation that many people in Helmand might wonder what all the fuss was about, just because some buildings fell down in a place called 'New York': 'Where is this New York? Is it in the next valley? Buildings are for ever falling down in this country – not because aircraft crash into them, but because aircraft drop bombs on them.'[49]

This view is amply borne out by the evidence. In 2010, nine years into the campaign, the International Council on Security and Development (ICOS), a respected NGO, conducted an extensive survey of opinion in Afghanistan, with hundreds of interviews held in Helmand and Kandahar provinces.[50] The interview base was far larger than anything attempted by NATO (500 interviewees in Helmand alone) and the survey was far more reliable, since it was carried out by an independent NGO without any political affiliation or agenda, not to prove a partic- ular propaganda point.

The results were not welcome to the international forces. Briefly, the resulting report showed that: 'Many Afghans remain hostile towards the international community, unsure of its objectives, and unaware of or untouched by tangible effects of development.'[51] This states the case rather mildly: in fact only 31 per cent of respondents believed that NATO protected civilians (48 per cent believed it did not), and 65 per cent believed that NATO killed more civilians than did the Taliban.[52] In Helmand overall, most people opposed further military operations against the Taliban.[53]

Some 43 per cent of Helmandis believed that foreigners were in Afghanistan for 'violence and destruction', as against 24 per cent who believed they were there to help rebuild Afghanistan; 7 per cent thought they were in the country for 'peace and security', another 7 per cent 'for their own defence', and 6 per cent felt they were there to occupy Afghanistan.

The answers were even more striking when the question of 9/11 arose. ICOS read its respondents an account of 9/11 and asked whether they had heard of the attack. The account concluded: 'The Americans asked the Taliban to hand over Osama bin Laden. They refused, so the Americans and their allies NATO attacked the Taliban and came into Afghanistan to look for Osama bin Laden and overthrew the Taliban.'

In Sangin, where the British had fought a bloody and largely futile campaign for three years until they were withdrawn in 2009, only 3 per cent had heard of the 'event which the foreigners call 9/11' or the reason for foreigners being present. The highest figure for those who were aware of 9/11 was to be found in the provincial capital of Lashkar Gah, where a princely 14 per cent of those questioned were able to identify the primary declared reason for the presence on their territory of large numbers of foreign troops.

In all, only 8 per cent of Helmandis said that they had heard of the attacks by Al Qaeda on New York. At this point it is worth reiterating that since 2001 many times more Afghan civilians have been violently killed than were murdered in the United States on 9/11. Indeed, as we have seen, it is highly likely that more people have been killed in just Helmand, either by the Taliban and their sympathizers or by foreign forces, than died on 9/11.

When informed of the details of 9/11 and asked whether those events justified the US and UK presence, 53 per cent of those questioned in Helmand did not consider them an adequate reason for the foreign presence. In Sangin and Garmsir, where the British had done a great deal of damage, the figures were 72 per cent and 63 per cent, respectively.[54] Across Southern Afghanistan as a whole, 51 per cent believed the foreigners' initial declared justification for their presence was inadequate.

One of the many other reasons offered for the Western presence has been the promotion of democratic values. When asked what that meant, 72 per cent of Helmandis were unable to give an answer.[55]

Rather ominously, 49 per cent of respondents in Helmand believed there should be an independent Pashtun state – bad news for those who will be striving for a unitary Afghanistan after the foreign occupation. While it is perhaps no surprise that 81 per cent of people believed the Afghan police either supported the Taliban now or would end up joining them, somewhat surprisingly 69 per cent believed the same of the Afghan army.[56] Some 61 per cent believed that the Afghan security forces would not be able to provide security if and when the foreign forces left.[57]

In fairness, these results were derived from interviews taken in 2010, and since then major changes may have occurred in the views of Helmandis. Or then again, in this intensely conservative and understandably suspicious part of Southern Afghanistan, maybe not. No such major independent survey of southern Afghan views on these issues has been undertaken since then.

The British legacy

An Afghan friend of mine from Helmand has worked for several years for NATO forces and various international agencies. In a phone call I asked him what the legacy of the British in Helmand would be: 'We were promised good governance: where is it? We were promised economic growth: where is it? We were promised stability: where is it? What can they show as their achievement? It is getting worse every day.'[58] He, like very many of those who have worked for us in this war, is desperate to leave. He can expect no help from the governments he worked for: they will leave him in danger, as they left so many in Iraq exposed.[59]

And what of Helmand as a whole? It is unlikely (though not impossible) that the Afghan army will be able to hold the major towns of the province on behalf of the Afghan government. The Afghan government itself, however, bears no real resemblance to any unitary state that a European would recognize, and it may well not survive even in its present ramshackle form. Even if the Afghan government does manage to hold on to the towns, the countryside – already largely under the sway of the Taliban or various tribal/narcotic gangs – will remain as it was in 2006 and as it always has been: beyond government control. The various groups will come to local arrangements or will fight over narcotics interests, just as they did before the arrival of the British. Helmand itself will remain a part of the Pashtun jigsaw, its opium making it perhaps more important than the neighbouring Nimruz or Ghor provinces. As General Richards, now chief of the defence staff, said in 2006, the really important province was and remains Kandahar.

For the British army and the few civilians who worked with it, Helmand will remain 'their war' and will dominate their consciousness, both corporate and individual; for many careers were made here and many lives were seriously damaged. For most Helmandis, the latest British intrusion will be remembered as just that – an intrusion. The Helmand of 2015 will, in all significant respects, resemble the Helmand of 2005. The only British legacy may be the long-vacated patrol bases, their remains scoured by some of the poorest people on the planet for old plastic bottles or ammunition boxes. Chief among these locations will be the traces of what was once Camp Bastion. Ambassador Sherard Cowper-Coles was not the first to compare Bastion with the colossi in the desert built by Shelley's Ozymandias. I believe he was the first, however, to produce his own version of that poem's final lines:

Look on the West's works, ye mighty, and despair
Nothing beside Bastion remains. Round the decay
Of that colossal base, boundless and bare
The lone and level sands stretch far away.[60]

And the Afghan perspective as a whole, what of that? One of the few Afghan women to have written in English about the war is the politician Fawzia Koofi, from Badakhshan in Northern Afghanistan:

Little if any thought was given to the ambitions, hopes, and welfare of ordinary Afghans. Ironically it was perhaps the Soviets who got closest, building hospitals and learning institutions to improve people's lives . . . Recently there have been many talks about Taliban reconciliation and reintegration into government. Much of this process has been led by the international community and its purpose is to serve the agenda of withdrawing their troops as quickly as possible. But that is a mistake. It is another short term quick fix that will do nothing to solve the world's problems, only store them up and make them worse for another day.[61]

CHAPTER 8

And For What? – Security

What was it all about?

So much for what we have done for Afghanistan. What, though, have we achieved for ourselves? Sometime in the summer of 2011, I had dinner with a friend of mine who is now a reasonably senior army officer. He, like many of his peers, had served with some distinction in Helmand, commanding a reconnaissance unit in the campaign. Over dinner, he was relating the story of one particular patrol that had got involved in a battle when he stopped, took off his glasses and rubbed his eyes: 'When I got home I sat down and said to myself "What the fuck was all that about?"'

It is part of good leadership and good strategy to make sure that if the question 'What is it all about?' is asked, there is a sound and coherent answer. When we send people to war, to kill and be killed, to maim and be maimed, we had better have a very good reason for doing so. There may come a time when the initial reason disappears or is no longer relevant; but reason there must be. Both law (in the shape of the international laws of war) and morality (in the form of the 'just war' traditions present in all societies) require an answer to the vital question:

'What is this all about?' Soldiers and the citizens who send them have an absolute right to ask this of their leaders and to demand an unequivocal and clear answer. Unfortunately, no such answer has been apparent to most of the soldiers who have fought in Helmand.

In the year since the publication of my previous book *Losing Small Wars*, which dealt with British military failure in recent conflicts, it has been my privilege to be invited to many military bases and barracks to discuss the book with service personnel, the vast majority of whom have served in Helmand, often many times over. Perhaps 10 or 15 per cent of those I have spoken to are of the view that we are succeeding and that it has been worth it (though even they are often unclear what it was that they had succeeded in doing). The majority expressed the same sentiment as my dinner companion.

The government's answer

What drove the Afghan War was, it is said, the perceived risk of terrorism. We were there ultimately to provide security for ourselves. It was vital after the 9/11 attack on the United States to ensure that there could never again be a safe haven for terrorists. This was the entire *casus belli*. And it remains so, with the political rhetoric continuing to stress the importance of 'stabilizing' Afghanistan, so that it no longer represents a threat to international security. The United States has been leading and totally dominating the political and military agendas. The United Kingdom has been a junior member, one of very many countries (between 47 and 49, depending on the year) in a coalition that has included Tonga and Mongolia.

While the UK government's strategies for the country have shifted and changed regularly, the stated principal reason for the UK presence has remained fairly constant. John Hutton, one of New Labour's six defence secretaries, summarized it thus:

[T]he decision to stay [in Afghanistan] was based on a hard-headed assessment of our clear national security interest in preventing the re-emergence of Taleban rule or Afghanistan's decline into a failing state again. Either of those outcomes would have allowed Al Qaida to return and recreate their terrorist infrastructure. The same calculations informed our later decisions to make a significant military contribution to the International Security and Assistance Force, and then to play a lead role in NATO's operations in the south, especially in Helmand Province.[1]

At the time of the initial intervention in Afghanistan, in 2001, it was not fully appreciated, of course, that the 'terrorist infrastructure' in Afghanistan was a ramshackle business and of very limited relevance to the 9/11 plot. The Taliban certainly were not aware of the 9/11 plot, and equally certainly would not have approved even if they had been. Mullah Abdul Salam Zaeef was the Taliban ambassador to Pakistan, one of the three countries that recognized the regime, when the attacks took place in the US. In his autobiography, *My Life with the Taliban*, he relates his shock at the attack – and his fears. He knew what would happen: 'The United States would seek revenge and they would turn to our troubled country.'[2]

It is worth recalling here the Taliban's response to the attacks:

We strongly condemn the events that happened in the United States and at the World Trade Center and the Pentagon. We share the grief of those who have lost their nearest and dearest in these incidents. All those responsible must be brought to justice and we want America to be patient and careful in their actions.[3]

They knew what was coming, and it duly came, with the able assistance of the United Kingdom.

At the time of the invasion of Afghanistan, it was not realized how the attacks were planned, by whom or where. We now know that they were conceived and initially planned in Germany, that the training was carried out in the US and that most of the hijackers were Saudi. The initial idea was Osama bin Laden's, and he may have conceived it in Afghanistan. Or he may not. We simply do not know. But *not a single Afghan* was involved at any stage.

Whether a different approach could have been taken is beyond the remit of this book.

Hindsight is a wonderful thing. But it is worth pointing out that alternatives were presented to the UK government in 2001. These have been examined by Lucy Morgan Edwards, a long-time Afghan resident and former political advisor to the EU Mission in Afghanistan. Her fascinating book, *The Afghan Solution*, looks at the strong advice given to the British government through MI6 *in September 2001* by several people who were very familiar with Afghanistan. One of these was the remarkable journalist and analyst Ken Guest, who was personally acquainted with the major figures of the Soviet–Afghan War, including Sirajuddin Haqqani (now causing the Afghan government a great deal of trouble) and Osama bin Laden (who now troubles no one). He offered clear advice that the correct approach was to engage with genuinely credible Afghan figures, rather than with the likes of Karzai and his clique.[4] Doing otherwise, and particularly engaging in extended foreign military operations, would, he warned, result in protracted war. Guest's friend, the former leader of the Liberal Democrats Paddy Ashdown, was familiar with the thinking of the British government at the time. He told Guest that, whatever the advice, 'there has to be a fireworks display . . . the Americans are demanding it'.[5]

But we are where we are.

What about Afghanistan as a 'haven for terrorism'?

So has international security been improved by having European and North American powers invade and occupy a Central Asian country for a decade and a half? Was the war relevant to our security at all? Members of the House of Commons Foreign Affairs Committee have taken a particular view:

> We conclude that there is evidence to suggest that the core foreign policy justification for the UK's continued presence in Afghanistan, namely that it is necessary in the interests of UK national security, may have been achieved some time ago, given the apparently limited strength of al-Qaeda in Afghanistan. Although the Government disputes this, we are concerned that this fundamentally important assessment appears to be based on intelligence that has not been subject to parliamentary scrutiny. We recommend that the Government makes this intelligence available to the Intelligence and Security Committee, which should then report, as appropriate, to the Foreign Affairs Committee on its veracity.[6]

Needless to say, no such intelligence was forthcoming. But the head of the CIA was less coy. In an interview with ABC News in 2010, Leon Panetta was asked: 'How many Al Qaeda, do you think, are in Afghanistan?' His answer came as something of a shock to many: 'I think the estimate on the number of Al Qaeda is actually relatively small. At most, we're looking at 50 to 100, maybe less.'[7]

Very few Al Qaeda operators have been killed or captured in Helmand. It would appear that Al Qaeda has a far greater hold elsewhere:

> [In 2008] Jonathan Evans, the head of MI5, estimated that there were 2,000 al-Qaeda sympathisers based in Britain – the largest concentration of al-Qaeda activists in any Western country. But American officials, who regularly refer to 'Londonistan' because of the high concentration of Islamic radicals in the capital, believe the figure is growing all the time.[8]

So there are far more dangerous concentrations of Al Qaeda in the UK than in Afghanistan. There is no 'safe haven' for Al Qaeda now in Afghanistan. There has been no such 'safe haven' since 2001 and there is no real risk of one developing. The real dangers lie elsewhere. As Professor Paul Rogers, the doyen of peace and conflict studies in the UK, told me: 'They [the UK government] did not pay any attention to what was happening in other countries throughout the period of this war – countries such as Somalia, Yemen, Mali, Nigeria, Zanzibar.'[9] That is where jihadist militants have built what might be called 'real and present' strongholds.

Almost none of the government 'narrative' of Afghanistan again being a potential haven for terrorists is true. Afghans have no interest in fomenting trouble abroad. A former NATO spokesman in Afghanistan, employed (as he put it) to 'put lipstick on a pig', summarized matters thus:

> [The Taliban] pose no threat to Britain and *not one Afghan* has ever been involved in any terror attack in Europe or the US. It is simply rubbish to assert that British soldiers are fighting impoverished opium farmers and low-grade US$10 a day gun-for-hire insurgents in Helmand Province to protect the British people from terror attacks. These Afghans are fighting our soldiers because they just don't like foreigners and infidels. They never have and never will.[10]

Why the Helmandis fight

Who are the 'Taliban'? Michael Martin, the Pashto-speaking British researcher we encountered in chapter 1, has this to say: 'The Taliban's rootedness in Helmandi society is something that ISAF have consistently failed to understand, or have deceived themselves over.' What was actually happening, as is luminously clear from Martin's research, is that the British had encountered a large group (or more accurately groups) of men who were motivated by a number of disparate but, from the British perspective, unfortunate motives: 'Every man had private reasons for fighting, but in a society where the threshold to violence was low, many men were fighting. In many cases people were fighting because of private feuds or inter-community violence, often generated or exacerbated by the warlords.'[11]

The British were under the impression that they were the representatives of the Afghan 'government'. It was only many years into the campaign, and after perhaps a dozen brigade rotations, that they began to appreciate that the government was, at best, little more than a loose and corrupt group of interests and individuals.

But this was very clear indeed to Helmandis, who regarded those the British supported, defended and fought for as rapacious thieves. The men the British called the 'Taliban' regarded the British, the hated 'Angrez', as carrying on their historical role as savage invaders and oppressors. The British army's intelligence was also manipulated by local officials, who regarded them as 'useful idiots', in much the same way as its Soviet predecessors had been manipulated. The British were led to believe that certain villages or groups were 'all Taliban'. All this in a society that, in Martin's words, 'was just too opaque to be understood by outsiders'.[12] The very last reason Helmandi guerrillas had for fighting the British was to support or further some notion of 'international caliphate', about which Helmandis, quite literally, could not care less.

Indeed, while the 'Taliban' clearly exists in the form of forces commanded by the Quetta Shura or other leaders, such as Sirajuddin Haqqani, it is highly questionable whether those that the Helmandis call *aslee* Taliban – 'real' Taliban, as opposed to the local guerrillas the British and Americans in Helmand call Taliban – actually exist as an effective unitary force in Helmandi politics. To the extent that they do exist, it is due to British failure to understand the complex roots of the 30-year conflict into which they had blundered. In treating local fighters as 'Taliban', they had in a sense created their own enemy: for in being treated as 'Taliban' those fighters became Taliban.

What is the perspective of the 'real' Taliban?

Leading US terrorism experts Robert Pape and James Feldman ask us 'to view occupation from the perspective of the resistance movement (e.g. terrorists)' because it is the behaviour of the local actors, and not the foreign power, that determines whether suicide terrorism occurs.[13] Whether the foreign power regards itself as a 'stabilizing ally' rather than an 'occupier' is not relevant.

So what is the view of our enemy in Afghanistan beyond Helmand? What do the 'real' Taliban think? Are they bent on building another terrorist state and dedicating their lives to the international struggle for a caliphate?

One way into their mindset is through their media presence. The Taliban website is very impressive – a constant stream of news, with film of Taliban attacks, statements and stories.[14] From the Western perspective, it is almost totally fictitious. The following example covers one day in 2012 when no NATO troops were in fact killed: '6 US NATO cowardly troops killed in fighting, 4 wounded . . . 3 puppets killed as enemy blown up in IEDs.' And there is a grand amalgam of the most choice phrases: '6 NATO/puppet cowardly troops killed in Paktika.'

To us, this is almost endearingly Soviet in style, and the language, with its 'puppets' and 'cowards' could just as easily have come from the Vietnam era. From an Afghan perspective, ideas of antiquated style are irrelevant (the website is, of course, a translation from the Pashto).

In not one of the speeches, statements or news stories is there any reference to the need for a world Islamic revolution. Interestingly, there are no laudatory references to any foreign jihadist terrorist attacks at all. The rhetoric is entirely based around the need for resistance. Rhetoric matters here: preaching international jihad does not appeal to Afghans of any tribes or groups.

In their study of the Taliban, *An Enemy We Created*, Alex Strick van Linschoten and Felix Kuehn point out that, while Al Qaeda is a priority for the West, 'This is not the case for the Taliban. The Al Qaeda issue is much lower down on their list of priorities ... The Taliban agenda focuses on a whole different set of local political concerns and of goals within the leadership.'[15] The authors take the view, on the basis of many years of close acquaintance with the organization, that the Taliban, as constituted now, is 'an enemy we created'.

Robert Pape and James Feldman make the point that Afghans have not been involved in international terrorism and there have been no Afghan Taliban attacks outside Afghanistan's borders: 'In many ways, the years since September 11 have been a difficult crash course for the political leadership of the Taliban in the realities of international relations.'[16] In other words, at least concerning links with Al Qaeda the Taliban have learned their lesson.

Fighting the wrong enemy and making more enemies in the process

It was a serious mistake to treat Al Qaeda as a military problem. The core of the organization has been hunted down by US forces worldwide, and it is a shadow of what it once was. The problem was primarily an intelligence one, and treating it as such – using signals and human intelligence, combined with well-prepared commando groups – has resulted in great success. The killing of Osama bin Laden was only one of many cases where terrorist operators were dealt with using those techniques.

The occupation of Muslim countries by huge, unwieldy and largely institutionally ignorant foreign armies has been less successful. Indeed, it is argued here that it has been actively counterproductive.

So have we been fighting the wrong enemy over the last decade or so? Almost certainly we have. The situation is even worse than that. We may very well have exacerbated the jihadist problem. The question has to be asked: 'Why do people decide to become "terrorists" anyway?'

President George W. Bush had an answer: 'Why do they hate us? They hate what they see right here in this chamber, a democratically elected government . . . they hate our freedoms: our freedom of religion, our freedom of speech, our freedom to vote and assemble and disagree with each other.'[17] Osama bin Laden dealt with this point briefly: 'Contrary to what Bush says and claims, that we hate [your] freedom– [So] why did we not attack Sweden?'[18]

In what is arguably the key text in the study of global suicide terrorism, Pape and Feldman make the point – obvious to some, perhaps, but clearly not to all – that the chief reason why terrorists are motivated to kill themselves lies in the one word 'occupation':

> Examination of the universe of suicide terrorism around the world
> from 1980 to 2003 shows that the principal cause of suicide terrorism
> is resistance to foreign occupation, not Islamic fundamentalism. Even
> where religion matters, moreover, it functions mainly as a recruiting
> tool in the context of national resistance.[19]

This is a theme taken up by almost all suicide terrorists.

Abu Al-Jaraah Al-Ghamidi, one of the Saudi hijackers of 9/11, is clear what motivated him and the other hijackers, and it had nothing to do with hating freedom: 'What is happening in Muslim countries today? Blatant occupation about which there is no doubt . . . there is no duty more obligatory after faith than to repel him.'[20]

Hamza Al Ghamdi, another hijacker, picked up the idea: 'And I say to America: if it wants its armies and people to be safe, then it must withdraw all of its forces from the Muslim lands and depart from all our countries. If not, then let it await the men, prepare its coffins and dig graves for its citizens.'[21]

One of the British suicide bombers in London, Mohammad Sidique Khan took a similar view:

> Your democratically elected governments continuously perpetuate
> [sic] atrocities against my people all over the world. And your support
> of them makes you directly responsible, just as I am directly

responsible for protecting and avenging my Muslim brothers and sisters. Until we feel security, you will be our targets. And until you stop the bombing, gassing, imprisonment and torture of my people we will not stop this fight. We are at war and I am a soldier. Now you too will taste the reality of this situation.[22]

With such views clearly prominent among terrorists and their recruits, one wonders whether further or continued invasions of Muslim countries are the best antidote. What about religion? Don't extremist interpretations of Islam play a part? Pape and Feldman are clear on this: 'Religion matters ... it functions mainly as a recruiting tool *in the context of national resistance*.'[23]

What is the Al Qaeda perspective?

From the perspective of Al Qaeda, of course, Afghanistan has been a tremendous success: a hundred or so of their operatives have succeeded in tying down tens of thousands of US and other troops, at virtually no cost to themselves. It does seem to have been an objective of Osama bin Laden to ensure that this happened. Abdel Bari Atwan, editor of the London-based Arabic-language newspaper *Al Quds al Arabi* and author of *The Secret History of Al Qaeda* met the organization's former leader.[24] Atwan said in an interview:

He [bin Laden] told me personally that he can't go and fight the Americans and their country. But if he manages to provoke them and bring them to the Middle East and to their Muslim worlds, where he can find them or fight them on his own turf, he will actually teach them a lesson.[25]

With hundreds of billions of US dollars and tens of billions of British pounds spent, with hundreds of soldiers killed and thousands wounded, and with a population now unwilling to engage in operations that may in fact be necessary, military historians might come to regard the Afghan campaign as the most effective 'asymmetric' campaign in the history of warfare.

Furthermore, the Western occupation of Afghanistan has been a quite excellent recruiting tool for the terrorist network, playing directly into its key selling point: that the West is bent on occupying and controlling Muslim lands.

So are we safer?

Even if the Taliban were, by some miracle, to be totally destroyed, would we be any 'safer'? It is very doubtful whether the last decade of military action in Afghanistan has had any positive effect in reducing either domestic or international terrorism.

But there are some believers. In the winter of 2011, I went to a dinner at which a very senior military officer spoke. He was reasonably well received by the well turned out and accomplished guests. The speech was witty and interesting, and the general held the attention of his audience as he spoke about UK defence policy and the present and future state of the UK armed forces. Then he turned to Afghanistan. At this point he lost his touch, saying that 'if by 2015 there has been no terrorist attack on the UK it will be because we have had troops in Helmand'.

According to Anatol Lieven, the writer, former journalist and acknowledged expert on Pakistan, there is a Russian school of philosophy which states that the fate of men is decided by the migration of fruit flies: 'And who is to say they are wrong?'[26] Who indeed? The point is that this kind of arbitrary connection cannot be disproved. Philosophers would call it the *post hoc ergo propter hoc* fallacy, confusing sequence with causality: if Manchester City wins the football premier league, and that is followed a month later by a rise in the stock market, the one has not necessarily caused the other. The truth is, of course, that our military activities in Helmand have no impact whatsoever on terrorist plots in the UK.

The real reason for the huge British presence in Afghanistan

The real reason we have expended so much blood and money on Afghanistan is simple and is accepted in private by most sensible politicians and senior soldiers. It is the same reason that prompted Tony Blair to lead Britain into the Iraq quagmire: the perceived necessity of retaining the closest possible links with the US. General Dannatt had a clear idea of the opportunities offered by an increased presence in Afghanistan. As we saw in chapter 1, after the somewhat less than successful performance of UK forces in Iraq:

> There is recognition that our national and military reputation and credibility, unfairly or not, have been called into question at several levels in the eyes of our most important ally as a result of some aspects of the Iraq campaign. Taking steps to restore this credibility will be pivotal – and Afghanistan provides an opportunity.[27]

The vital words here are '*credibility . . . in the eyes of our most important ally*'. This has been the silent elephant in the room throughout Britain's recent misadventures. This is not the place for a full discussion of the pros and cons of (or indeed the truth behind) the so-called 'special relationship' between the UK and the US. However, as every senior officer knows, a major reason for the UK's presence *in such numbers* is the 'special relationship'. There was a desire to show that the British could 'do something', and in so doing to preserve and, if possible, deepen the 'special relationship'.[28] Anyone with even a nodding acquaintance with the UK armed forces can be in no doubt that in military circles there is indeed an extraordinarily close relationship. There are historical links, a constant flow of exchange officers and a genuine feeling of closeness between the UK and US militaries. From the British perspective, this appears unique; from the US perspective less so – such relationships exist with many countries all over the world: Canadian generals on exchange programmes provide deputy commanders for major US military formations, for example. Nevertheless, with its relatively large armed forces (relative to countries such as Peru or Jordan), Britain is probably at or very near the top of the list.

The same pathology exists with the intelligence services, which have the ear of senior politicians far more regularly than our soldiers could ever hope to have. There is an intelligence relationship between the five major English-speaking countries of Australia, Canada, the UK, the US and New Zealand (the 'five eyes' or AUSCANUKUS system). Most intelligence information is shared by these countries. Most, but by no means all. When I worked in Iraq for a largely US military organization, reports I had written would be classified (for whatever reason) SECRET US NOFORN – meaning that no foreigner could read it, not even the British writer.

Senior British military and intelligence officers believe that the 'special relationship' is vital to national security and are determined, at almost any cost, for cooperation to continue at the same level: it plugs them into a much larger and more powerful organization than their own, and provides access to intelligence, equipment and training of which they could otherwise only dream. The effects of this are toxic and go far beyond the military. One evening, after a conference, I was privileged to meet a very senior and well-known military officer who has been deeply involved in both the Iraq and the Afghanistan campaigns. He took serious issue (as well he might) with certain assertions made during the conference about the lack of strategy in both those campaigns. 'Don't you see?' he grumbled. 'We cannot have a separate strategy for the very simple reason that we are in a coalition.'

Of course this is little short of nonsense. The 'coalition' is not a coalition of equals; it is not even the kind of alliance where one party is *primus inter pares*. I suppose that was the general's point: the campaigns we have been involved in are US operations, to which others, including the British, have signed on. No decision on Afghanistan – for example, on drawdown – is made by the UK without reference, indeed permission, from the United States. To that extent, the general was right. That is the way it is.

However, it is not the way it should be, and nor is it how other nations have handled their alliance with the US. They have taken robust views as to the nature and degree of their involvement in the campaign, with explicit and active reference to their own national interest: Canada withdrew its forces from Kandahar in 2011; the Netherlands, which had fought an often innovative (militarily far more so than the UK in Helmand) if ultimately largely pointless campaign in the province of Uruzgan, left in 2010. France – of whom President Obama said 'we have no stronger friend and stronger ally'[29] – withdrew her forces from Afghanistan in late 2012, having decided that her national interests were not served by continuing to take casualties and to spend vast quantities of money in Central Asia.

These other countries took strategic decisions. What they did not have was some almost unquestioned idea that they were in some form of 'special relationship', which absolved them from independent thinking. In the years since 2001, the British military leadership has had what might be described as an 'unconscious barrier to thinking about strategy at all'.[30] That a senior officer would express the view that the UK cannot have a separate Afghan strategy as 'we are in a coalition' is surely evidence of this.

Perhaps it is time for this 'special relationship' to be looked at dispassionately. Our threats and concerns are absolutely *not* those of the United States, any more than they should be identified with those of France, Germany or Thailand. There may be *common* interests, but they are not identical. In the end, we may indeed be well served by retaining strong links to US intelligence – particularly US signals intelligence capability – which is a key silent driver of the 'special relationship'. But this is a two-way street, as our own capabilities have a value of their own. We may well need the US as a 'special ally', but do we need to give lives for it? Maybe we do. But if so, how many? The awful paradox of Britain's failure in Helmand (and indeed Basra) is that it may have actually damaged the relationship, since the UK may no longer be seen as an ally of first resort. In the longer term, of course, that may be no bad thing for the UK.

As matters stand, the UK's military and political leaders have a long way to go before they realize that the US needs the UK almost as much as the UK needs the US (particularly in terms of bases and intelligence). Perhaps the debacle of Helmand may cause our political leaders to assess coolly what exactly the United Kingdom's national interests require, in the same way as France appraises her own interests and follows her own path – evidently, as President Obama's comments show, with no damage to Franco-US relations. Doing so may open the way for the UK to begin thinking seriously about strategy.

The real front line – the UK and Pakistan

The so-called 'special relationship' has led Britain into the invasion of two Islamic countries. Her confused and inconsistent strategy (or the lack of any strategy) in the ensuing wars and her over-enthusiastic and totally uncritical following of US policy have been intensely damaging to British (and indeed Afghan) interests. The policies pursued have been entirely counterproductive and literally self-defeating.

As Anatol Lieven says:

If by 2015 it is just a question of £30 billion and 400 dead, it could be seen as simply another Isandlwana [the famous defeat of a British army by Zulus in 1879] – an embarrassment, but with little serious consequence. If, however, we have succeeded in destabilizing Pakistan, it will have far more serious consequences that will hit us very close to home.[31]

Pakistan is as critical to UK interests as Afghanistan is peripheral. Yet it has been sidelined by the US and by a UK that is in thrall to the US. With the UK's large population of Pakistani expats and their descendants who retain close links with the 'old country', Pakistan is far more important to our national security than Afghanistan. Nothing demonstrates quite so powerfully the divergence between US and British interests.

In April 2009, on a visit to Afghanistan, Prime Minister Gordon Brown spoke of the 'crucible of terrorism' in the mountainous border between Afghanistan and Pakistan. He added that 'three-quarters of the terrorist activities that happened in Britain arise from *the areas around here*. The safety of people on the streets of Britain is immediately being safeguarded by the action being taken here.'[32]

In late 2012, David Cameron attempted a similar formulation: 'When I sit in No 10 Downing Street and look at where the plots that we face in terms of terror, where they come from, far fewer come from *this part of the world* than used to be the case when we first came to Afghanistan, so we have made real progress.'[33] As both prime ministers must have known, the truth was that the areas they were talking about were located exclusively in Pakistan – certainly in 'this part of the world', but not in Afghanistan. No government official has ever claimed that terrorists in Helmand were plotting against the United Kingdom.

Anything the British armed forces were doing had limited or no positive impact on what was or is going on in Pakistan. The British armed forces had and have no presence at all in Pakistan. Indeed, the Pakistani armed forces themselves have only the most tenuous hold on those areas from which real terrorist plots are said to be hatched. Nonetheless, the accomplished and ruthless Pakistani intelligence service – the Inter-Services Intelligence or ISI – has assisted the British security services greatly.

However, that assistance may be at risk. Anatol Lieven, author of the magisterial *Pakistan: A hard country*,[34] believes that:

There would be very serious damage if what we have done, and our support for the US, produces a collapse between ISI and US/UK. The ISI does give a lot of help concerning the comings and goings of people who really do present a threat to the UK. But that cooperation has not broken down despite the controversies of recent years ... What we surely can say is that UK policy has been an absolute disaster in the perception of the Muslim population and has produced a significantly increased terrorist threat.[35]

And a very large proportion of the Muslim population of the United Kingdom is of Pakistani origin.

As was observed above, the Afghan aspect of the Afghan War is pretty well irrelevant to terrorism in the UK (save for the fact that the war may have acted as an aid to recruitment). But there is a Pakistani aspect that is far more dangerous. For the US is increasingly using drones to kill militants across the border from Afghanistan – against the express wishes of the Pakistan government. Any increased instability in Pakistan will have consequences that will be felt in the UK – and not solely (perhaps not at all) in the form of terrorism. For if Pakistan were to descend into chaos, it is to their close relatives in Britain that tens of thousands of refugees will turn.

Yet the money pumped into Helmand by the UK is many orders of magnitude greater than the amount of aid delivered to Pakistan, which is strategically far more important to the UK: 'A great deal of money is poured away in Pakistan, it is true. But even if you cannot build anything, you can buy a great deal of influence.'[36]

A more serious point is the economic helplessness of large parts of the UK. A major tranche of investment in new industry in parts of Lancashire and Yorkshire could be very effective in reducing the chronic poverty (by UK standards) among large sections of ethnic Pakistani youth. 'The real front line against terrorism in the UK is in the UK.'[37] That is surely incontrovertible in the light of the July 2005 bombings in London and subsequent attempted attacks, many of them mounted by UK citizens of Pakistani origin.

Wider security implications of the UK's Afghan campaign

The somewhat less than victorious campaigns in the various deserts of the east have focused much of the defence effort on the needs of the army – it, after all, was doing most of the fighting. Moving away from what has been seen as the dominant priority will be difficult and expensive. In military parlance, this shift away from a distraction and back to what the armed forces are supposed to do – defend the national interests – is called 'reset'. Such change is difficult enough in a rational organization like a large business or a bank, and indeed it has spawned a business discipline called 'change management'. But in the world of British defence, with its chaotic organization and bloated hierarchy of senior officers, things are even more complicated, as those officers jostle to uphold the interests of their respective services.

Traditionally we are a maritime nation. The focus on counterinsurgency in Central Asia has diverted our gaze from the perennial national interest of preserving our lines of communication and safeguarding our lines of supply. There is a sense among military officers that the way things are is the way they will always be. Consequently, despite the end of the Afghan War (for the UK), officers will continue to be trained in 'counterinsurgency' theory, just as they continued to be instructed in how to repel Soviet tank units long after the collapse of the Soviet Union. This tendency is dubbed 'presentism', which was defined by one leading strategist as 'assuming that the shape and nature of the campaign you are in represents the shape and nature of all future campaigns against which you should be preparing'.[38] Others simply call it 'fighting the last war'.

The Libyan campaign was exactly the sort of expeditionary campaign for which the British armed forces like to think they are equipped and trained. Yet Libya showed just how much the UK lacks any such effective and independent capability.

I was privileged to serve with the UK mission in Libya for several months in 2011–12. As he emerges from the somewhat chaotic arrivals hall at Benghazi airport into the Libyan sun, the first thing the flustered traveller sees is a large billboard. It stands on a roundabout that is much like those at hundreds of provincial airports all over the world. On the hoarding is a picture of a revolutionary, swathed in green cloth and brandishing a rifle in one hand. With the other hand he is making a V-sign. At the top, in metre-high lettering, is written 'Merci la France' – 'Thank you, France'.

I searched in vain for a similar expression of gratitude to the UK. The poster is not a testament to the PR skills of the French embassy (although anyone who has had dealings with the French will know that they are masters of presentation). It simply reflects what every Benghazawi knows – that the aircraft that stopped Gadhafi's armoured brigade from entering Benghazi and destroying Libya's nascent revolution were French. That particular mission was flown from the French mainland by Mirage aircraft. Indeed, for most of the conflict, if you were fortunate enough (or unlucky enough, depending on your view) to see a NATO aircraft, it was more than likely to be French, probably from the French navy. For rarely was the nuclear aircraft carrier *Charles de Gaulle* more than 20 miles off the coast of Libya. The significant point is that the aircraft were not British.

Around a third of air strikes (bombing missions) were French. Indeed aircraft of the French air force carried out those first air strikes on Gadhafi's forces outside Benghazi. And it was French forces that saved the citizens of Benghazi from the kind of savagery meted out in several Syrian cities in 2012–13. They also conducted the last decisive raid that destroyed the dictator's convoy of vehicles outside Sirt, and allowed his capture and eventual killing. In terms of the proportions of air strikes carried out by NATO aircraft, the NATO figures are revealing:

the RAF delivered about 10 per cent, as did Italy, Norway and Canada; they were just behind Denmark (11 per cent); while the US carried out 16 per cent.[39]

Meanwhile a fleet of no fewer than 26 British warships and auxiliaries – almost all the remaining Royal Navy ships available – steamed up and down the coast, occasionally popping shells off at Libyan coastal positions (and being fired on in return) and stopping suspicious fishing vessels. Apart from the single 4.5-inch gun of HMS *Liverpool*, the best support they could offer the campaign on the shore was a flight of much-heralded army helicopters, comprising four Apache helicopters, which managed a total of 26 strike missions.[40] Due to the perceived capabilities of Libyan air defences, the helicopters were not permitted to cross the coastline. A far cry from the genuinely powerful French task force headed by the *Charles de Gaulle*, with its strike and fighter aircraft. Painful as it is for a former British officer such as myself to admit, from the first operations to the last the French were in the lead. The reason is that France has not recalibrated its armed forces to the requirements of wars in Central Asian deserts. Rather it has adjusted its commitment to that conflict according to what it can do with what it has. Consequently it retains far more flexible and capable armed forces than the UK.

Over the years of the Afghan War (and indeed the Iraq War) there has been a great focus on the needs of the army, to the exclusion of the Royal Navy in particular. The result is that, as former Royal Navy Admiral Terry Loughran put it when interviewed on the BBC: 'We've now reduced . . . to such a low level that this maritime nation can no longer sustain a tin-pot operation like Libya.'[41]

By emasculating the Royal Navy to pay for the army and its operations in the Afghan desert, the UK has jeopardized the defence of our island nation's vital interests. Protecting our transport arteries, our trade and energy, and preserving security in Europe – that is the ultimate role, the *raison d'être*, of our defence forces.

It is the job of strategy to ensure that the defence of our vital interests is balanced with the means available. Commodore Steven Jermy, formerly commander of the Royal Navy's Fleet Air Arm, is author of the contemporary classic *Strategy for Action*, a study of recent strategic thinking as well as a prescription for improved strategy. He believes that: 'Politicians feel as though they have been hoodwinked by the military's faith in itself; this is a faith which is founded in ignorance.'[42] This in turn reflects a failure of the political nation as a whole to clarify where our key national interests lie and to ensure their security.

Whatever the views of much of our military hierarchy, whether or not we are in a 'coalition', a proper appreciation of national strategy is of absolutely fundamental importance. How can we develop that in practice if we are to be dragged into almost every US campaign – including those, such as Helmand, that have no bearing whatsoever on British national interests, or indeed that actively damage them.

Improving our strategic thinking and practice will require firm political control over senior officers and their ambitions. As we saw above, the Helmand debacle was, to a great degree, motivated by the perceived need to restore the army's reputation in the eyes of the US. Retaining such firm control may require some very brave decisions, one of which would be to encourage Britain to revert to a realistic approach to its national interests. That may mean denying the armed forces the wherewithal to conduct extended military operations in areas that are not our own, at the same time as increasing our capabilities to defend our vital interests (which surely do not lie in Central Asian deserts).

The 2012 cuts in the army are a positive step towards rebalancing our defence forces and encouraging a more pragmatic posture. However, the emaciated state of the navy remains a national disgrace and a serious danger. Traditionally, the United Kingdom has not retained a large land-force capability (at least not relative to other countries). The exception was during the Cold War in Europe, when the UK armed forces were configured to resist an attack from the Soviet Union in

Germany. No one was in any doubt then about the function of the armed forces. The question they were designed to address was the Soviet Union's Third Shock Army, which was poised to invade West Germany. What question has our involvement in Afghanistan been addressing?

We still live in a very dangerous world, where terrorism is only one of many potential risks, and by no means the greatest. Climate change, coupled with declining natural resources, could open up the possibility of conflict in the Arctic. The discovery of oil, combined with the ongoing Falklands dispute with Argentina, offers a great potential for naval rivalry. In the Arabian Gulf and the Mediterranean, perennial insecurity and conflict – and in the Indian Ocean even pirates! – present a constant threat to our lines of fuel supply. And our own regional back-yard in the Balkans still poses the risk of conflict – and of having others drawn into that conflict, as in 1914.

None of these problems are new. Attempting to predict the exact nature of future conflict is a fool's errand. We cannot forecast what will happen. What we can do is control what it is we get involved in and calibrate that precisely and clearly with reference to our national inter-ests. We must then do all we can to ensure that the gains are commen-surate with the costs.

Conclusion

'Do not ask me if it was worth it, because it was not . . . All we want is a country we can forget about.'[1] Unnamed British diplomat, to BBC reporter, October 2012

The achievement in Helmand

Britain's efforts have resulted in the 'stabilization' (i.e. the temporary pacification) of 3 of the 14 districts that make up the province of Helmand – just one of 34 provinces in a country with a population that is half that of the UK. In terms of overall political significance, this might be the equivalent of three large market towns in rural Lincolnshire.

Before the British burst onto the scene, Helmand was 'stable', in the sense that there was almost no Taliban presence and little prospect of any. After three years of British presence, the province was the most savage combat zone in the world. With British forces and their commanders out of their depth, it was only the intervention of a powerful US force of marines that brought some level of control to the situation.

Before the British arrived with the avowed intention of combating narcotics, Helmand produced just under 40 per cent of Afghanistan's opium. Immediately after the British entry, opium production rose considerably. Helmand now produces about 49 per cent of Afghanistan's opium crop.[2]

No significant Al Qaeda presence has been reported in Helmand since 2001.

How much has it cost?

Financial costs

Military expenses	£31.1 billion
Future care of veterans	£3.8 billion
Civilian development costs	£2.1 billion
Total	**£37 billion**

These figures do not include interest, which must be added as a cost.[3] This will run at £1 billion per year on the (at least) £33.2 billion of disbursed costs (i.e. military and development costs already spent).[4] Interest costs will rise even further as such liabilities as increased health costs become due.

By 2020, Britain will have spent at the very least **£40 billion** on its Afghan campaign, some 90 per cent of it on military activities. That represents an investment of about £650 by every resident of the United Kingdom, or over £2,000 by every taxpaying household.

Put another way, over £25,000 will have been spent for every single one of the roughly 1.5 million inhabitants of Helmand province (no one knows the exact population) – more than most of them will earn in a lifetime. Of course, for most of the campaign, the UK has only been working in three districts, with a combined population of about 400,000. So the figure works out at roughly £100,000 for each Helmandi 'beneficiary'.

Remember: all these are *minimum baseline figures*.

To take some random comparisons, £40 billion is enough to:

- pay for two-thirds of a NASA manned mission to Mars,[5] or to fund several UK manned missions to the moon;
- run 1,000 primary schools for 40 years;
- fund free tution for *all* students in British higher education for 10 years;
- pay for the entire overseas development budget for five years; or
- recruit over 5,000 new police officers or nurses and pay for them *for their entire careers*.

Or, in a military context, it is enough to:

- equip the Royal Navy with a full, up-to-date aircraft carrier group, complete with an aircraft carrier, an air wing consisting of 50 of the latest F-35 Lightning II aircraft and some helicopters, and four Daring Class destroyers with an attendant submarine – and to run them all for ten years;
- replace the UK's nuclear deterrent; or
- recruit and equip three full army or Royal Marine brigades and fund them for ten years, including full capitation (through-career pay, housing and pensions) for all troops.

Human costs

British casualties:

- Dead: 440[6]
- Wounded: over 2,600
- Psychologically injured: unknown but upwards of 5,000.

Afghan (Helmandi) non-combatants:

- Dead, killed by British/NATO forces: at least 542
- Wounded and disabled caused by British/NATO forces: unknown, but in a *single* month, 158 civilians wounded in fighting were admitted to just *one* hospital in Lashkar Gah
- Refugees and internally displaced Helmandis: 20,000 in Kabul alone.

How did this happen?

On a balmy, late summer's evening, two soldiers, both working in military intelligence and one of them an accomplished Arabic-speaker, sat chatting after a patrol on the banks of the Shatt-al-Arab River in Basra, Iraq.

- You know, before I went to war, I wanted to be the guy in the know, the one who, what with all the chaos and confusion, really understands what is going on.
- I know the feeling. I want to be the soldier who has all the answers.
- In this war that's supposed to be us, isn't it? We're the ones that everyone else thinks are in the know.
- We are indeed. We're the ones supposed to be in the know. That's us all right.
- We don't have a clue, do we?
- Not a clue.

I was one of those soldiers (not the Arabic-speaker!). We really did not have a clue what was going on in Basra, or indeed why it was going on. We were the men looking for the weapons of mass destruction, with a sideline in counter-terrorism. If anyone should have known, it surely should have been us. That was certainly the attitude of the ordinary fighting troops.

So we had 'no clue' what was going on. *But* we believed (or at least were supposed to believe) that someone else did: the soldiers or (more likely) civilians 'above our pay grade'. They were the grown-ups, the ones we had been taught to believe were 'the guys in the know' about what was happening around us and to us. We soldiers sitting on the banks of the Shatt-al-Arab were at the tactical level – the level where things actually happen. It was those at higher levels – at the 'operational' and 'strategic' levels, according to military doctrine and parlance – who understood things. Maybe the generals knew, or maybe the civilians who drove around in bullet-proof SUVs, armed to the teeth with dossiers. They were the grown-ups. Or maybe MI6 – they might know something. After all, someone *must* know.

My next deployment was to Helmand. I was one of those civilians who sat at the 'operational' level, where people look at big maps and think; where PowerPoint presentations are made about plans that are being hatched. I drove around in a bullet-proof SUV, armed with files. I briefed generals and politicians.

For the sake of balance or symmetry, it would be nice to be able to relate a 'someone must know' conversation between civilians in the PRT. But it became perfectly clear early on that no one actually did know. Certainly not us. Maybe those politicians: they might have an insight denied to us soldiers and civilians ...

So what about them? What of the views and the approach of our political leadership? In his recent book on his successful and wide-ranging career, *Ever the Diplomat*, Britain's former ambassador to Afghanistan makes a point that escaped the reviewers and interviewers, but that is of huge importance. Sir Sherard Cowper-Coles, a man who always expresses himself very carefully, has this to say: this has been 'a war in which almost no-one – certainly not the senior politicians – really believes'.[7]

This is a view I have heard expressed regularly by politicians of varying degrees of seniority. I had dinner with one very senior politician in early 2012. He had to leave early to give an interview to a leading news programme about casualties that the army had taken that day. 'What are you going to say?', I asked. 'The usual', he replied. 'These men died to keep Britain secure.' 'But you don't believe that', I countered. 'No one really believes that, do they?' His answer was instructive: 'What else can I say?'

In late 2012, while preparing this book, I emailed every politician who has held the post of defence secretary since 2006, when British forces entered Helmand. I was hoping for some clarification. This is what I wrote to each of them:

> As well as researching the costs, I am interested in what people think might have been gained. Accordingly, I am writing to former defence secretaries to ask what you think may be the legacy of Helmand, positive or negative. If you could spare the time for an interview, I am at your disposal. Otherwise, your written thoughts, however brief, would be more than welcome.

Unfortunately, none could spare the time either for an interview or to provide their brief written thoughts on the war over which they presided.[8] Those who replied said they were otherwise engaged. All, of course, are busy men.[9]

So why, if it was evident that little was to be achieved by staying in Helmand, did we stay there? It has already been argued in this book that the principal reason for being in Afghanistan in such numbers was to preserve and cement the 'special relationship'. Obviously this played a key part in ensuring that, unlike other countries with a rather clearer view of their true national interests, Britain 'stayed the course' (as the generals might say), however hopeless and expensive that course was. Nonetheless, other – deeper – factors may be at play and may have exacerbated the 'special relationship' problem.

Sunk costs

In a previous book, *Losing Small Wars*, I argued that one of the driving forces behind the failure of the British armed forces in Iraq and Afghanistan to succeed in any of their objectives (insofar as any could be identified) was a deeply embedded culture of 'cracking on' – of pressing on with an endeavour without proper thought or consideration, on the grounds that, by doing so, sooner or later something positive might happen.

A young officer in the Welsh Guards who served hard time in Helmand reflected on the inability of the British to accept failure:

> The British are very good at whipping ourselves up into a sense of achievement . . . We almost have to, to make it bearable. You can't do something like this and analyse it all the way through and think: 'Actually we got that wrong.' You just can't. It takes so much emotional investment. I'm not saying we lie to ourselves but there's an element of telling yourself that it's all right and it's going well, just to keep going.[10]

To keep going. No *successful* general would argue in favour of hopeless action. The gain must always be recognizably proportionate to the loss. There is no virtue in 'pressing on regardless', 'keeping going' or 'cracking on' when objective analysis demonstrates that the actions are highly likely to fail. There lies the road to defeat. Unfortunately, so I argued in that previous book, for several reasons the British have been somewhat lacking in successful generals in recent years.

Yet when so much has already been expended, when so many lives have already been lost, it is a natural human response to say: 'We have to make it worthwhile, we must persevere.' This kind of thinking seeps insidiously into all military thinking. There is a perverse, but entirely understandable logic in the idea that if we spare no expense in striving to achieve our goals, then we must press on, regardless of cost, until those goals are achieved.

The unfortunate corollary of this is the so-called 'sunk cost fallacy'. Sunk costs are those disbursements on any given task or project that are gone and cannot be recovered. The trouble is that human psychology attaches an irrational value proportional to the investment made. At the most basic level, the more they have paid, the more inclined people are to shy away from objective analysis of value. If I use all my savings to buy an old oil painting because I really believe it to be the lost painting by the seventeenth-century baroque master Gian Lorenzo Bernini that I have always wanted to find, I will take a great deal of persuading that it was, in fact, painted down the road in Peterborough by a talented forger just a few years ago. In economics, this approach is also called the 'escalation of commitment' – a term used to justify an ever-increasing investment due to the large financial commitment already made. Experiments have shown that it is very difficult to deal with.

It is the same impulse that drives a compulsive gambler to keep pouring money into a game of cards: 'I've spent so much already that I might as well carry on.' Rationally, the gambler knows that his chances of winning are no better than they ever were. But reason plays little part in his decision.

When we come to military endeavour, the combination of the two related impulses of 'cracking on' and 'escalation of commitment' can become very pronounced. Insistence beyond all reasonable hope that success is yet possible if we make just one more push is a common feature of military thinking. It can go beyond the realms of the acceptable and is all too often seen as a virtue. There is a view that anything is possible, if only the will is there. One of Napoleon's famous adages was: 'If you set out to take Vienna, take Vienna.' Of course, unlike the people running our societies, Napoleon was genuinely prepared to do 'whatever it took' (as politicians are so fond of saying) to achieve his aims. He was also a general who, at least until 1812 and his over-optimistic invasion of Russia, had a keen appreciation of what was possible. In the case of senior officers who lack perspective, the traditional military virtue of 'cracking on' until something positive happens is toxic.

Clearly, in some circumstances, the approach of 'pressing on regardless' can bear fruit. What would have happened had the naysayers been heeded before the Battle of Britain? The struggle against the 'might of the Luftwaffe' is often presented as the epitome of victory against overwhelming odds. However, when we analyse conflicts such as the Battle of Britain in detail, we almost invariably discover a fine and entirely rational appreciation of reality on the part of the eventual victors, as well as careful and brutally realistic preparation.

Let us take the Battle of Britain as an example. The pilots of the RAF are often presented as dashing and recklessly brave, fighting an almost hopeless, last-ditch battle against all the odds. Their opponents in the Luftwaffe are seen as embodying German efficiency and ruthlessness. But the truth is quite different. While a few of the combat aircrew were in the 'tally-ho' mould, none of the RAF's successful commanders were: instead they were intensely and bluntly realistic. Aware of the vital importance of the task in hand, they were equally conscious of the losses that would have to be sustained if success was to be assured.

Britain's air defence system had been prepared with grim and efficient determination. It was commanded by calculating and realistic senior officers. By contrast, the German effort was relatively slapdash, poorly planned and unrealistic. It was the Luftwaffe that adopted the 'just one more push' philosophy, despite considerable evidence that this could not help it achieve its objective of 'wiping the RAF from the skies'.

The flip side of the 'press on regardless' approach adopted by the Luftwaffe and many armed forces before and since is the well-known military maxim: 'Don't reinforce failure.' In other words once it becomes clear that failure is inevitable – or that success, however defined, cannot be achieved by the military means you have adopted – stop what you are doing and think again. Insanity, said Albert Einstein, is 'doing the same thing over and over again and expecting different results'.

Looking to the future

Chinese Premier Zhou Enlai is supposed to have mused in 1971 that it was probably too early to assess the impact of the French Revolution of 1789. But we can probably draw some conclusions about the significance of the Helmand campaign. For a start, it is almost certainly the last time that a British army will be deployed in large numbers so far away for so long. In that sense it is the last imperial war.

In late 2011, I was at a conference where the discussion had turned to the future and to the global roles that the British armed forces might be able to develop, particularly after 2020, by which time the army would be reformed and the navy would have its carriers, if not necessarily its carrier aircraft. One of the participants, perhaps significantly an arms company executive, pulled everyone up short:

> Look, by 2020 we will have maybe 20 major navy surface vessels and a few submarines. India's navy will have about 100 capable major surface warships, three carrier groups and 400 aircraft. That's just the navy. Their army is huge and their air force is impressive. That's India. China will be even more powerful. Get real and ask yourselves where 20 major surface warships, of which we might be able to deploy 7, an aircraft carrier, some submarines and a deployable brigade of 5,000 men might fit in there.

With an emaciated army, a depleted treasury and no public appetite at all for foreign military expeditions, it may well be that we have reached the end of the road for large-scale global adventures. Will the Afghan campaign, along with its evil twin the Iraq campaign, come to be regarded as the death throes of a post-imperial power? One that – at a time when the West was prepared to blow trillions of dollars on forlorn efforts in the Middle East and Central Asia – had more money than sense? These are huge questions that are well beyond the remit of this book.

Now, as major British involvement draws to a close, if we cannot assess the overall significance of the war, we can at least tell ourselves the truth. For Jonathan Steele, a journalist and Afghanistan expert, the shadows of the Vietnam War, from which Harold Wilson kept us, and of the Afghan-Soviet War loom large: 'It is completely accepted in Russia that the young men of the Soviet war died in vain. It was the same in the United States after the Vietnam War. Here in the UK it is much harder for many professionals to accept that they have failed and that it was in vain.'[11] As citizens and soldiers, we must be mature enough as a nation to accept that we did our best but that, in the words of 'Peter', the seriously injured veteran we met in chapter 2, it 'didn't work out'.

If we are ever again involved in this kind of 'war among the people' – perhaps as part of a UN mission to Syria or other countries far away of which we know nothing – there needs to be a focus on the people among whom we are fighting. We talk the talk about 'protecting the people', but in war things go badly wrong. People get maimed and killed who should not get maimed or killed. That's the way it is. If we are serious about this kind of work – and our military surely is – then we need to learn to take care of the people who get in our way. We need to act as if our words mean something.

Thousands of people – we called them 'innocent civilians' but all too often treated them as a mere backdrop to our own little dramas – got in our way in Helmand. They did not mean to do so: they were simply, as the saying goes, 'in the wrong place at the wrong time'. But those people are suffering even now, as you come to the end of this book. They are mourning their lost children; living – if it can be called that – in agony in dark corners of hot shacks; shivering in squalid refugee camps in Kabul . . .

It is no good talking of 'protecting the people' if we then shove responsibility for those we have not merely failed to protect but have actually hurt onto a ramshackle and corrupt government and say 'goodbye'. We need to make sure that those people are treated decently; that we know who they are, however difficult that may be; and that they are properly compensated.

The same applies – and for the same reasons – to the brave professionals we send out to try to do what we ask of them. We need to take proper care of our veterans.

The bitter irony is that none of this would cost more than a tiny fraction of what we have spent on bullets, air transport and aid consultants.

Notes

Introduction

1. Sherard Cowper-Coles, *Ever the Diplomat: Confessions of a Foreign Office mandarin*, HarperPress, London, 2012, p. 300.
2. Keith Hartley, 'The costs of conflict: the UK experience in Afghanistan and Iraq', in Manas Chatterji et al., *Frontiers of Peace Economics and Peace Science*, Emerald Press, Bingley, 2011, p. 74.

Chapter 1: Helmand and the 'Angrez'

1. Tony Blair, Camp Bastion 21 November 2006.
2. Rodric Braithwaite, *Afgantsy*, Profile Books, London, 2011.
3. 'In Afghanistan, a Soviet past lies in ruins', *New York Times*, 11 February 2012, available at: www.nytimes.com/2012/02/12/world/asia/kabuls-soviet-ruins-offer-a-reminder-of-imperial-ambitions.html?pagewanted=all
4. See Tariq Ali's review of Rodric Braithwaite's *Afgantsy* in 'Andropov was right', *London Review of Books*, 12 June 2011, available at: www.lrb.co.uk/v33/n12/tariq-ali/andropov-was-right
5. 'The unexamined Iraqi dimension of UK involvement in Iraq', Iraq Body Count, 22 May 2011, available at: www.iraqbodycount.org/analysis/beyond/uk-involvement/ The authoritative and very conservative Iraq Body Count has documented 5,720 killed and 11,174 wounded civilians in the rest of Iraq.
6. Interview with Nadene Ghouri, June 2012.
7. See, inter alia, Frank Ledwidge, *Losing Small Wars*, Yale University Press, London, 2011 (passim) for further details of the effect of this diversion of resources.
8. 'Part-time soldier dies in bombing', BBC News, 29 January 2004, available at: http://news.bbc.co.uk/1/hi/england/devon/3441409.stm. Three soldiers had died in Afghanistan before Private Kitulagoda, but as a result of accident and suicide, not enemy action.
9. Conversation with very senior military officer, September 2012.

10. Matt Cavanagh, 'Ministerial decision-making in the run-up to the Helmand deployment', *RUSI Journal*, 157:2 (2012), pp. 48–54, available at: www.rusi.org/downloads/assets/201204_Jnl_Cavanagh.pdf (italics in original).

11. Supplementary written evidence from Sir Sherard Cowper-Coles to the Foreign Affairs Committee, 23 December 2010, available at: www.publications.parliament.uk/pa/cm201011/cmselect/cmfaff/514/514we10.htm

12. General Sir Richard Dannatt, lecture to Chatham House, 'A perspective on the nature of future conflict', 15 May 2009, available at: www.chathamhouse.org/events/view/155699

13. Rajiv Chandrasekaran, *Little America: The war within the war for Afghanistan*, Bloomsbury, London, 2012, p. 45.

14. Quoted in James Fergusson, *A Million Bullets: the real story of the British army in Afghanistan*, Bantam, London, 2008, p. 172.

15. This story was researched by Nick Cullather of Indiana University, in cooperation with Adam Curtis, a BBC journalist. His series of blogs on little-known aspects of Afghan history includes this one, 'The lost history of Helmand', which tells the story of the US in Helmand in the immediate post-war period. It is well worth reading and is available at: www.bbc.co.uk/blogs/adamcurtis/2009/10/kabul_city_number_one_part_3.html There is also an excellent account of this period in Chandrasekaran, *Little America*.

16. Curtis, 'The lost history of Helmand'.

17. Michael Martin, 'War on its head: an oral history of the Helmand conflict 1978–2012'. Unpublished thesis for King's College London, 2013, p. 64.

18. Antonio Giustozzi and Noor Ullah, '"Tribes" and warlords in Southern Afghanistan, 1980–2005', Crisis States Research Centre Working Paper no. 7, 2006, p. 11, available at: www2.lse.ac.uk/internationalDevelopment/research/crisisStates/download/wp/wpSeries2/wp72.pdf

19. Martin, 'War on its head', p. 97.

20. ibid., p. 405.

21. ibid., p. 115.

22. ibid., p. 123.

23. ibid., p. 162.

24. ibid., p. 165.

25. ibid., p. 191.

26. We use the word 'Taliban' as shorthand for often highly disparate groups of resistance fighters with often very differing motivations and backgrounds, ranging from local farmers to well-organized and disciplined groups of trained fighters with a clear command structure.

27. Conversation with UK special forces officer, September 2010.

28. Damian McElroy, 'Afghan governor turned 3,000 men over to Taliban', *Daily Telegraph*, 20 November 2009, available at: www.telegraph.co.uk/news/worldnews/asia/afghanistan/6615329/Afghan-governor-turned-3000-men-over-to-Taliban.html

29. Ministry of Defence, *Security and Stabilisation: The military contribution*, Annex 10A, 2010, available at: http://webarchive.nationalarchives.gov.uk/20121026065214/www.mod.uk/NR/rdonlyres/18FD9BF8-3FFB-4917-9C3F-5FDB7BD4278C/0/JDP340A4.pdf

30. Ben Anderson, *No Worse Enemy: The inside story of the chaotic struggle for Afghanistan*, Oneworld, Oxford, 2011, p. 13.

31. McElroy, 'Afghan governor turned 3,000 men over to Taliban'.

32. ibid.

33. Martin, 'War on its head', p. 263.

34. Interview with senior British official, September 2010, and confirmed by discussions with senior army officers, 2012.

35. Martin, 'War on its head', p. 244.

36. Personal communication, January 2012.

37. This was 52 Brigade, deployed from October 2007 until March 2008. It suffered fewer casualties than any other brigade deployed before 2011, despite having engaged in some large-scale operations.

38. Leo Docherty, *Desert of Death: A soldier's journey from Iraq to Afghanistan*, second edition, Faber and Faber, London, 2008, p. 192.

39. Martin, 'War on its head', ch. 5 (passim).

40. UK operational mentoring liaison team commander, Afghanistan, 2009. Quoted in *British Army Field Manual*, vol. 1, part 10, *Countering Insurgency*, October 2009, pp. 3–10, available at: http://news.bbc.co.uk/1/shared/bsp/hi/pdfs/16_11_09_army_manual.pdf

41. Martin, 'War on its head', p. 206.

42. 'More than 150 UK casualties in a week in Helmand', *Guardian*, 21 July 2009, available at: www.guardian.co.uk/uk/2009/jul/21/record-uk-casualties-helmand-taliban

43. Martin, 'War on its head', p. 265.

44. Cavanagh, 'Ministerial decision-making'.

45. Chandrasekaran, *Little America*, p. 59.

46. ibid., p. 206.

47. 'US embassy cables: UK "not up to task" of securing Helmand, says US', *Guardian* website, 2 December 2010, available at: www.guardian.co.uk/world/us-embassy-cables-documents/181930

48. Ministry of Defence, 'UK forces: operations in Afghanistan', available at: www.gov.uk/uk-forces-operations-in-afghanistan

49. Discussion with senior Afghan army officer, June 2012.

50. 'Pentagon says Afghan forces still need assistance', *New York Times*, 10 December 2012, available at: www.nytimes.com/2012/12/11/world/asia/afghan-army-weak-as-transition-nears-pentagon-says.html?ref=asia&_r=0 Detail is available at US Department of Defense, *Report on Progress toward Security and Stability in Afghanistan*, 2012, Figure 22, p. 93, available at: www.globalsecurity.org/military/library/report/2012/afghanistan-security-stability_201212.pdf

51. 'NATO Afghan strategy in disarray after joint ground operations suspended', *Guardian*, 18 September 2012, available at: www.guardian.co.uk/world/2012/sep/18/nato-scales-back-operations-afghans

52. 'President Karzai sacks Helmand governor in blow to British influence', *Daily Telegraph*, 20 September 2012, available at: www.telegraph.co.uk/news/worldnews/asia/afghanistan/9555376/President-Hamid-Karzai-sacks-Helmand-governor-in-blow-to-British-influence.html

53. Martin, 'War on its head', p. 306.

54. Harry G. Summers, Jr., *On Strategy: A critical analysis of the Vietnam War*, Presidio Press, Novato, Calif., 1982, p. 1. Related in Richard Halloran, 'Strategic communication', *Parameters* (Autumn 2007), available at: http://www.carlisle.army.mil/usawc/parameters/Articles/07autumn/halloran.pdf

55. Cowper-Coles, *Ever the Diplomat*, p. 300.

56. For full and up-to-date figures, see http://icasualties.org/oef/ByProvince.aspx

57. Interview with Jean MacKenzie, October 2007.

58. Martin, 'War on its head', p. 348.
59. ibid., p. 351.
60. Informal conversation with senior British army officer, September 2012.
61. 'Hamid Karzai suggests security in Helmand better before British troops arrived', *Guardian*, 13 February 2013, available at www.guardian.co.uk/world/2013/feb/03/ hamid-karzai-security-helmand-british-troops.

Chapter 2: Military Suffering

1. Interview with Caroline Wyatt, May 2012.
2. J. Stiglitz and L. Bilmes, *The Three Trillion Dollar War: The true cost of the Iraq conflict*, Penguin, Harmondsworth 2009, p. 61.
3. 'Blood, sweat and . . . a game of cards: Inside Camp Bastion's trauma clinic where lives of British soldiers rest in hands of elite medics', *Daily Mail*, 27 June 2012, available at: www.dailymail.co.uk/news/article-2165225/Photos-reveal-life-Camp-Bastions-trauma-clinic.html
4. ibid.
5. Official definition in Ministry of Defence statistics, available at: www.gov.uk/uk-forces-operations-in-afghanistan#medical-facilities-and-classifying-injuries For a regular update, see: www.dasa.mod.uk/applications/newWeb/www/index.php?page=48&thisc ontent=1360&pubType=0&date=2012-12-18&PublishTime=09:30:00
6. See: www.dasa.mod.uk/applications/newWeb/www/index.php?page=48&thiscontent= 1360&pubType=0&date=2012-12-18&PublishTime=09:30:00
7. ibid. A full breakdown is available at: www.gov.uk/government/uploads/system/ uploads/attachment_data/file/49970/20130115_Op_Herrick_to_31_Dec_12.pdf (as of 18 January 2013).
8. Glen Owen, 'Army major's despair at our "pointless war": senior officer's damning emails reveal plummeting morale at heart of Afghan campaign that has cost 409 British lives', *Daily Mail*, 21 April 2012, available at: www.dailymail.co.uk/news/article-2133204/Army-majors-despair-pointless-war-Senior-officers-damning-emails-reveal-plummeting-morale-heart-Afghan-campaign-cost-409-British-lives.html
9. The Defence Analytical Services Agency produces quarterly statistics on amputations. They are available at: www.dasa.mod.uk/applications/newWeb/www/index.php?page=48&pubT ype=0&thiscontent=1380&PublishTime=09:30:00&date=2012-07-31&disText=7%20 Oct%202001%20-%2031%20Jun%202012&from=listing&topDate=2012-07-31
10. Personal communication, September 2012. I am very grateful to Dr Lee for his time and patience in discussing his research.
11. Ministry of Defence letter to Dr Peter Lee, dated 27 July 2012.
12. See Ledwidge, *Losing Small Wars*, pp. 252–3.
13. M. Taylor, 'MOD reveals scale of brain injuries among Iraq and Afghanistan veterans', *Guardian*, 16 January 2008, available at: www.guardian.co.uk/uk/2008/jan/16/iraq.iraq
14. C.W. Hoge et al., 'Mild traumatic brain injury in US soldiers returning from Iraq', *New England Journal of Medicine*, 358 (2008), available at: www.nejm.org/doi/full/10.1056/ NEJMoa072972
15. Taylor, 'MOD reveals scale of brain injuries'.
16. ibid.
17. I am obliged to 'Peter' for his account; that is not his real name and some minor details have been changed.
18. Stephen Weiss, *Second Chance*, Military History Publishing, 2011, and interview with author.

19. See Combat Stress website: www.combatstress.org.uk/

20. 'Symptoms of trauma', Combat Stress website, available at: http://www.combatstress.org.uk/veterans/symptoms-of-trauma/

21. Combat Stress website, available at: www.combatstress.org.uk/about-us/

22. B.C. Frueh and J.A. Smith, 'Suicide, alcoholism, and psychiatric illness among union forces during the US Civil War', *Journal of Anxiety Disorder*, 26:7 (2012), pp. 769–75.

23. Interview with Dr Ian Palmer, July 2012. The charity Combat Stress suggests 13 years from discharge as an average.

24. 'Research … suggests that 10–18% of OEF/OIF [Operation Enduring Freedom/Operation Iraqi Freedom] troops are likely to have PTSD after they return.' US Department of Veterans Affairs, 'Mental health effects of serving in Afghanistan and Iraq', available at: www.ptsd.va.gov/public/pages/overview-mental-health-effects.asp

25. Interview with Dr Ian Palmer, July 2012.

26. See written evidence of Robin Short, Martin Kinsella and David Walters to House of Commons Select Committee on Defence, July 2008, available at: http://www.publications.parliament.uk/pa/cm200708/cmselect/cmdfence/424/424we13.htm

27. 'Combat stress: 50,000 British veterans of Iraq and Afghanistan "to develop mental health problems"', *Daily Telegraph*, 7 September 2011, available at: www.telegraph.co.uk/health/8745388/Combat-stress-50000-British-veterans-of-Iraq-and-Afghanistan-to-develop-mental-health-problems.html

28. See the regularly updated 'UK Armed Forces Mental Health Report – Quarterly Report', available at: www.dasa.mod.uk

29. 'Mental health statistics: UK and worldwide', Mental Health Foundation website, available at: www.mentalhealth.org.uk/help-information/mental-health-statistics/UK-worldwide/?view=Standard

30. 'Terrible legacy of a decade of war: 500 troops a month seek mental help as endless fighting in Afghanistan and Iraq takes its toll', *Daily Mail*, 8 July 2012, available at: www.dailymail.co.uk/news/article-2170353/Afghanistan-Iraq-500-troops-seek-mental-health-help-ceaseless-fighting-takes-toll.html#ixzz208EfrAjb

31. Interview with Dr Ian Palmer, military psychiatrist, July 2012.

32. Allan Mallinson, 'As thousands of servicemen are made redundant, how many will be turned away from homeless shelters that are packed full of immigrants?', *Daily Mail*, 24 June 2012, available at: www.dailymail.co.uk/debate/article-2164042/As-thousands-servicemen-redundant-turned-away-homeless-shelters-packed-immigrants.html

33. A. Travis, 'Revealed: the hidden army in UK prisons', *Guardian*, 24 September 2009, available at: www.guardian.co.uk/uk/2009/sep/24/jailed-veteran-servicemen-outnumber-troops

34. Howard League for Penal Reform, *Report of the Inquiry into Former Armed Service Personnel in Prison*, 2011, p. 4, available at: www.howardleague.org/fileadmin/howard_league/user/pdf/Veterans_inquiry/Military_inquiry_final_report.pdf

35. *The Lancet*, 381:9870 (March 2013), pp. 907–17, available at: www.thelancet.com/journals/lancet/article/PIIS0140-6736(13)60354-2/abstract

36. '"Violence risk" after military tours', BBC news, 15 March 2013, available at: www.bbc.co.uk/news/health-21790348

37. Hugh Milroy, CEO of Veterans Aid, speaking on 'Prison and veterans', available at: www.youtube.com/watch?v=jbSoqCYYg_A&feature=plcp

38. As of 17 January 2013.

39. See Bomber Command Campaign Diary, March 1944, available at: www.raf.mod.uk/bombercommand/mar44.html

Chapter 3: Killing the Wrong People

1. Conversation with British army officer friend, October 2011.
2. Depending on the year. In 2010 it was 75 per cent; in 2011 – 77 per cent; and in 2012 probably in the region of 90 per cent. See, for example, Susan G. Chesser, 'Afghanistan casualties: military forces and civilians', US Congressional Research Paper, December 2012, available at: www.fas.org/sgp/crs/natsec/R41084.pdf or the annual UN Assistance Mission to Afghanistan reports on 'Protection of Civilians in Armed Conflict', available at: http://unama.unmissions.org/default.aspx?/
3. 'Civilian deaths threaten US pact, says Karzai', *The Nation* (Pakistan), 8 May 2012, available at: www.nation.com.pk/pakistan-news-newspaper-daily-english-online/national/ 08-May-2012/civilian-deaths-threaten-us-pact-says-karzai
4. See www.iraqbodycount.org/
5. John Bohannon, 'Counting the dead in Afghanistan', *Science*, 331 (March 2011), available at: www.sciencemag.org/content/331/6022/1256.full.pdf
6. Interview with Colonel Wilson by John Bohannon, available as a podcast at: www. sciencemag.org/content/331/6022/1256/suppl/DC2
7. 'Afghanistan: The war logs', *Guardian* website, 25 July 2010, available at: www.guardian. co.uk/world/afghanistan/warlogs/6534E42B-16A2-4E7B-988F-BDFDA246EF3A
8. At that time there had been no serious casualties sustained by women.
9. 'Senior officer relives "grim" moment US bomb hit British platoon in Afghanistan', *Daily Mail*, 20 April 2010, available at: www.dailymail.co.uk/news/article-1267559/Senior-officer- relieves-grim-moment-U-S-bomb-hit-British-platoon-Afghanistan.html#ixzz1ypHKCYvQ
10. Enoch Powell, Speech on the Hola Camp in Kenya, House of Commons, 27 July 1959, available at: www.newstatesman.com/uk-politics/2010/02/powell-speech-kenya-hola
11. A start can be made with the Helmand PRT's information sheet 'Our achievements', British Embassy Kabul website, available at: http://ukinafghanistan.fco.gov.uk/en/ about-us/working-with-afghanistan/prt-helmand/Our-achievements
12. 'Troops in contact', Human Rights Watch website, available at: www.hrw.org/ reports/2008/09/25/troops-contact
13. Anderson, *No Worse Enemy*, pp. 4–5.
14. See his books *The Junior Officers' Reading Club*, Penguin, London, 2010; *Kandak*, Allen Lane, London, 2012.
15. Anderson, *No Worse Enemy*, p. 32.
16. Interview with Danish-Afghan journalist Nagieb Khaja, June 2012.
17. Usually attributed to economics expert Roger Brinner. The original does seem to be the more instinctively correct 'the plural of anecdote *is* data', coined by Ray Wolfinger in the early 1970s.
18. MOD reply to Freedom of Information request by author, MOD Ref D/CLC and P/12- 01-08, July 2012.
19. ibid.
20. The Armed Forces and Reserve Forces (Compensation Scheme Order) 2011, available at: www.legislation.gov.uk/uksi/2011/517/schedule/3/made (Table 5).
21. MOD reply to Freedom of Information request by author, MOD Ref D/CLC and P/12- 01-08, July 2012.
22. The Armed Forces and Reserve Forces (Compensation Scheme Order) 2011, Table 7.
23. The Armed Forces and Reserve Forces (Compensation Scheme Order) 2011, Table 2.

24. MOD reply to Freedom of Information request by author, MOD Ref D/CLC and P/12-01-08, July 2012.

25. MOD reply to Freedom of Information Request, FOI Request 23-04-2007-121537-004, 20 April 2007, available at: http://webarchive.nationalarchives.gov.uk/20121026065214/www.mod.uk/NR/rdonlyres/2AE71FF9-D7A6-4A1F-842F-226F947AC086/0/civilian_casualties_and_claims.pdf

26. ibid.

27. 'Afghan casualties: number of UK payouts "treble"', Channel 4 News website, 24 June 2010, available at: www.channel4.com/news/articles/uk/afghan%2Bcasualties%2Buk%2Bpayouts%2Bfor%2Bcivilian%2Bdeaths%2Bapostrebleapos/3690482.html

28. ibid.

29. For full data see 'Afghan civilian compensation; the sums received from UK forces', *Guardian*, 28 March 2011, available at: www.guardian.co.uk/world/datablog/2011/mar/28/afghanistan-civilian-compensation

30. MOD reply to Freedom of Information request by author, MOD Ref D/CLC and P/12-01-08, July 2012.

31. See spreadsheet of compensation claims pursuant to *Guardian* Freedom of Information request, available at: https://docs.google.com/spreadsheet/ccc?key=0AonYZs4MzlZbdE9hbTh3LTBVVExickZKMnBvVENIOWc#gid=0

32. Jon Boone, 'Caught in the crossfire: the forgotten casualties of war in Afghanistan', *Guardian*, 7 September 2009, available at: http://www.guardian.co.uk/world/2009/sep/06/forgotten-casualties-war-afghanistan

33. MOD reply to Freedom of Information request, FOI Request 23-04-2007-121537-004, 20 April 2007.

34. Personal communication, September 2012.

35. Personal communication, September 2012.

36. Interview with Aziz Ahmad Tassal, September 2007.

37. 'Senior Taliban commander captured', CBS News website, 8 August 2009, available at: www.cbsnews.com/2100-224_162-3814983.html

38. 'Helmand: precision strike or reckless bombing?', IWPR website, 9 August 2007, available at: http://iwpr.net/report-news/helmand-precision-strike-or-reckless-bombing

39. 'Nato rockets kill 12 Afghan civilians', *Guardian*, 14 February 2010, available at: www.guardian.co.uk/world/2010/feb/14/nato-rockets-kill-afghan-civilians

40. Jean MacKenzie and Aziz Ahmad, 'Afghanistan: in search of the true civilian toll', Global Post website, 9 August 2010, available at: www.globalpost.com/dispatch/afghanistan/100806/civilian-death-toll-taliban

41. 'Afghan civilians killed by RAF drone', *Guardian*, 5 July 2011, available at: www.guardian.co.uk/uk/2011/jul/05/afghanistan-raf-drone-civilian-deaths?INTCMP=SRCH

42. 'British soldiers in Afghanistan "kill three civilians"', *Guardian*, 6 April 2011, available at: www.guardian.co.uk/world/2011/apr/06/british-soldiers-afghanistan-kill-civilians%20British%20soldiers%20in%20Afghanistan%20'kill%20three%20civilians

43. 'Afghan civilians reported killed in Helmand air strike', *Guardian*, 29 May 2011, available at: www.guardian.co.uk/world/2011/may/29/afghans-civilians-reported-killed-air-strike

44. 'Airstrike reportedly kills civilians in Southern Afghanistan', *New York Times*, 6 August 2011, available at: www.nytimes.com/2011/08/07/world/asia/07helmand.html

45. See spreadsheet of compensation claims pursuant to *Guardian* Freedom of Information request.

46. ibid.

47. 'Karzai: Afghan civilian deaths could undermine US pact', Voice of America, 8 May 2012, available at: http://blogs.voanews.com/breaking-news/2012/05/08/karzai-afghan-civilian-deaths-could-undermine-us-pact

48. 'MoD compensation log illustrates human cost of Afghan war', *Guardian*, 1 January 2013, available at: www.guardian.co.uk/world/2013/jan/01/mod-compensation-log-afghan-war

49. 'Children killed in Nato attack: Afghan officials', Dawn.com (Pakistan) reporting Agence France Presse, 15 October 2012, available at: http://dawn.com/2012/10/15/children-killed-in-nato-attack-afghan-officials/

50. House of Commons Defence Committee Examination of Witnesses (Questions 66–112), Q85, available at: www.publications.parliament.uk/pa/cm201012/cmselect/cmdfence/554/10110302.htm

51. Karl Marlantes, *What it is Like to Go to War*, Atlantic, New York, 2011, p. 109.

52. 'UK troops in huge turbine operation', BBC News, 2 September 2008, available at: http://news.bbc.co.uk/1/hi/7593901.stm The turbine was intended to provide power to Kandahar and Southern Helmand. No one had given any consideration as to how the laboriously transported turbine could be installed, and it now sits, still in its plastic wrapping, beside the dam.

53. This particular detail was told to me by the reporter who investigated the story, the almost incredibly intrepid Jean MacKenzie, shortly after the story broke.

54. For further details, see 'Foreign troops accused in Helmand raid massacre', IWPR website, 15 January 2008, available at: http://iwpr.net/report-news/foreign-troops-accused-helmand-raid-massacre

55. Conversation with Jean MacKenzie, August 2011. She had interviewed the commander of ISAF at the time, General Dan McNeill, who denied that ISAF forces were involved. He did, however, indicate that MacKenzie might wish to speak to US national assets: at the time a large force of US troops was not under NATO command, which often caused confusion. The only US forces operating in Helmand under US national command, as opposed to NATO command, at the time were US Marine Corps 'Force Reconnaissance'. It is worth mentioning that Afghan forces did not then have any helicopter capability.

56. Not least article 2(1) of the European Convention on Human Rights.

57. 'Every Nato kill-capture mission in Afghanistan detailed and visualised', *Guardian* website datablog, 12 October 2011, available at: www.guardian.co.uk/news/datablog/2011/oct/12/afghanistan-nato-kill-capture-raids-isaf-petraeus

58. Conversation with member of UK military unit, September 2012.

59. Interview with Jonathan Steele, June 2012.

60. 'Afghanistan: huge rise in war-wounded civilians', Channel 4 News, 30 November 2010, available at: www.channel4.com/news/afghanistan-huge-rise-in-war-wounded-civilians

61. ibid.

62. I am obliged to Rebecca Stewart for her time. See Rebecca Stewart, 'Afghanistan: voiceless and displaced', *World Policy Journal* (Summer 2012), available at: http://www.worldpolicy.org/journal/summer2012/afghanistan-voiceless-and-displaced

63. Interview with Rebecca Stewart, February 2012.

64. Human Rights Watch, *'Troops in Contact': Airstrikes and civilian deaths in Afghanistan*, New York, 2008, p. 22, available at: www.hrw.org/sites/default/files/reports/afghanistan0908webwcover_0.pdf

65. See, for example, the debate at the UN Security Council on the Protection of Civilians in Armed Conflict on 25 June 2012. Speech by UN secretary-general available at: www.un.org/apps/news/infocus/sgspeeches/search_full.asp?statID=1585

66. See, for example, Elizabeth Minor, 'Towards the recording of every casualty: analysis and policy recommendations from a study of 40 casualty recorders', Oxford Research Group paper, October 2012, available at: www.oxfordresearchgroup.org.uk/publications/briefing_papers_and_reports/recording_practice_policy_paper

67. See Hamit Dardagan, John Sloboda and Richard Iron, 'In everyone's interest: recording all the dead, not just our own', *British Army Review*, 149 (Summer 2010), available at: www.oxfordresearchgroup.org.uk/sites/default/files/In%20everyones%20interest.pdf

68. James Jeffrey, 'Drone warfare's deadly civilian toll: a very personal view', *Guardian*, 20 September 2012, available at: www.guardian.co.uk/commentisfree/2012/sep/19/drone-warfare-deadly-civilian-toll

69. ibid., quoting Hannah Arendt, *On Revolution*, Penguin, Harmondsworth, 1963, p. 15.

Chapter 4: Military Costs

1. Dwight D. Eisenhower, 'The chance for peace', speech given to the American Society of Newspaper Editors, 16 April 1953, available at: http://en.wikisource.org/wiki/The_Chance_for_Peace

2. Conversation with senior army officer, March 2010.

3. Conversation with MOD official, August 2012.

4. Conversation with RAF officer, August 2012.

5. Band 5 point 20 is the salary of a staff nurse in mid-career – the kind of nurse who will work as a practice nurse in a GP's surgery or a senior nurse in a major hospital. See NHS pay rates at: www.nhscareers.nhs.uk/working-in-the-nhs/pay-and-benefits/agenda-for-change-pay-rates/

6. Written evidence from the Ministry of Defence to the House of Commons Defence Committee report 'Securing the future of Afghanistan', available at: www.publications.parliament.uk/pa/cm201012/cmselect/cmdfence/554/554.pdf

7. House of Commons Defence Committee, *Operations in Afghanistan: Fourth Report of session 2010–12*, 2011, para 108, available at: www.publications.parliament.uk/pa/cm201012/cmselect/cmdfence/554/554.pdf

8. House of Commons Defence Committee, *Operations in Afghanistan: Government response to the Committee's Fourth Report of session 2010–12*, 2011, para 23, available at: www.publications.parliament.uk/pa/cm201012/cmselect/cmdfence/1525/1525.pdf

9. National Audit Office, 'Report of the Comptroller and Auditor General on the 2010–11 annual accounts of the Ministry of Defence', July 2011, available at: www.nao.org.uk/publications/1012/mod_account_2010-11.aspx

10. Interview with military officer, August 2012.

11. Interview with Neil Davies, former chief economist at the Ministry of Defence, September 2012.

12. Interview with Neil Davies, September 2012.

13. Interview with Professor Keith Hartley, June 2012.

14. Ministry of Defence, *Annual Report and Accounts 2011–2012*, p. 10, available at: www.official-documents.gov.uk/document/hc1213/hc00/0062/0062.pdf

15. ibid., p. 51, Table 8.1, column 2.

16. ibid., p. 10.

17. Question from David Winnick to defence secretary, 24 April 2012, available at *Hansard*: www.publications.parliament.uk/pa/cm201212/cmhansrd/cm120424/text/120424w0001.htm (my italics).

18. 'Afghan war will cost British taxpayers £20 billion by time mission is complete', *Daily Telegraph*, 19 May 2012, available at: www.telegraph.co.uk/news/worldnews/asia/afghanistan/9275712/Afghan-war-will-cost-British-taxpayers-20-billion-by-time-mission-is-complete.html

19. House of Commons Defence Committee, *Operations in Afghanistan: Government response.*

20. Evidence of Sir Sherard Cowper-Coles to Parliamentary Committee on Foreign Affairs, 9 November 2010, available at: www.publications.parliament.uk/pa/cm201011/cmselect/cmfaff/c514-iii/c51401.htm Confirmed in *Ever the Diplomat*, p. 289.

21. Tony Blair at Camp Bastion, November 2006.

22. Major General Jeff Mason, quoted in Geoff Till, 'Back to basics: British strategy after Afghanistan', Corbett Paper No. 6, King's College London, 2011, p. 4, available at: http://www.kcl.ac.uk/sspp/departments/dsd/research/researchgroups/corbett/corbettpaper6.pdf

23. Nick Hopkins, 'Inside Camp Bastion', *Guardian*, 15 August 2011, available at: www.guardian.co.uk/uk/2011/aug/15/inside-camp-bastion

24. 'Among the costs of war: billions a year in AC?', NPR News, 25 June 2011, available at: www.npr.org/2011/06/25/137414737/among-the-costs-of-war-20b-in-air-conditioning

25. Ministry of Defence, *Annual Report and Accounts 2011–2012*, paras 8.13 and 8.16.

26. MOD reply to Freedom of Information request by author, FOI 29-05-2012-154021-011, May 2012.

27. National Audit Office figures support the commonly held assertion that the RAF has less than exemplary punctuality. The National Audit Office found in 2009 that 16.9 per cent of flights are subject to a delay of six hours *or more* in returning to the UK. See National Audit Office, *Support to High Intensity Operations*, 2009, available at: http://www.nao.org.uk/publications/0809/high_intensity_operations.aspx

28. Personal communication with military logistics officer.

29. First to Xe Services and now Academi.

30. 'How to make a killing in Kabul: Western security and a crisis in Afghanistan', *Daily Mail*, 28 February 2011, available at: www.dailymail.co.uk/home/moslive/article-1360216/How-make-killing-Kabul-Western-security-crisis-Afghanistan.html

31. National Audit Office, *Support to High Intensity Operations*, p. 35.

32. Owen, 'Army major's despair at our "pointless war"'.

33. ibid.

34. ibid.

35. A US gallon is about 20 per cent less than its 'imperial' equivalent.

36. Roxana Tiron, '$400 per gallon gas to drive debate over cost of war in Afghanistan', The Hill website, 15 October 2009, available at: http://thehill.com/homenews/administration/63407-400gallon-gas-another-cost-of-war-in-afghanistan-

37. Ministry of Defence, *Annual Report and Accounts 2011–2012*, para 8.9.

38. See Gavin Berman, 'The cost of international military operations', House of Commons Library Standard Note SN/SG/3139, available at: www.parliament.uk/briefing-papers/SN03139 The total cost of urgent operational requirements for Iraq and Afghanistan is stated to be £6.8 billion.

39. Ministry of Defence, *Annual Report and Accounts 2011–2012*, p. 11.

40. Interview with military officer, August 2012.

41. National Audit Office, *Support to High Intensity Operations*, p. 12.

42. 'MPs say MoD's army vehicle spending was "failure"', BBC News, 9 December 2011, available at: www.bbc.co.uk/news/uk-politics-16101242

43. 'Our war legacy to Afghans: £1bn of military vehicles will be given to national army when British troops pull out', *Daily Mail*, 11 May 2012, available at: www.dailymail.

co.uk/news/article-2143220/Our-war-legacy-Afghans—1bn-military-vehicles-given-national-army-British-troops-pull-out.html#ixzz1ul8x3cgJ

44. Conversation with senior Foreign Office official, June 2010.
45. 'RAF aircraft: C-17 Globemaster', Royal Air Force website, available at: www.armed-forces.co.uk/raf/listings/l0030.html
46. 'MOD to buy extra C-17 aircraft', UK Government News website, 8 February 2012, available at: www.gov.uk/government/news/mod-to-buy-extra-c-17-aircraft
47. ibid.
48. 'Future Force 2020: considerations on NATO', UK Armed Forces Commentary blog, 1 February 2012, available at: http://ukarmedforcescommentary.blogspot.co.uk/2012/02/future-force-2020-considerations-on.html
49. 'MOD to buy extra C-17 aircraft', UK Government News website, 8 February 2012.
50. 'Britain adds to its C-17 fleet', Defence Industry Daily website, 28 May 2012, available at: www.defenseindustrydaily.com/britain-to-buy-4-leased-c17s-add-a-5th-02506/
51. Interview with Neil Davies, former chief economist at the MOD, September 2012.
52. In fairness, there was a gap in the RAF's airlift capability. It was to have been filled by the European Airbus A400M. The RAF was understandably keen to get its hands on the superior C-17 earlier than it would have received the A400M, which has yet to go into service anywhere. Afghanistan provided that opportunity.
53. 'MoD to buy 14 new Chinook helicopters in £1bn deal', BBC News, 22 August 2011, available at: www.bbc.co.uk/news/uk-14616028
54. 'Army to lose 17 units amid job cuts', BBC News, 5 July 2012, available at: www.bbc.co.uk/news/uk-18716101
55. Chris Summers, 'The time when the British army was really stretched', BBC News Magazine, 22 July 2011, available at: www.bbc.co.uk/news/magazine-14218909
56. 'Army cuts: how have UK armed forces personnel numbers changed over time?', Guardian website datablog (drawing on Defence Analytical Services Agency figure), 1 September 2011, available at: www.guardian.co.uk/news/datablog/2011/sep/01/military-service-personnel-total#data
57. MOD reply to Freedom of Information request by Mr Hird MP, FOI 23-04-2012-153746-019, 25 April 2012, available at: www.whatdotheyknow.com/request/114311/response/276607/attach/html/3/FOI%20Hird.pdf.html
58. Such a figure would, in the usual run of things, comprise the 'full capitation costs'. These figures are no longer used in the MOD as a basis for calculation.
59. Evidence of Francis Tusa to House of Commons Defence Committee, 26 June 2012, available at: www.publications.parliament.uk/pa/cm201213/cmselect/cmdfence/c413-i/c41301.htm
60. Defence Minister Peter Luff in answer to a parliamentary question, 3 September 2012, available at: www.publications.parliament.uk/pa/cm201213/cmhansrd/cm120903/text/120903w0002.htm#12090322003084
61. ibid.
62. Evidence of Francis Tusa to House of Commons Defence Committee, 26 June 2012.
63. Conversation with a British officer with extensive experience of Afghanistan, July 2012.
64. Vanessa Allen, 'Taliban fighters get £100 per month to stop shooting our troops', Daily Mail, 28 November 2011, available at: www.dailymail.co.uk/news/article-2066938/Taliban-fighters-100-month-stop-shooting-troops.html

65. Gilles Dorronsoro, 'Who are the Taliban?', Carnegie Endowment for International Peace website, 22 October 2009, available at: http://carnegieendowment.org/2009/10/22/who-are-taliban/161

66. Evidence of Francis Tusa to House of Commons Defence Committee, 26 June 2012.

67. 'Afghanistan "Sandhurst in the Sand" academy announced by Philip Hammond', *Daily Telegraph*, 29 March 2012, available at: www.telegraph.co.uk/news/uknews/defence/9173032/Afghanistan-Sandhurst-in-the-sand-academy-announced-by-Philip-Hammond.html

68. Ministry of Defence Business Plan 2012–15, available at: www.mod.uk/NR/rdonlyres/21363C3C-5452-435D-9D6C-7B73069B6E27/0/mod_plan_final_11_06_12_P1.pdf

Chapter 5: Financial Element of Death and Injury

1. 'As US agencies put more value on a life, businesses fret', *New York Times*, 16 February 2011, available at: www.nytimes.com/2011/02/17/business/economy/17regulation.html?_r=3 See also Rebecca Goldin and Cindy Merrick, 'What's the value of a statistical life?', Stats.org, 27 June 2011, available at: http://stats.org/stories/2011/value_statistical_life_jun27_11.html

2. At the time of writing, the department is looking at new ways of calculating this figure. For those of a serious mathematical bent, see NERA Economic Consulting, *Updating the VPF and VPIs – Phase 1: Final Report Department of Transport*, 2011, available at: http://assets.dft.gov.uk/publications/pgr-economics-rdg-updatingvpfvpi-pdf/vpivpfreport.pdf

3. Reply to Freedom of Information request by author, July 2012.

4. 'AFCS: An overview', Veterans UK website, available at: www.veterans-uk.info/pensions/afcs_overview.html

5. The Armed Forces and Reserve Forces (Compensation Scheme) Order 2011, available online at: www.legislation.gov.uk/uksi/2011/517/schedule/3/made

6. The data is updated quarterly. The latest figures can be accessed at the Defence Analytical Services and Advice website at: http://www.dasa.mod.uk/applications/newWeb/www/index.php?page=67&pubType=0&thiscontent=1330&date=2012-06-0700

7. Answer to a parliamentary question to defence secretary, 10 September 2012, available at: www.publications.parliament.uk/pa/cm201213/cmhansrd/cm120910/text/120910w0003.htm#12091037000069

8. MOD reply to Freedom of Information request by author, FOI 29-05-2012-154021-011, May 2012.

9. This figure will include Iraq casualties.

10. Answer to a parliamentary question to the defence secretary, 14 October 2009, available at: www.publications.parliament.uk/pa/cm200809/cmhansrd/cm091014/text/91014w0014.htm

11. MOD reply to Freedom of Information request by author, FOI 03-10-2012-134122-007, October 2010.

12. Parliamentary Office of Science and Technology, 'Explosive injury', Postnote No. 395, December 2011, available at: www.parliament.uk/briefing-papers/POST-PN-395.pdf

13. National Audit Office, *Treating Injury and Illness Arising on Military Operations*, 2010, available at: www.nao.org.uk/publications/0910/injury_on_military_operations.aspx

14. ibid., para 3.1.

15. 'Op Herrick casualty and fatality tables' (regularly updated), available at: www.gov.uk/ government/publications/op-herrick-casualty-and-fatality-tables

16. From January 2006 to December 2012, some 6,375 service and civilian personnel were admitted to the field hospital for all causes, 4,309 for non-battle injuries. There were 6,377 aeromedical evacuations in that period. Clearly some of the sick were placed straight on the aircraft home.

17. Stiglitz and Bilmes, *The Three Trillion Dollar War*, p. 82.

18. See, for example, the case of 'ND' where a 23-year-old claimant in the High Court received a structured settlement of £4 million. It can be found in the case notes of leading personal injury barrister Bill Braithwaite QC, available at: www.billbraithwaite. com/cases/Brain_pdfs/ND%20(Brain).pdf

19. Conversation with 'Peter', October 2012.

20. Answer to a parliamentary question to the defence secretary, 16 April 2012, available at *Hansard*: www.publications.parliament.uk/pa/cm201212/cmhansrd/cm120416/text/ 120416w0003.htm#12041630000029

21. MOD reply to Freedom of Information request by author, FOI 29-05-2012-154021-011, May 2012.

22. 'Management of mental health in veterans: the role of the third sector charity Combat Stress', presentation by Dr Walter Busuttil, 14 May 2010, Royal College of Psychiatry website, available at: www.rcpsych.ac.uk/pdf/6-WBusuttil.pdf

23. Department of Health reply to Freedom of Information request by author, DE00000732409, November 2012.

24. See www.prosthetic-limbs.co.uk/prosthetic-limb-faq%27s.html

25. 'Help for Heroes set to raise £100m', BBC News, 5 June 2011, available at: www.bbc. co.uk/news/uk-13663355

26. For a look at the wide range of services offered by the Royal British Legion, see www. britishlegion.org.uk/about-us/what-we-do

27. See Help for Heroes website at: www.helpforheroes.org.uk/

28. See US Department of Veterans Affairs website at: www.va.gov/

29. This is the budget for 2010. See: www.whitehouse.gov/omb/fy2010_department_ veterans/

30. See Service Personnel and Veterans Agency website at: www.veterans-uk.info/

31. See Department for Veterans Affairs website at: www.va.gov/vetdata/Veteran_ Population.asp

32. Interview with Hugh Milroy, CEO of Veterans Aid, May 2012.

33. Interview with Hugh Milroy, May 2012.

34. Some veterans' charities have huge endowments. Some senior executives – very commonly retired senior military officers supplementing often large pensions – are very well paid indeed. For example, Blind Veterans UK raises £23 million per year and has assets in one form or another of £150 million. Its best-paid employee (the accounts do not specify who this is) receives over £100,000 per year, roughly the salary of a two-star general. Three others are paid between £60,000 and £70,000. By comparison, Oxfam, with over 4,000 staff worldwide, huge numbers of ongoing projects and an annual income of over £135 million, in 2010–11 had a single member of staff paid over £100,000.

35. Charity Commission, 'Charity overview: Alzheimer's Society', 2012, available at: www. charitycommission.gov.uk/Showcharity/RegisterOfCharities/CharityWithPartB.aspx? RegisteredCharityNumber=296645&SubsidiaryNumber=0

36. Charity Commission, 'Charity overview: Alzheimer's Research UK', 2012, available at: www.charitycommission.gov.uk/Showcharity/RegisterOfCharities/CharityWithPartB. aspx?RegisteredCharityNumber=1077089&SubsidiaryNumber=0

37. Interview with Professor Keith Hartley, May 2012.

38. QALY is used in the field of health economics rather than statistics to put an economic value on the loss of welfare associated with injury and incapacity relative to normal health. It is used, for example, by the National Institute for Health and Clinical Excellence (NICE) to judge whether to approve the general prescription of new medicines. I am obliged to Neil Davies for making this clear.

39. The derivation of the £40,000 figure is the product of many arbitrary judgements and is very much at the conservative (i.e. low) end of the range.

40. Interview with Neil Davies, former chief economist at the Ministry of Defence, September 2012.

41. That is 20 per cent of 2,500 × 40 × 40,000.

42. The QALY could be used to place a value on this.

43. See Help for Heroes website for up-to-date figures of how much it has disbursed and how much it is seeking to raise: www.helpforheroes.org.uk/

Chapter 6: Developing Afghanistan

1. Colonel Wade, political agent on the North West Frontier, before the First Afghan War. I am obliged to Major Ian Gordon for referring me to this.

2. Foreign Office reply to Freedom of Information request by author, 0776-12, August 2012. No figures are available for the total expenditure from 2001. The Foreign Office wrote that determining such a figure would result in the cost of replying to the FOI request exceeding the statutory limit of £600.

3. Statement by a DFID official, quoted in 'DFID increases funding for Afghanistan', Devex website, 7 August 2009, available at: www.devex.com/en/blogs/231/blogs_ entries/61396

4. Independent Commission for Aid Impact, *The Department for International Development: Programme controls and assurance in Afghanistan*, March 2012, p. 22, available at: http://icai.independent.gov.uk/wp-content/uploads/2012/03/ICAI-Afghanistan-Final-Report_P11.pdf

5. Transparency International, *Corruption Perceptions Index 2011*, available at: http://issuu.com/transparencyinternational/docs/ti_cpi2011_report_print?mode=window&backgroundColor=%23222222

6. Implicit in the 'amber-red' mark awarded; see the 'traffic light' key on the Contents page of Independent Commission for Aid Impact, *The Department for International Development: Programme controls and assurance in Afghanistan*.

7. ibid., p. 1.

8. Answer to a parliamentary question to the international development secretary, 16 June 2011, available at *Hansard*: www.publications.parliament.uk/pa/cm201011/cmhansrd/cm110616/text/110616w0003.htm#11061650000003

9. 'Want to stop foreign aid fraud? Scrap foreign aid', Bob Shepherd's blog, 20 October 2011, available at: http://bobshepherdauthor.com/2011/10/20/want-to-stop-foreign-aid-fraud-scrap-foreign-aid/

10. Matt Waldman, 'Falling short: aid effectiveness in Afghanistan', ACBAR Advocacy Series paper, 2008, available at: www.oxfam.org/sites/www.oxfam.org/files/ACBAR_aid_effectiveness_paper_0803.pdf

11. 'Overview of Provincial Reconstruction Team', British Embassy Kabul website, available at: http://ukinafghanistan.fco.gov.uk/en/about-us/working-with-afghanistan/prt-helmand/overview-prt-helmand

12. Naina Patel, 'The long road to justice in Afghanistan', *Guardian*, 15 September 2011, available at: www.guardian.co.uk/world/2011/sep/15/long-road-justice-afghanistan

13. Chandrasekaran, *Little America*, p. 211.

14. ibid., p. 210.

15. Patel, 'The long road to justice in Afghanistan'.

16. '"Poverty barons" who make a fortune from taxpayer-funded aid budget', *Daily Telegraph*, 16 September 2012 , available at: www.telegraph.co.uk/news/politics/9545584/Poverty-barons-who-make-a-fortune-from-taxpayer-funded-aid-budget.html

17. DFID, 'Business case: province based district delivery programme', July 2011, available at: http://projects.dfid.gov.uk/project.aspx?Project=202190

18. ibid. See link to annual review.

19. Rory Stewart and Gerald Knaus, *Can Intervention Work?*, Norton, New York, 2011, p. 20.

20. 'Where we work: Afghanistan', DFID website, available at: www.dfid.gov.uk/Where-we-work/Asia-South/Afghanistan/?tab=4

21. See International Development Act 2002 S 1 (1). 'The Secretary of State may provide any person or body with development assistance if he is satisfied that the provision of the assistance is likely to contribute to a reduction of poverty.' Text available at: www.legislation.gov.uk/ukpga/2002/1/section/1

22. See the ARTF Business Case (2011), p. 5, available on the Afghanistan Reconstruction Trust Fund web page, at: http://projects.dfid.gov.uk/project.aspx?Project=114525

23. ibid.

24. ibid, p. 5.

25. 'Supporting Employment and Enterprise Development', DFID Projects website, available at: http://projects.dfid.gov.uk/project.aspx?Project=200898

26. 'Afghanistan Infrastructure Trust Fund', DFID Projects website, available at: http://projects.dfid.gov.uk/project.aspx?Project=202297

27. 'National Solidarity Programme', DFID Projects website, available at: http://projects.dfid.gov.uk/project.aspx?Project=107181

28. 'Microfinance Investment Support Programme', DFID Projects website, available at: http://projects.dfid.gov.uk/project.aspx?Project=107196

29. 'Strengthening Tax Administration', DFID Projects website, available at: http://projects.dfid.gov.uk/project.aspx?Project=113362

30. See list at: http://projects.dfid.gov.uk/Default.aspx?countrySelect=AF-Afghanistan

31. 'Strengthening Civil Society in Afghanistan', DFID projects website, available at: http://projects.dfid.gov.uk/project.aspx?Project=201000

32. 'Logical framework', downloadable at ibid.

33. ibid. See 'Indicator' column.

34. DFID/FCO/MOD, *Conflict Pool Annual Report 2009/10*, p. 44, available at: www.fco.gov.uk/resources/en/pdf/publications/annual-reports/conflict-pool-report-09-10

35. 'UK fund to prevent global conflict fails to make major impact', *Guardian*, 13 July 2012, available at: www.guardian.co.uk/global-development/2012/jul/13/uk-fund-prevent-conflict-impact

36. Independent Commission for Aid Impact, *The Department for International Development: Programme controls and assurance in Afghanistan*.

37. 'Where we work: Afghanistan', DFID website, available at: www.dfid.gov.uk/Where-we-work/Asia-South/Afghanistan/?tab=4
38. 'Summary of DFID's work in Afghanistan 2011–2015', DFID website, June 2012, available at: www.dfid.gov.uk/Documents/publications1/op/afghanistan-2011-summary.pdf
39. Figures confirmed in DFID reply to Freedom of Information request by author, DFID F2012-242, July 2012. See DFID figures available at: http://collections.europarchive.org/tna/20100423085705/dfid.gov.uk/documents/publications/sid2006/table-12.3.xls (for 2001–06) and: www.dfid.gov.uk/Documents/publications1/sid2011/Table%2014.3%20-%20Asia_P1.xls (for 2007–12).
40. 'Overseas aid shake-up: how DfID plans to spend abroad', BBC News, 1 March 2011, available at: www.bbc.co.uk/news/uk-12606665
41. Increasing daily. It is worth checking the website to see how quickly these figures rise.
42. As mentioned above, the cost of running the embassy is currently in the region of £35 million a year (Foreign Office reply to Freedom of Information request by author, 0776-12, August 2012). It may well be that this figure was not as high in the early days of the mission from 2001 to 2006. In those circumstances a figure of £300 million is a reasonable, if low figure.

Chapter 7: And For What? – Afghanistan

1. Junior member of UK government in conversation with the author, June 2012.
2. Interview with Nagieb Khaja, Danish-Afghan journalist, June 2012.
3. Professor Paul Collier, in evidence to House of Lords Economic Committee, 29 March 2012, para 70, available at: www.publications.parliament.uk/pa/ld201012/ldselect/ldeconaf/278/27808.htm
4. See Brown University's Costs of War Project website, available at: http://costsofwar.org/article/economic-cost-summary
5. 'Factsheet of Human Development Report 2009: Afghanistan ranked 181 out of 182 countries', RAWA News, 5 October 2009, available at: www.rawa.org/temp/runews/2009/10/05/human-development-report-2009-factsheet-afghanistan-ranked-181-out-of-182-countries.html
6. Kavitha Viswanathan et al., 'Infant and under-five mortality in Afghanistan: current estimates and limitations', *Bulletin of the World Health Organization*, 88:8 (2010), pp. 576–83, available at: http://www.who.int/bulletin/volumes/88/8/09-068957.pdf
7. 'Afghanistan: food still unaffordable for millions', IRIN Humanitarian News, 12 March 2009, available at: www.irinnews.org/Report/83417/AFGHANISTAN-Food-still-unaffordable-for-millions
8. Interview with Jonathan Steele, June 2012.
9. Written evidence from David James to the House of Commons Defence Committee report 'Securing the future of Afghanistan', available at: www.publications.parliament.uk/pa/cm201213/cmselect/cmdfence/writev/413/m01.htm
10. Interview with Norwegian military officer, September 2012.
11. Interview with John Hilary, executive director of War on Want, April 2012.
12. Kate Fearon, *City of Soldiers: A year of life, death and survival in Afghanistan*, Signal Books, Oxford, 2012.
13. Evidence of Liam Fox, in House of Commons Defence Committee, *Operations in Afghanistan: Fourth Report of session 2010–12*, Q314.

14. Patel, 'The long road to justice in Afghanistan'.
15. 'Gunmen kill Afghan government prosecutor', *The Hindu* (India), 21 August 2011, available at: www.thehindu.com/news/international/article2379032.ece
16. Jonathan Steele, *Ghosts of Afghanistan: The haunted battleground*, Portobello Books, London, 2011, p. 28.
17. Nick Hopkins, 'Afghan schools and clinics built by British military forced to close', *Guardian*, 27 September 2012, available at: www.guardian.co.uk/world/2012/sep/27/afghan-schools-clinics-built-british-close
18. Sherard Cowper-Coles, *Cables from Kabul: The inside story of the west's Afghanistan campaign*, Harper Press, London, 2011, p. 240.
19. 'US efforts fail to curtail trade in Afghan opium', *New York Times*, 26 May 2012, available at: www.nytimes.com/2012/05/27/world/asia/drug-traffic-remains-as-us-nears-afghanistan-exit.html?_r=1&ref=asia
20. United Nations Office on Drugs and Crime, *Afghanistan Opium Survey 2010: Summary findings*, available at: www.unodc.org/documents/crop-monitoring/Afghanistan/Afg_opium_survey_2010_exsum_web.pdf
21. 'The good and bad news about Afghan opium', Council on Foreign Relations Expert Brief, 10 February 2010, available at: http://www.cfr.org/afghanistan/good-bad-news-afghan-opium/p21372
22. United Nations Office on Drugs and Crime, 'The global heroin market', in *World Drug Report 2010*, available at: www.unodc.org/documents/wdr/WDR_2010/1.2_The_global_heroin_market.pdf
23. Joshua Partlow, 'UN report cites sharp drop in opium cultivation in Afghanistan', *Washington Post*, 2 September 2009, available at: www.washingtonpost.com/wp-dyn/content/article/2009/09/01/AR2009090103223.html
24. Nigel Inkster, 'Drugs: a war lost in Afghanistan', *Foreign Policy* AfPak Channel, 29 May 2012, available at: http://afpak.foreignpolicy.com/posts/2012/05/29/drugs_a_war_lost_in_afghanistan
25. 'Taliban's ban on poppy a success, US aides say', *New York Times*, 20 May 2001, available at: www.nytimes.com/2001/05/20/world/taliban-s-ban-on-poppy-a-success-us-aides-say.html
26. Martin, 'War on its head', p. 168.
27. United Nations Office on Drugs and Crime, *Afghanistan Opium Survey 2007: Executive summary*, available at: www.unodc.org/pdf/research/AFG07_ExSum_web.pdf At that time, Afghanistan accounted for 85 per cent of the world's production. Helmand produced 62 per cent of that and therefore 51.5 per cent of the global crop.
28. Conversation with owner of Helmandi poppy field, November 2007.
29. Antonio Giustozzi (ed.), *Decoding the New Taliban: Insights from the Afghan field*, Hurst, London, 2010, p. 144.
30. Interview with British military officer, May 2012.
31. US Department of State/UK Foreign and Commonwealth Office, 'Fighting the opium trade in Afghanistan: myths, facts, and sound policy', 11 March 2008, available at: http://kabul.usembassy.gov/media/afghan_opium_myths_and_facts-final.pdf
32. United Nations Office on Drugs and Crime, *Afghanistan Opium Survey 2012: Summary findings*, p. 6, available at: www.unodc.org/documents/crop-monitoring/Afghanistan/Summary_Findings_FINAL.pdf
33. ibid., p. 13.
34. ibid.
35. Interview with British military officer, May 2012.

36. UN Office on Drugs and Crime, *World Drug Report 2011*, available at: www.unodc.org/documents/data-and-analysis/WDR2011/WDR2011-ExSum.pdf

37. 'US efforts fail to curtail trade in Afghan opium', *New York Times*, 26 May 2012.

38. 'Why Britain's pledge to end Afghanistan's deadly heroin trade has failed', *Daily Telegraph*, 21 May 2012.

39. United Nations Office on Drugs and Crime, *World Drug Report 2011*.

40. Inkster, 'Drugs: a war lost in Afghanistan'.

41. Fawzia Koofi (with Nadene Ghouri), *The Favored Daughter: One woman's fight to lead Afghanistan into the future*, Palgrave, New York, 2012.

42. 'Radio address by Mrs Bush', American Presidency Project website, 17 November 2001, available at: www.presidency.ucsb.edu/ws/index.php?pid=24992#axzz1ynz15ubh

43. 'Cherie Blair attacks Taleban "cruelty"', BBC News, 19 November 2001, available at: http://news.bbc.co.uk/1/hi/uk_politics/1663300.stm

44. Steele, *Ghosts of Afghanistan*, p. 364.

45. Conversation with senior British officer, September 2012.

46. 'Afghanistan passes "barbaric" law diminishing women's rights', *Guardian*, 14 August 2009, available at: www.guardian.co.uk/world/2009/aug/14/afghanistan-womens-rights-rape

47. 'Hamid Karzai backs clerics' move to limit Afghan women's rights', *Guardian*, 6 March 2012, available at: www.guardian.co.uk/world/2012/mar/06/hamid-karzai-afghanistan-womens-rights?newsfeed=true

48. Marlantes, *What it is Like to go to War*, p. 253.

49. Interview with senior military officer, July 2012.

50. ICOS, *Afghanistan Transition: Missing variables*, 2010, available at: www.icosgroup.net/static/reports/afghanistan_transition_missing_variables.pdf

51. ibid., p. 12.

52. ibid., p. 20–1.

53. ibid., p. 22.

54. ibid., p. 29.

55. ibid., p. 31.

56. ibid., p. 35–6.

57. ibid., p. 37.

58. Personal communication.

59. '60 Iraqi interpreters murdered working for UK', *Daily Telegraph*, 12 August 2007, available at: www.telegraph.co.uk/news/worldnews/1560112/60-Iraqi-interpreters-murdered-working-for-UK.html See also 'Afghanistan "not safe" for interpreters', BBC Newsbeat website, 2 August 2011, available at: www.bbc.co.uk/newsbeat/14368889 There is no sign of the Afghans who served as interpreters for the UK forces being accorded the same asylum rights as were given to some Iraqi interpreters.

60. Cowper-Coles, *Ever the Diplomat*, p. 290.

61. Koofi, *The Favored Daughter*, p. 248.

Chapter 8: And For What? – Security

1. Speech at the International Institute for Strategic Studies, 11 November 2008, quoted in House of Commons Foreign Affairs Committee, *Global Security: Afghanistan and Pakistan*, 2009, para 264, available at: www.publications.parliament.uk/pa/cm200809/cmselect/cmfaff/302/30210.htm#n428

2. Abdul Salam Zaeef, *My Life with the Taliban*, Hurst/Columbia University Press, New York, 2010, p. 141.

3. ibid., p. 144.

4. Lucy Morgan Edwards, *The Afghan Solution: The inside story of Abdul Haq, the CIA and how Western hubris lost Afghanistan*, Bactria Press, London, 2011, pp. 262ff.

5. ibid., p. 266.

6. House of Commons Foreign Affairs Committee, 'The UK's foreign policy approach to Afghanistan and Pakistan: formal minutes', para 182 (corrected and amended to para 184), available at: http://www.publications.parliament.uk/pa/cm201011/cmselect/cmfaff/514/51420.htm

7. 'CIA: At most, 50–100 Al Qaeda in Afghanistan', ABC News, 27 June 2010, available at: http://abcnews.go.com/blogs/politics/2010/06/cia-at-most-50100-al-qaeda-in-afghanistan/

8. 'Al-Qaeda threat: Britain worst in western world', *Daily Telegraph*, 15 January 2010, available at: www.telegraph.co.uk/news/uknews/terrorism-in-the-uk/6996655/Al-Qaeda-threat-Britain-worst-in-western-world.html

9. Interview with Professor Paul Rogers, October 2012.

10. Personal communication.

11. Martin, 'War on its head', p. 266.

12. ibid., p. 267.

13. Robert Pape and James Feldman, *Cutting the Fuse: The explosion of global suicide terrorism and how to stop it*, University of Chicago Press, Chicago, 2010, p. 20.

14. http://shahamat-english.com/

15. Alex Strick van Linschoten and Felix Kuehn, *An Enemy We Created*, Hurst, London, 2011, p. 335.

16. ibid.

17. George Bush, Address to Congress, 20 September 2001, transcript available at: http://edition.cnn.com/2001/US/09/20/gen.bush.transcript/

18. From video address played on Al Jazeera, 29 October 2004. Quoted in Peter Bergen, *The Osama bin Laden I Know*, Free Press, New York, 2006, p. 378.

19. Pape and Feldman, *Cutting the Fuse*, p. 20.

20. ibid., p. 23.

21. ibid.

22. 'London bomber: text in full', BBC News, 1 September 2005, available at: http://news.bbc.co.uk/1/hi/uk/4206800.stm

23. Pape and Feldman, *Cutting the Fuse*, p. 20 (my italics).

24. Abdel Bari Atwan, *The Secret History of Al Qaeda*, University of California Press, Berkeley, 2008.

25. Abdel Bari Atwan, interviewed by Australian Television ABC News, 24 August 2007, transcript available at: www.abc.net.au/news/2007-08-24/bin-laden-wanted-us-to-invade-iraq-author-says/648888

26. Interview with Professor Anatol Lieven, June 2012.

27. General Sir Richard Dannatt, lecture to Chatham House, 'Perspectives on the nature of future conflict'.

28. Interview with Professor Paul Rogers, October 2012.

29. Barack Obama's welcoming address to French President Sarkozy, Washington, DC, 10 January 2011.

30. I am obliged to Anatol Lieven for this phrase.

31. Interview with Anatol Lieven, June 2012.

32. Gordon Brown, quoted in 'Gordon Brown unveils plan to tackle "crucible of terrorism" between Afghanistan and Pakistan', *Daily Telegraph*, 27 April 2009, available at: http://www.

telegraph.co.uk/news/politics/gordon-brown/5228654/Gordon-Brown-unveils-plan-to-tackle-crucible-of-terrorism-between-Afghanistan-and-Pakistan.html (my italics).

33. 'David Cameron visits troops in Afghanistan amid tight security', *Guardian*, 21 December 2012, available at: www.guardian.co.uk/world/2012/dec/20/david-cameron-afghanistan-tight-security (my italics).

34. Anatol Lieven, *Pakistan: A hard country*, Penguin, London, 2012.

35. Interview with Anatol Lieven, June 2012.

36. Interview with Anatol Lieven, June 2012.

37. Interview with Anatol Lieven, June 2012.

38. Till, 'Back to basics', p. 4.

39. 'What percent of NATO strikes in Libya were carried out by the US?', CNN World, 22 August 2011, available at: http://globalpublicsquare.blogs.cnn.com/2011/08/22/what-percent-of-nato-strikes-in-libya-were-carried-out-by-the-u-s/ Figures are correct as of late August 2011, by which time the bulk of air strikes had been delivered.

40. Discussion with Royal Navy officers, February 2012.

41. Quoted in Andrew Mackay and Steve Tatham, *Behavioural Conflict: Why understanding people and their motives will prove decisive in future conflict*, Military Studies Press, Saffron Walden, 2011, p. 182.

42. Interview with Commodore Steven Jermy, June 2012.

Conclusion

1. Quentin Sommerville, 'Afghanistan's "green on blue" collapse of trust', BBC News, 6 October 2012, available at: www.bbc.co.uk/news/world-south-asia-19834021

2. United Nations Office on Drugs and Crime, *Afghanistan Opium Survey 2012: Summary findings*, p. 6.

3. Personal communication with Neil Davies, former chief economist at the Ministry of Defence.

4. This figure, again, is a minimum. It is rare for interest rates on the government gilts that support debt over a ten-year period to fall below 3 per cent.

5. 'Should NASA ditch manned missions to Mars', Space.com website, 5 August 2012, available at: www.space.com/16918-nasa-mars-human-spaceflight-goals.html

6. As at 17 January 2013.

7. Cowper-Coles, *Ever the Diplomat*, p. 286.

8. Only one had the courtesy to reply in any but the most peremptory fashion. He did not feel able to comment.

9. They have all prospered since their departure from office. All but two were elevated to the House of Lords. The two who remain in the House of Commons are Bob Ainsworth, the minister most respected by the officers with whom he worked, and Liam Fox, who left office (or was removed) following a misunderstanding concerning a close friend.

10. Quoted in Toby Harnden, *Dead Men Risen*, Quercus, London, 2011, p. 558.

11. Interview with Jonathan Steele, May 2012.

Bibliography

Books and articles

Anderson, Ben, *No Worse Enemy: The Inside Story of the Chaotic Struggle for Afghanistan*, Oneworld, Oxford, 2011

Atwan, Abdel Bari, *The Secret History of Al Qaeda*, University of California Press, Berkeley, 2008

Belesco, Amy, 'The cost of Iraq, Afghanistan and other Global War on Terror operations since 9/11', Congressional Research Service, 29 March 2011, available at: www.fas.org/sgp/crs/natsec/RL33110.pdf

Bergen, Peter, *The Osama bin Laden I Know*, Free Press, New York, 2006

Berman, Gavin, 'The cost of international military operations', House of Commons Library Standard Note SN/SG/3139, available at: www.parliament.uk/briefing-papers/SN03139

Bohanon, Jon, 'Counting the dead in Afghanistan', *Science*, vol. 331, March 2011, available at: www.sciencemag.org/content/331/6022/1256.full.pdf

Braithwaite, Rodric, *Afgantsy*, Profile Books, London, 2012

Cavanagh, Matt, 'Ministerial decision-making in the run-up to the Helmand deployment', *The RUSI Journal*, 157(2), 2012, pp. 48–54

Chandrasekaran, Rajiv, *Little America*, Bloomsbury, London, 2012

Chesser, Susan G., 'Afghanistan casualties: Military forces and civilians', U.S. Congressional Research Paper, December 2012, available at: www.fas.org/sgp/crs/natsec/R41084.pdf

Council for Foreign Relations, Expert Brief, 'The good and bad news about Afghan opium', 10 February 2010, available at: www.cfr.org/afghanistan/good-bad-news-afghan-opium/p21372

Cowper-Coles, Sherard, *Cables from Kabul: The Inside Story of the West's Afghanistan Campaign*, Harper Press, London, 2011

Cowper Coles, Sherard, *Ever the Diplomat; Confessions of a Foreign Office Mandarin*, Harper Press, London, 2012

Curtis, Adam et al., 'The lost history of Helmand', available at: www.bbc.co.uk/blogs/adam-curtis/2009/10/kabul_city_number_one_part_3.html

Dardagan, Hamit, John Sloboda and Richard Iron, 'In everyone's interest: Recording all the dead, not just our own', *British Army Review*, No. 149, Summer 2010

Docherty, Leo, *Desert of Death: A Soldier's Journey from Iraq to Afghanistan*, second edition, Faber and Faber, London, 2008

Dorronsoro, Giles, 'Who are the Taliban?', Carnegie Endowment for International Peace website, 22 October 2009, available at: http://carnegieendowment.org/2009/10/22/who-are-taliban/161

Fearon, Kate, *City of Soldiers: A Year of Life, Death and Survival in Afghanistan*, Signal Books, Oxford, 2012

Fergusson, James, *A Million Bullets: The Real Story of the British Army in Afghanistan*, Bantam Press, London, 2008

Fergusson, James, *Taliban*, Bantam Press, London, 2010

Frueh, B.C and J.A Smith, 'Suicide, alcoholism, and psychiatric illness among union forces during the U.S. Civil War', *Journal of Anxiety Disorder*, 26(7), 2012, pp. 769–75

Giustozzi, Antonio and Ullah Noor, 'Tribes and warlords in Southern Afghanistan', Crisis States Research Centre, Working Paper No. 7, 2010, available at: www2.lse.ac.uk/internationalDevelopment/research/crisisStates/Home.aspx

Giustozzi, Antonio (ed.), *Decoding the New Taliban*, Hurst, London, 2010

Goldin, Rebecca and Cindy Merrick, 'What's the value of a statistical life?', Stats.org, 27 June 2011, available at: http://stats.org/stories/2011/value_statistical_life_jun27_11.html

Harnden, Toby, *Dead Men Risen*, Quercus, London, 2011

Hartley, Keith, 'The costs of conflict: The UK experience in Afghanistan and Iraq' in Manas Chatterji et al., *Frontiers of Peace Economics and Peace Science* (*Contributions to Conflict Management, Peace Economics and Development*, vol. 16), Emerald Press, Bingley, 2011, pp. 74ff

Hennessey, Patrick, *The Junior Officers' Reading Club*, Penguin, London, 2010

Hennessey, Patrick, *Kandak*, Allen Lane, London, 2012

Hoge, C. W. et al., 'Mild traumatic brain injury in U.S. soldiers returning from Iraq', *New England Journal of Medicine*, 358, 2008, available at: www.nejm.org/doi/full/10.1056/NEJMoa072972

Human Rights Watch, 'Troops in Contact', available at: www.hrw.org/reports/2008/09/25/troops-contact

ICOS, 'Afghanistan Transition: Missing Variables', available at: www.icosgroup.net/static/reports/afghanistan_transition_missing_variables.pdf

Iraq Body Count, 'The unexamined Iraqi dimension of UK involvement in Iraq', 22 May 2011, available at: www.iraqbodycount.org/analysis/beyond/uk-involvement/

Koofi, Fawzia with Nadene Ghouri, *The Favored Daughter: One Woman's Fight to Lead Afghanistan into the Future*, Palgrave, New York, 2012

Ledwidge, Frank, *Losing Small Wars: British Military Failure in Iraq and Afghanistan*, Yale University Press, London, 2011

Lia, Brynjar, *Architect of Global Jihad*, Hurst, London, 2007

Lieven, Anatol, *Pakistan: A Hard Country*, Penguin, London, 2012

Mackay, Andrew and Stephen Tatham, *Behavioural Conflict: Why Understanding People and Their Motives Will Prove Decisive in Future Conflict*, Military Studies Press, Saffron Walden, 2011

Marlantes, Karl, *What It Is Like to Go to War*, Atlantic Monthly Press, New York, 2012

Martin, Michael, 'War on its Head: An Oral History of the Helmand Conflict, 1978–2012', unpublished thesis for King's College London, to be published by Hurst, London, 2013

Minor, Elizabeth, 'Towards the recording of every casualty: Analysis and policy recommendations from a study of 40 casualty recorders', Oxford Research Group paper, October 2012, available at: www.oxfordresearchgroup.org.uk/publications/briefing_papers_and_reports/recording_practice_policy_paper

Morgan Edwards, Lucy, *The Afghan Solution: The Inside Story of Abdul Haq, the CIA and how Western Hubris lost Afghanistan*, Bactria Press, London, 2011

NERA Economic Consulting, 'Updating the VPF and VPIs – Phase 1: Final Report Department of Transport', 2011, available at: http://assets.dft.gov.uk/publications/pgr-economics-rdg-updatingvpfvpi-pdf/vpivpfreport.pdf

Pape, Robert and James Feldman, *Cutting the Fuse: The Explosion of Global Suicide Terrorism and How to Stop It*, Chicago University Press, Chicago, 2010

Robinson, Paul and Jay Dixon, *Aiding Afghanistan: A History of Soviet Assistance to a Developing Country*, Hurst, London, 2013

Steele, Jonathan, *Ghosts of Afghanistan: The Haunted Battleground*, Portobello Books, London, 2011

Stewart, Rebecca, 'Afghanistan: Voiceless and Displaced', *World Policy Journal*, Summer 2012, available at: www.worldpolicy.org/journal/summer2012/afghanistan-voiceless-and-displaced

Stewart, Rory and Gerald Knaus, *Can Intervention Work?*, W. W. Norton & Company, New York, 2011

Stiglitz, Joseph and Linda Bilmes, *The Three Trillion Dollar War*, Penguin, London, 2008

Strick van Linschoten, Alex and Felix Kuen, *An Enemy We Created: The Myth of the Taliban/ Al Qaeda Merger in Afghanistan, 1970–2010*, Hurst, London, 2012

Summers, Harry G. Jr., *On Strategy: A Critical Analysis of the Vietnam War*, Presidio Press, New York, 1982

Till, Geoff, 'Back to basics: British strategy after Afghanistan', Corbett Paper No. 6, King's College London, 2011, pp. 4, available at: www.kcl.ac.uk/sspp/departments/dsd/research/researchgroups/corbett/corbettpaper6.pdf

Waldman, Matt, 'Falling short: Aid effectiveness in Afghanistan', ACBAR Advocacy Series paper, March 2008, available at: www.oxfam.org/sites/www.oxfam.org/files/ACBAR_aid_effectiveness_paper_0803.pdf

Weiss, Stephen, *Second Chance*, Military History Publishing, Saffron Walden, 2011

Zaeef, Abdul Salam, *My Life with the Taliban*, Hurst, London, 2009

Selected Parliamentary Documents

House of Commons Defence Committee Fourth Report of Session 2010–12, 'Operations in Afghanistan', available at: www.publications.parliament.uk/pa/cm201012/cmselect/cmdfence/554/10110302.htm

House of Commons Defence Committee, 'Operations in Afghanistan: Government Response to the Committee's Fourth Report of Session 2010–12', available at: www.publications.parliament.uk/pa/cm201012/cmselect/cmdfence/1525/152504.htm

House of Commons Defence Committee, 'Securing the Future of Afghanistan; oral evidence taken before the Defence Committee', 26 June 2012, available at: www.publications.parliament.uk/pa/cm201213/cmselect/cmdfence/c413-i/c41301.htm

House of Commons Foreign Affairs Committee Report, 'The UK's foreign policy approach to Afghanistan and Pakistan', available at: www.publications.parliament.uk/pa/cm201011/cmselect/cmfaff/514/51406.htm#n12

House of Lords Economic Committee Sixth Report, 'The Economic Impact and Effectiveness of Development Aid', 21 March 2012, available at: www.publications.parliament.uk/pa/ld201012/ldselect/ldeconaf/278/27802.htm

Government Papers and Resources

Afghanistan casualty and fatality tables are updated regularly and are available at: www.gov.uk/government/publications/op-herrick-casualty-and-fatality-tables

Armed Forces and Reserve Forces (Compensation Scheme) Order 2011, Tariff of awards, available at: www.legislation.gov.uk/uksi/2011/517/schedule/3/made

Armed Forces Compensation Scheme, 'An Overview', Veterans UK website, available at: www.veterans-uk.info/pensions/afcs_overview.html

Armed Forces Statistics, The Defence Analytical Services Agency, available at: http://dasa.mod.uk/

Department for International Development (DFID), 'Operational plan 2011–15', June 2012 revision, available at: www.dfid.gov.uk/Documents/publications1/op/afghanistan–2011.pdf

DFID, 'Summary of DFID's work in Afghanistan 2011–2015', June 2012, available at: www.dfid.gov.uk/Documents/publications1/op/afghanistan–2011-summary.pdf

DFID, 'Where we work: Afghanistan', available at: www.dfid.gov.uk/Where-we-work/Asia-South/Afghanistan/?tab=4

DFID/Foreign and Commonwealth Office (FCO)/Ministry of Defence (MOD), 'Conflict Pool Annual Report 2009/10', available at: www.fco.gov.uk/resources/en/pdf/publications/annual-reports/conflict-pool-report–09–10

DFID/FCO/MOD, Helmand PRT's information sheet, 'Our achievements', available at: http://ukinafghanistan.fco.gov.uk/en/about-us/working-with-afghanistan/prt-helmand/Our-achievements

DFID/FCO/MOD, 'Overview of Provincial Reconstruction Team', available at: http://ukin-afghanistan.fco.gov.uk/en/about-us/working-with-afghanistan/prt-helmand/overview-prt-helmand

House of Commons Library Standard Note, 'Cost of International Military Operations', 2011, available at: www.parliament.uk/briefing-papers/SN03139

MOD, 'Annual Report and Accounts 2010–11', available at: www.gov.uk/government/uploads/system/uploads/attachment_data/file/27067/mod_ara1011.pdf

MOD, 'Annual Report and Accounts 2011–12', available at: www.gov.uk/government/uploads/system/uploads/attachment_data/file/27067/mod_ara1011.pdf

MOD, 'Business Plan 2012–15', available at: www.mod.uk/NR/rdonlyres/21363C3C–5452–435D–9D6C–7B73069B6E27/0/mod_plan_final_11_06_12_P1.pdf

MOD, 'Security and Stabilisation: The Military Contribution', Annex 10A, 2010, available at: http://webarchive.nationalarchives.gov.uk/20121026065214/www.mod.uk/NR/rdonlyres/18FD9BF8–3FFB–4917–9C3F–5FDB7BD4278C/0/JDP340A4.pdf

MOD, 'UK forces: operations in Afghanistan', available at: www.gov.uk/uk-forces-operations-in-afghanistan

MOD British Army Field Manual, 'Countering Insurgency', Volume 1, Part 10, October 2009, pp. 3–10, available at: http://news.bbc.co.uk/1/shared/bsp/hi/pdfs/16_11_09_army_manual.pdf

National Audit Office (NAO), 'Ministry of Defence: Treating injury and illness arising on military operations', 2010, available at: www.nao.org.uk/publications/0910/injury_on_military_operations.aspx

NAO, 'Report of the Comptroller and Auditor General on the 2010–11 Annual Accounts of the Ministry of Defence', available at: www.nao.org.uk/publications/1012/mod_account_2010–11.aspx

NAO, 'Review of the Conflict Pool', March 2012, available at: www.nao.org.uk/report/review-of-the-conflict-pool

NAO, 'Support to High Intensity Operations', 2009, available at: www.nao.org.uk/publications/0809/high_intensity_operations.aspx

NAO, 'Treating injury and illness arising on military operations', 2010, available at: www.nao.org.uk/publications/0910/injury_on_military_operations.aspx

Parliamentary Office of Science and Technology, 'Explosive injury', Postnote No. 395, December 2011, available at: www.parliament.uk/briefing-papers/POST-PN–395.pdf

U.S. Department of State/UK FCO, 'Fighting the opium trade in Afghanistan: myths, facts, and sound policy', 11 March 2008, available at: http://kabul.usembassy.gov/media/afghan_opium_myths_and_facts-final.pdf

U.S. Department of Veteran Affairs, 'Mental Health Effects of Serving in Afghanistan and Iraq', available at: www.ptsd.va.gov/public/pages/overview-mental-health-effects.asp

United Nations Resources

'The global heroin market', available at: www.unodc.org/documents/wdr/WDR_2010/1.2_The_global_heroin_market.pdf

United Nations Assistance Mission to Afghanistan (UNAMA), 'Annual Report 2012: Protection of Civilians in Armed Conflict', available at: http://unama.unmissions.org/default.aspx?/

United Nations Office on Drugs and Crime (UNODC), 'Afghanistan Opium Survey 2007: Executive Summary', available at: www.unodc.org/pdf/research/AFG07_ExSum_web.pdf

UNODC, 'Afghanistan Opium Survey 2010: Executive Summary', available at: www.unodc.org/documents/crop-monitoring/Afghanistan/Afg_opium_survey_2010_exsum_web.pdf

UNODC, 'Afghanistan Opium Survey 2012: Summary findings', available at: www.unodc.org/documents/crop-monitoring/Afghanistan/Summary_Findings_FINAL.pdf

UNODC, 'World Drug Report 2011', available at: www.unodc.org/documents/data-and-analysis/WDR2011/WDR2011-ExSum.pdf

Other Useful Sources

Brown University in the U.S. has an ongoing comprehensive 'Costs of War Project'. Its website is available at: http://costsofwar.org/article/economic-cost-summary

Channel Four has also done excellent work on civilian casualties, for example: www.channel4.com/news/afghanistan-huge-rise-in-war-wounded-civilians

The *Guardian*'s work on these matters has been superb. Some of the results of the work of its researchers and journalists are available as follows:

Guardian, 'Afghanistan War Logs: Wikileaks Afghanistan files', available at: www.guardian.co.uk/world/datablog/2010/jul/25/wikileaks-afghanistan-data

Guardian, 'Afghanistan civilian compensation', 2010, available at: www.guardian.co.uk/world/datablog/2011/mar/28/afghanistan-civilian-compensation; 'MoD compensation log

illustrates human cost of Afghan war', available at: www.guardian.co.uk/world/2013/jan/01/
mod-compensation-log-afghan-war

Guardian, 'Army cuts: how have UK armed forces personnel numbers changed over time?',
drawing on Defence Analytical Services Agency figures, 1 September 2011, available at:
www.guardian.co.uk/news/datablog/2011/sep/01/military-service-personnel-
total#data

ICAI (Independent Commission on Aid Impact) report 'Department for International
Development: Programme Controls and Assurance in Afghanistan', March 2012, avail-
able at: http://icai.independent.gov.uk/wp-content/uploads/2012/03/ICAI-Afghanistan-
Final-Report_P11.pdf

Transparency International, the leading anti-corruption NGO, produces the invaluable
'Corruption Perceptions Index'. The latest, for 2011, is available at: http://issuu.com/
transparencyinternational/docs/ti_cpi2011_report_print?mode=window&backgroundC
olor=%23222222

Index